12 Steps To Natural Gardening

Alfred H. Krautter

To James S Atkinson

Thank you for your support and friendship through the years. From pounding the pavement to gardening its people like you that have made this long journey such a pleasant one.

Happy Organic Gardening
Al Krautter
July 26, 2011.

Published by FastPencil, Inc.

Published by FastPencil, Inc.
3131 Bascom Ave.
Suite 150
Campbell CA 95008 USA
(408) 540-7571
(408) 540-7572 (Fax)
info@fastpencil.com
http://www.fastpencil.com

First Edition

I dedicate this book to my wonderful family. My parents convinced me to become part of the family business; taught me how to grow, care and communicate with plants; and bond with nature in a way I never thought could exist. My wife, Heidi, has played an integral part in managing the family business. My children, Tonja and Torsten, grew up at Sprainbrook Nursery and spent many hours playing and working there. My sister, Norma, grew up with me where we spent our teenage years among flowers, plants and a family atmosphere that fosters love for horticulture. They all have encouraged and inspired me to write a book on Natural Gardening.

Acknowledgements

I am a nurseryman who finds great meaning in nature's gifts. I feel honored and privileged to work in the horticultural field. In addition, I am a husband, father and grandfather who finds great meaning in securing the health and well-being of my family members through the use of natural gardening. Both my family and my career are priorities in my life. I feel blessed to have created a balance between them.

The identification and understanding of the dangers involved in using a chemical approach to gardening can leave a family feeling frustrated, confused and frightened. Toxic pesticides are harmful to our children, our pets and our environment. My greatest hope in writing this book is to provide knowledge about the necessity to switch to a natural gardening approach. If we as a society make this switch, we will begin to preserve the health and well-being of our loved ones and our planet. We are witnessing first hand a dramatic environmental phenomenon circled around toxins, pesticides and poor health. By acknowledging this phenomenon, we are able to gain a better understanding of the complexities involved with it and offer the opportunity to help our environment and ourselves in both positive and healthy ways.

I would like to acknowledge the contributions of several people, without whom, I would not have completed this book.

To my editor, Charlotte Rodziewicz. Thank you for your interest and commitment to this book project. You encouraged me to add personal stories into the book and the book would not be the same without them. I could not have finished this book without you.

To my good friend, Steve O'Deegan and my son Torsten Krautter, for their continued hard work and commitment throughout the book project. You helped create a wonderful finalized product.

To my talented illustrators Rolf Svensson, Rosa Mendoza, Tavo Figueroa, Marcos Hernandez, Torsten Krautter, Tyler Pearson and Brody Pearson. Rolf your incredible black and white illustrations have made this book unique. A picture is worth a thousand words and you conveyed a powerful message without the use of color. Rosa thank you for filling in with illustrations on pages where we still needed a last minute drawing. Tavo – your artistic talent helped make the book complete. Torsten – you have always been the talented artist in our family and now your nephews are following in your footsteps. Tyler and Brody – thank you for creating such beautiful illustrations to put in this book. I cannot believe how talented you both are at the ages of eight and six. All of the illustrations have added interest and perspective to the nursery business.

To my dedicated readers, Heidi Krautter, Fred Fritts, Rosella Zaglio and Al Sarnotsky. Thank all of you for your time and effort in reviewing all of the material in this book. It is an honor and privilege to have your support and guidance.

To the many people who supported me in my efforts and convinced me that this book was a must read for individuals in society today: Jeff Frank whose course at the Nature Lyceum changed my outlook on life; the amazing staff at Sprainbrook Nursery (past and present), who through the years have helped me improve and maintain a family business, write and sort out my recommendations and formulas and inspired me to develop new directions as a nurseryman; my running friends, who have been a sounding board for me during our morning runs; my peers and competitors who have given me honest answers to difficult questions; and my enthusiastic customers who have shared my love for gardening and joined me in my search for answers. It is all of you who have given me the drive and desire necessary to write this book.

Lastly, I would like to thank my wonderful family members who have always given me tremendous support. To my amazing wife, Heidi Krautter, who has stuck with me through thick and thin. You have worked by my side for over four decades in the horticultural field. Thank you for all your love and support. To my son, Torsten Krautter, whose foresight helped me see the importance of changing my focus to an organic gardening approach. To my daughter, Tonja Krautter, who encouraged and inspired me to write this book after she wrote some of her own. To my sister, Norma Weisbrich, who has always supported me in my endeavors. To Jason, Tyler, Brody, Kim and Jake for your many kind words of encouragement. To my parents, Alfred and Hermine Krautter (R.I.P.) who encouraged me to get an education in the field of horticulture, follow in their footsteps and build a business we could be proud of. It has been a long, hard journey, but a beautiful one.

Thank you all!!

Contents

INTRODUCTION: ALL ABOUT MY JOURNEY INTO NATURAL GARDENING

I have spent my whole life in the horticultural field. I took over the family greenhouse business, which I was involved in since childhood. From a greenhouse operation we developed into a full-service horticultural operation, becoming known as a Garden Center, Nursery and Landscape Design and Installation company. I am 76 years old now and I have decided it is time to write a book on organic gardening. Once I made the switch to natural gardening I knew I had to get the word out to tell everyone that we need to follow Nature's lead, that our philosophical outlook must change. Plants have sent us a message and we need to listen. We need to work with Nature and not against her.

In the late 1950s I studied Horticulture at an agricultural land grant college which, like most agricultural colleges, was a part of a university system. Agricultural colleges at the time focused on chemical fertilizers and the development of the best growing programs for each crop. World War II had supplied us with a source for inexpensive chemical fertilizers. The belief of the agricultural community was that we could use cheap fertilizers to outproduce the rest of the world. There was talk that America could save the world from famine and become the largest agricultural-producing nation in the world.

We based everything on NPK as the foundation of any fertilizer: N = Nitrogen, P = Phosphorus and K = Potassium. The numbers were manipulated for each crop and, as time went by, programs were written on how to best grow each crop. The chemical companies became very rich and powerful and plants grew rapidly and lush. Chemical fertilizers, although stimulating growth, weakened plants, making them more susceptible to insects and disease. Programs were developed and pesticides were manufactured as cures for the things that plagued each crop. Production was increased and farmers were making money. The direction was to greater mechanization, as small farms were bought up by larger farms, and farming became big business with the bottom line becoming the driving force.

Throughout all these times there were signs of problems cropping up as dead soils and unhealthy drinking water developed in our farm belt. Despite these signs, we plowed along, entrenched in our ways and our new-found science, which was breeding "success." Our colleges constantly came up with newer and better plant programs to increase the bottom line for farmers. This usually came at the expense of quality as we added toxic substances to our soils and plants and as seeds were genetically enhanced–all to increase production. Our food chain has suffered terribly–and many feel the chain is broken. The health of our nation is at risk. It is going to be a struggle to correct it.

Horticulture training, following the same line of thinking, continued in a similar path of destruction. We were taught in college that for each plant crop we grew there was a specific fertilizer formulation and a recommended program to follow. Chemical spray programs were set up to prevent insect damage to each specific plant crop. Chemical companies developed a four-step program for creating a beautiful lawn. Vegetable gardeners believed strongly in their 5-10-5 chemical fertilizer, and miracle liquid chemical fertilizers were the rage for those who wanted beautiful flowers. Plants weakened by these chemical fertilizer programs required more pesticides and fungicides and new programs were developed to deal with issues caused by additional chemicals.

Homeowners were brainwashed by the advertising of these products, and guys like me were taught through the schooling we received that this was the right way to teach gardening. Universities were supported by grants from rich chemical companies and professors were writing up in journals the findings they discovered through their grants. They were hailed as great intellects in the horticultural world. They were toasted at dinners and rewarded with honors. I was a firm believer in the universities' recommendations and sprayed my greenhouses weekly. Growing a large diversity of crops, I needed to vary my spray program to control all of my many pest problems and to deal with resistant strains. Each week I would suit up in my yellow rubberized suit, black rubber gloves and a dual respirator mask. In 2002 I came down with prostate cancer even though this was not inherent in our family. My doctors were concerned that the many years of exposure to toxic sprays was catching up to me.

In the 21st century I made the best decision in my life–to switch my operation to natural gardening. My switch to an organic approach came about when my son refused to use pesticides on the crops he was growing for us on our upstate farm. He switched to beneficial insects instead of insecticides, convincing me to do the same. I went to a three-day seminar at the Nature Lyceum in Long Island, New York, where I saw things in a different light. Something clicked in my mind and the organic seminar focused me on things that made sense. As a grower who lived his life close to his plants, I understood.

I read feverishly about the simple path Mother Nature has set out for us to follow. Being a marathon runner and born a Taurus, I became obsessed with my new direction. Realizing that I owed a different gardening approach to my customers, I wrote programs tying in my many years of growing experience to develop an easy-to-follow homeowner program using organic gardening. I found that the greater the mix of plants in the garden and the greater the mix of organic material in the soil, the greater the results. I tested the programs and installed them on landscape jobs with excellent success. Through the years I tweaked the programs, with my customers providing me with important feedback. Many have marveled at how beautifully developed their gardens have become by following my advice.

My mother was 95 years old when she passed away. She worked every day of her life. She was the first one out in the morning tending to her watering chores; in the spring, she joined the night crew workers who planted small seedlings for spring sale, Mondays through Thursdays 5-10 p.m. She enjoyed the camaraderie of the women who worked with her. By 9 o'clock in the evening they would tell her that she needed to go home and get a good night's sleep, tomorrow is another day. Her little long-haired dachshund who followed her around all day would agree. Since she lived in a brick house on the nursery property, the two of them would walk home, heading for bed, after she reluctantly said goodnight. Gardening keeps both the mind and the body active and we are sure this is what kept her so young and fit at her age. She was in tune with her plants and with Nature. She loved every aspect of gardening.

Gardening is a wonderful pastime. It is therapeutic, keeping the body active and the mind alert. Many of us live a hectic life and we need to spend some quality time alone. To work hard and create beauty is a very rewarding activity, which gardening provides. This book is a guide to gardening success. It is a product of a lifetime, which I spent in the horticultural field growing plants, designing gardens, diagnosing problems, developing formulas, producing a yearly catalogue, writing monthly newsletters and weekly e-mails with garden tips and giving lectures and handouts to customers for specific problems. I enjoy my work but spend much too much time working. Luckily, my commute is only down a set of stairs. My audience is my customers who benefit from my guidance. It is for this reason that I had a burning desire to write this book and pass on what I have learned and worked so hard to produce, much in the form of handouts to my customers. I hope that this advice can help you understand the basic principles for good gardening.

My father bought Sprainbrook Nursery, the nursery where we live, in 1944. There were three greenhouses on the property which were put up in the thirties to grow wholesale floral crops. I was in the third grade when we moved here. As a kid I worked Saturdays and summers. The blue laws were still in effect and we were able to observe the Sabbath. Later, the retail chains moved in and got the laws changed to be open on Sunday. One had to follow suit or go out of business.

In 1958, I graduated from Cornell University Floricultural Department with a BS degree, having taken all of the Horticultural and Landscape Design courses they offered. They have served me well throughout the years. A close friend and classmate of mine at Cornell said to me "Soon we will graduate from college but then we will have to go to the school of hard knocks and that is when the learning curve will really kick in."

After graduation I entered the family business and realized how right he was as each day offered a different challenge. Because I had a Cornell education, I got asked all the technical questions. Customers came in with insect or disease problems, questions with what to do with their lawns, how to prepare their soil, when to plant, what to prune and how to prune, and on and on. The questions varied from easy to complex and I never pretended to know all the answers. But if I didn't know an answer to a question I would always try to find out the answer. I equipped myself with the best reference books, sent samples to the Cornell labs, and I would discuss problems with peers or experts in certain fields. I constantly drew upon my day-to-day experiences of growing and propagating plants.

I had a father who was one of the best growers on the east coast. He learned his trade in Dresden, Germany. He taught me what made a plant grow. His plants would sit on a bench like soldiers, each one had to be a perfect specimen. There was a specific time to pinch, a specific time to space, a specific time to feed and a specific time to spray. Watering was an art; too much or too little was not tolerated. Overhead watering on the flowers was not allowed. Weeds were the enemy and were never to be seen. One soon learned that roots were more important than top growth. There were never enough hours in the day to accomplish the tasks that needed to be done.

I think the most enjoyable part of my day is the early morning hours when I do my watering in the quiet of a greenhouse, surrounded by beauty and always trying to grow the perfect plant. This is also the most important task of the day. Customers ask why I don't get someone else to do the watering, since I have more important things to do. There is no more important job than watering. The importance of proper watering is the most difficult thing to master. I have struggled to teach this to my staff and to my customers throughout the years. More plants die from either over-watering or under-watering than any other single cause.

The late 1970s and 1980s were my favorite years. They were also our most profitable years. The big-box stores had still not hit our market; flower shops were still the main source for selling potted plants, and a plant boom had hit our market area. The rage was to decorate your home with lots of foliage and flowering plants. Decorating with plants came before putting up curtains. There was a tremendous demand for interior plants, which had not existed before. Digging back into the past, unusual and exotic varieties of houseplants were finding popularity. Small plant shops were popping up throughout Manhattan. Business was thriving as the historically slow winter season became a very busy one. Outdoor plants were also gaining in popularity as new varieties emerged. The better varieties performed well in the garden, creating greater success and more repeat sales the following years.

During these years I spent a lot of time answering questions, perfecting and expanding my catalogue, and writing informational handouts for my customers. I learned much from my customers' questions, problems and experiences. Forced to do research, I developed a desire to provide information. We started our Saturday morning winter lecture series, providing talks on Houseplants, Perennials, Annuals and Roses. We had a spring weekend filled with hands-on demonstrations. We would show how to prune, seed and propagate; how to grow a beautiful container combination; teach how to grow a beautiful lawn; the maintenance of perennials; watering techniques; landscape design and organic gardening. Each year we would add new topics that might be of timely interest. These activities taxed my brain and made me come up with more and more handouts. The handouts met an urgent demand to answer customers' questions. Writing them put me in tune with what homeowners wanted to know and what problems they needed help in solving. I became involved in the New York Nursery and Landscape Association and eventually became President. This took a lot of my time and opened my eyes to many of the problems our industry faced.

A great sadness came in the 1980s when my father suddenly passed away from a heart attack. A lot more responsibility was placed upon my shoulders. I needed to take over more of the growing, propagating, seeding and scheduling. Being a family business, it put a lot of extra pressure on my wife, who was running the office and the business. My mother was a trooper and pitched in even more, but without Dad, things were never the same. Two generations in a business like this gives you some leeway and a sense of freedom–being tied down is never a good feeling.

During the 90s and going into the next century, I developed some strong opinions on what direction our country was taking. The small retailer who had built this country was taking a tremendous hit. Great incentives were given to bring big-box stores into our area. Ten-year deals on tax savings were the kind of offers often negotiated by the town fathers, creating an unfair playing field. The big boxes bought aggressively on price and forced our manufacturing market overseas. Millions of Americans lost jobs that they had worked so hard for all of their lives. "Made in the USA" became hard to find. Stores that had been in towns for years went out of business and "for rent" signs made business districts look like ghost towns.

Americans are resilient and, over time, we have filled many of these vacancies with new kinds of businesses. But I wonder if we have ever thought, when we bought that incredibly low-priced appliance made in a foreign country, what negative effects we were causing our fellow Americans. When I see more and more flowers sold in supermarkets, fruit markets and the big-box stores, it saddens me. Many of the big boxes pay the grower only what is rung up on the cash register. The growers are pushed to the limit and once this happens the whole industry suffers. It pushes prices down for the consumer but causes profits in the industry to crumble. Quality is reduced as the big growers needed to find ways to cut costs in order to meet the demands of their large customers.

To be competitive, small retail growers can't charge the prices they need to make a profit. Garden centers are also going out of business, and with them go the knowledgeable staff that can teach and help individuals garden. Enrollment is down in the horticultural schools as young people look for different professions to make a living in. Neither of my children chose to enter the family business. I often think of all the things we need to know to grow a good plant how much advice we give out for free, whereas many other professions make a living on giving advice. Customers jokingly come in and say "I need to see the Plant Doctor." Knowledge is so important in our industry.

It is easy to put the blame on the gardener when things go wrong. Firing him and getting another one will not solve the problem. One needs to take control over one's own garden by getting involved and doing some of the work. Bring in professionals to do the technical tasks when you feel the need for help on pruning, planting, designing and spraying. But to have a beautiful garden with meaning, you have to be part of it. Your garden is you, an expression of your love and creativity. This is what has made gardening so popular and the rewards so great. You can't get it and reap its bounties unless you are a part of it. We need more people to learn and study the field of horticulture—and we need that information passed on to us. Hopefully this book will help to accomplish this mission.

I often wish we could know what impact we have each time we make a purchase. The ripple effect laid out on a spreadsheet would shock us. We can make a difference in making America a stronger society. We need the small businesses, the competitive market, the quality product and the knowledgeable staff. We need to support our local merchants. This is what makes America great. So much has changed so fast it is difficult to understand the direction we are heading. It is important to understand the consequences of our actions. Short-term gains often lead to long-term losses.

The 20th century brought its own challenges. In retailing one has to keep reinventing the wheel. Under pressure, many good garden centers have become great garden centers while others have succumbed and fallen by the wayside. Others have said that since the supermarkets are selling flowers, they are going to sell produce—and they have been successful in this venture. It has changed the complexion of our industry; and being a purist, I am appalled at the thought of selling vegetables and insecticides at the same counter.

Others have expanded their horticultural base by expanding the line of products they sell and the services they offer. This has allowed them to increase sales. A common adjustment made by many is to expand their landscape design and installation services. In modern society, and particularly in affluent communities, two heads of the household are working. These families require daycare, nannies, baby sitters, gardeners and house cleaners. Yet through all of this, gardening is growing. It is still America's number one pastime activity. New plants and better varieties hit the market and capture the attention of a hungry public. The greater the stress of the job, the more immersed one can get into gardening. Hired gardeners need to cut the grass weekly, but the creativity and the beauty of the garden should be the product of the individual who lives there. Gardens are an ongoing process. Each year large or small changes are made as we strive to improve our creation. The body is kept physically fit and the mind is kept keenly alert. Knowledge is important and will make the task that much more successful.

When you reach 76, you realize that there are not that many good years left. You wonder what happened to them and why they went by so fast. I woke up one morning and realized I had put a lot into the informational aspect of the business. My horticultural life had gone through a transition. I found that the answers to all my questions were answered by my plants. I found that Nature had laid down a path to follow. I learned we cannot control Nature; we need to work with her. In order to be on her side and help her in whatever way we can, our focus must change. When we live in harmony with Nature, we will live in harmony with ourselves. I have the burning desire to pass this information on. That is why I wrote this book, hoping that it will help someone else become a better gardener and live a healthier more fruitful life.

.....WHY MY PARENTS GOT MARRIED

My mother came to this country leaving Germany when she was 16 years old. She was sponsored by an uncle who lived on Long Island and got her a job in a household. She ended up working for a very lovely family who took her in and treated her as their own. She was a very good housekeeper and cook and was told she was to eat all her meals with them. They had horses and they had an extra horse that needed riding so she joined in the fun and exhilaration of this daily event. My mother spent a lot of her free time with the family. She became very close to the two daughters. Two times a week she attended night school where she learned English.

My father came to this country from Germany after he finished his apprenticeship at the age of 21. He went to Lockport, New York and worked in a greenhouse range where he was head grower. The opportunity arose to go into business with a Long Island associate. He went for it. The associate had the money and my father had the knowledge.

During the depression the business failed and my father ended up without a job. He lived in Bayport, New York, the same town my mother was working in. They attended classes together, hung out with a large German group and dated each other. My father soon landed a great job in Chappaqua, New York, as head grower. The position was for a couple. The job came with a house and required a married person to live on the premises. In the greenhouse business you need a person to be there at all times. If the boiler goes out on a cold winter night unnoticed, you are out of business. During the interview my father assured his potential boss that he was married. He was hired on the spot. Dad drove back to Long Island, proposed to my mother, got married that weekend and drove to Chappaqua to start his new job the following Monday.

The greenhouse operation grew Lily of the Valley pips, which they shipped into the New York market. When that market was ruined due to cheaper imports, the business went under. My father was well known in the industry and found a job as head grower in Stamford, Connecticut. This was a very large operation with a night watchman. Dad rented a small house. Two years later a well-to-do client, for whom my father grew the bedding plants, offered my parents housing in exchange for maintaining his estate. They had the choice of the huge house or the cottage. He and my mother chose the cottage. The owner, getting on in years, moved out and built a new house on one level across the bay. With my mother's help, and working two jobs, my father was able to save money.

My dog Blackie, a Labrador Retriever, got run over shortly after we moved to this estate. At our former house on Newfield Avenue, Blackie would meet me each day at school; and walk me home for lunch and again after school. He knew the safe route, crossing at the light where the crossing guard was and following the sidewalk home. I couldn't stop crying when he was killed. Blackie was exploring a new road and didn't know the area.

When the owner of the estate, Mr. Carter, saw how sad I was, he gave me his new Bull Terrier. He said it was too much of a dog for him to train at his age. This was an expensive breed. My mother thanked him but couldn't get over what an ugly dog it was. "It looks like a pig," she told my father. We had two beaches to swim from and Bull Terriers hate water. But whenever my sister and I went swimming, the bull terrier would swim in circles around us until we were safely back on land. We grew so fond of this breed that we continued owning them.

These were great times for us, having a big estate to ourselves. But this beautiful property eventually drew buyers. In 1944, when it was close to being sold, my parents started to look for a place of their own. My father and mother had saved enough money to get a mortgage and buy a three-greenhouse operation in Scarsdale, New York, with a red brick house to live in. The property was being foreclosed and the bank offered it at a great price. At that time, my father was working three jobs—defense at night, a grower during the day and cutting lawns on a large estate between shifts. The deal was made with the bank and the move took place quickly. My father started growing crops in the greenhouse but continued to work defense until after the war.

ADD YOUR GARDEN STORY HERE

1. PART ONE: 12 STEPS TO NATURAL GARDENING

1. planning
2. Planting
3. Watering
4. Weeding
5. Feeding
6. Mulching
7. Pruning
8. Composting
9. Grooming
10. Observing
11. Transplanting
12. Enjoying

Without plants we cannot exist. Societies are built around them. The strength of any plant is in its roots and the soil it grows in. The more nutritious the soil, the healthier the plant. This is a miraculous system where life springs forth from the earth. When we try to control nature, we destroy it; when we work with nature, we live in harmony with it.

In an attempt to control nature, powerful chemical companies have emerged and have taken over our way of thinking. Universities have followed with a path of learning that has supported chemical fertilizers. This, in turn, has led to the development of harsh pesticides, herbicides and fungicides, which kill bugs, weeds and fungus while poisoning our soils. Health problems are emerging from this process. In a push for increased production, we have mechanized our growing operations and ruined our food chain. The destruction we have created can only be understood when we understand the important

1

role nature plays in our lives. Making changes on our own properties and following a path back to natural gardening is a first step in acquiring this knowledge.

Once we work with nature, and not against her, we will learn lessons from plants and their surroundings that we can never acquire from a textbook. Each person will learn differently. Everything in our universe is connected and we all play a part in it. Modern civilization is based on a path of controls–controls that will eventually lead to self-destruction. My personal view is that we have created laws that don't work and have placed many people in prison who don't belong there. We fight wars because of differences when we should embrace differences rather than condemn them. We have created systems where a few flourish and where the masses struggle to survive.

What I have learned in my journey may not be the same thing you will learn in yours. Once you understand the miraculous workings of nature, the systems that exist, the beauty that emerges from the earth and the bond that man has with plants, your perspective on life will change. Once you learn to live with the forces of nature rather than living to control them, you will live in harmony. You will reap the benefits the earth can supply. I am convinced there is more in life that we don't know than what we do know. There is a simple path that has been laid out for us to follow – all we need to do is find it. We need to live it and walk it to understand it.

I have written my 12 Steps to help you become a natural gardener. It will do more than teach you about gardening. It will provide you with a path that will open your eyes to many things, as it has mine. Take the step, sow the seed and reap the benefits you will harvest as you flourish in harmony with a greater force.

I am a horticulturist who has spent his whole life with plants, most of it trying to propagate and grow a superior crop. As a result, I have become an advisor to many homeowners trying to do the same. For most of my life I followed the chemical approach that my agricultural university taught me. In my journey, I learned there was another way, a better way. I wasted too much time with recommendations that were not good for our earth and our health. My guilt has motivated me to set the record straight. I have a driving desire to write what I believe will make a difference. Each day I follow the organic approach and as new revelations occur to me, I am utterly amazed at how differently I now see things.

EMBRACING DIFFERENCES

My life is built on serving the horticultural world. I marvel at how beautiful gardens are filled with a great mixture of plants and how each one plays an important role in the overall design of nature. From the majestic oak, which grew from a little acorn, to the miniature crocus whose early bloom inspires us with feelings of spring, what makes gardens beautiful are the differences that exist and the blending of these differences into a harmonious landscape.

Things keep changing in the garden and it is filled with excitement. I am amazed at how important a part each plant plays in developing the beauty, harmonizing the diversity and maintaining interest … it has taught me that differences are important and the greater the mix the greater the success. If we all learn to appreciate differences, life will become easier. We will appreciate the role each of us plays.

I have also carried this philosophy of mixing when I condition my soil. I believe the greater the mix of organic material you put into your soil the greater the results. You will find that all of my formulas for conditioning soil embrace this concept. Those using my recipes have come back and raved at the results. Here again, the differences make the difference.

FEELING AT PEACE

When I am surrounded by the beauty of plants and bond with them, I am at peace. I feel no anger and am happy to be alive. I feel there is hope and that life can be beautiful. I feel the sun, breathe the fresh air, see the flowers that fill me with their inspiration and feel the warmth of a garden–a garden I have created and which gives me great satisfaction, a garden that I have worked with nature to sustain. I am thankful that from the earth emerges beauty. My father was happiest when he watered the plants in his greenhouses. He would sing each morning to his plants. I think the plants liked that since he grew great crops.

EATING HEALTHY FOOD

The earth supplies us with food. There is a relationship with the microbial activity in the soil, the roots of the plants and the nutrients the roots are able to extract from the ground. If we condition our soil with a mixture of organic amendments, a plant will be able to fill all of its nutrient needs. This is the secret to growing great plants.

At the Nursery we developed an exceptional organic planting mix that draws people from great distances to buy. We follow up by growing our plants using an organic program. The same principle of developing an exceptional mix is important in growing nutritious food. Force feeding a plant with chemical fertilizers will not give us the nutritional value that we need. There is more to fertilizer than NPK and there is more to nutrition than these three elements. An organic approach provides us not only with toxic-free food but it also supplies us with greater nutrition. Supply a plant with all its needs and it will be strong, healthy and nutritious. Supply the human body with nutritious food and it will become strong and healthy.

VALUING THE EARTH WE LIVE ON

It is difficult to understand what takes place in the soil. The drama within an organic soil is fascinating to study. Healthy soil is productive–teeming with life. When we kill this life by overusing chemical fertilizers, pesticides, herbicides or fungicides, we end up with dead soils. In the process, we not only kill our soils but we contaminate our waterways.

Plant life struggles to grow and often ends up dying. Plants need carbon to survive, which is why we add organic matter. A great deal of contamination has taken place both by homeowners and industries. We need to protect the microbial activity within our soils and help nature sustain it. We can play a vital role in maintaining healthy soil.

CONTAMINATING SOILS

Many large manufacturers have contributed to large-scale contamination. We have also contributed to the contamination of soils in our quest for a beautiful lawn. By responding to chemical ads on how to grow a beautiful lawn, we have poisoned our soils and killed the microbes. However, contaminated soils CAN be cleaned up. The solution to the problem of contamination is to build up the microbial activity by following an organic approach to developing a beautiful lawn. Microbes will rid your soils of toxins by digesting them and making them available for plant use. Microbes are the silent workers that labor for us day and night. We need to protect them and nourish them. They are the key to developing healthy and productive soils.

HEALING PLANTS

Medicinal and healing plants are almost too numerous to count. My two favorites are Aloe vera and Wheatgrass. It is incredible what they can do for you, and there are healing stories of the benefits they have provided for thousands of people. These are just two of many plants with medicinal powers. There needs to be more time and research put into exploring natural cures.

I have been known to advocate the benefits of plants to my friends. I tell them everything can be remedied by going for a run each day, eating Aloe vera and Wheatgrass. They laugh at me and my enthusiasm, but when they get into trouble they often find that I am right. In my chapter Focus on Prevention Rather than Cure, you'll read a number of stories on the healing capabilities of Aloe vera and Wheatgrass. Remember, these are just two plants of many that have great healing powers to read up on and explore. Many of us spend our lives surrounded with prescription drugs. I come from a family where my mother, father, sister, wife and children have stayed away from them and have stuck to a natural approach. I feel that we've enjoyed better health than many of our friends who have not tried this approach.

MAKING TOO MANY LAWS

Many of us have not been kind to each other. We have created a hurtful environment. Retaliation to this hurt has caused an excessive number of laws. Our jails are filled with more people than most other countries. Often, people who love plants are loving people. If we lived in a society of loving people and kind people, we would not need as many laws. Loving people know how to nourish and care. They have learned that the more they give, the more they get in return. Nature teaches a path of hard work resulting in great rewards.

I know a gardener in Scarsdale, New York, who does all of his own yard work. He has the most beautiful front yard in his neighborhood. People walk by, stop and admire and then come back to take pictures. He has brought happiness to lots of people, and by recognizing his accomplishments they have brought him happiness in return. He has bonded with nature and has achieved amazing results. He constantly finds new methods and better ways to improve his garden. His mind is constantly working. Many of us have extra help to do these chores and miss out on this important bond with nature.

Westchester County and then New York State passed a 0 phosphate law for turf. I fought the law hard but lost the fight. Phosphates are a problem in our waters but phosphates entering the streams come from many sources. Blaming all lawn fertilizers containing phosphates for this problem is wrong. Lawns are beneficial in and of themselves as they are a good ground cover that prevents erosion. Erosion is a big problem in phosphate contamination.

I agree that chemical lawn fertilizers have soluble phosphates that can wash into our streams and soluble nitrates that can leach into our waterways. Organic fertilizers have neither of these things and using them rather than chemical fertilizers eliminates the problem of water pollution. Chemical companies can take the phosphates out by simply changing their formula. Organic fertilizers all have phosphates in them since all organic matter contains phosphates. Organic fertilizers are the solution not the problem.

I remember the day the county legislators had all the big wigs from New York State come in to meet with the full board. They talked eloquently about phosphates being a big problem in our water, a fact none of us challenged. It took a long time for them to speak and when they finished, a portion of the board left. The chemical people next presented their arguments and more people left. By the time the organic people presented their case there was no one on the board left, only the chair and vice chair.

At a later date the legislators passed the 0 phosphate law, which favors the powerful chemical companies. The law bans all phosphates from lawn fertilizers. They did not understand natural gardening. The board did not do what was right for our soils. Rather, they played to their constituents. This is a perfect example of how we make laws that can be detrimental instead of beneficial. In my mind, education is more important in solving problems than creating new laws. The laws we need to learn and follow are laid out by nature and have persisted for centuries.

PHILOSOPHICAL DIFFERENCE

I have listed some of the things that I have learned that have shaped my way of thinking. I now look at things differently because I am in tune with nature and feel I understand things better. I know there is more to learn. I have just begun to unravel nature's messages. She teaches us many things. Listen, observe and respond. I believe if our minds are set in the right direction we will make proper decisions. It is a philosophical approach that will mold our way of life.

In summation, I hope I can get you to involve yourself in gardening, do it the natural way and reap the benefits. Follow the 12 STEPS TO NATURAL GARDENING. The rest will take care of itself. Nature will become the teacher. You will not only enjoy a beautiful garden and be able to bond with nature, but you will also live a fuller life.

My programs list a lot of products. I do not recommend any one brand because I strongly believe the greater the mix, the greater the results. Since this is a book about my personal experiences and conclusions, I am listing the products I have used successfully. Organic products for the garden are usually local in nature and product names and labeling will vary in different parts of the country. If you follow my outline and logic, you can substitute and write your own program. Timing is sequential and based on the New York Metropolitan area. Spread the sequence out in a longer growing season and condense it in a shorter one in order to meet your personal needs.

NOTES & OBSERVATIONS

.....F. A. YOUNG LIVED ACROSS THE STREET FROM THE NURSERY

When we first moved to Scarsdale, New York, across the road lived Frank A. Young, already in his nineties. He farmed a small plot of land and called it Happy Valley. Mr. Young, as was the proper name for us children to call him, had originally lived farther up Underhill Road. His house burned down to the ground in a huge fire that lit up the whole valley. He rebuilt down the road directly across from what is now Sprainbrook Nursery. He never drove a car but he did drive a horse and buggy. He built a small house, drew his water from a well fed by a brook, built an outhouse and had a potbellied stove to keep himself warm in the winter. He fed the potbellied stove with wood collected in the surrounding woods.

When we knew him, he no longer had any horses or other animals. He spent his whole day on his hands and knees farming and weeding his crops. He farmed long before the time of chemical fertilizers and grew all of his crops with organic products because that was the way things were done in those days. He collected cow manure from local farmers and composted all of his weeds and leftover plants. He ground up leaves and mixed them into his compost pile. He collected his own seeds.

Mr. Young walked with a cane and we, as children, would bring in buckets of water for him. He would give us each a gingersnap cookie and tell us interesting stories of how things were done in the old days to take back to our parents. He told us how construction crews built the aqueduct that carries water to New York City and how they had to change Underhill Road, which was a very steep drop, to an S curve. He told us that where all the new houses and the country club are was once farmland. He told us where the Indians once lived and where Rochambeau built his swimming pool. When you farm land, stories about the land get handed down.

Mr. Young's son came once a month from Connecticut to stock him up with supplies. In his old age, Mr. Young barely made enough to live on. Old customers were old friends to him and he would give half of his produce to them. My mother was always upset with these so-called friends. How could they come and take advantage of an old, kind man who had barely enough money to live on. Once a week my mother would cook and send him a warm meal. Farming is a way of life and working with nature made him a very humble and happy man. Each day he battled the weeds on his hands and knees and grew beautiful produce. I remember the pride he took in his raspberry patch. He always wanted to give us baskets of raspberries. My mother would scold him and say, "You need to sell them not give them away." It was an innocent time. Marketing was not important, but growing a good tasty crop and having people visit him was.

There came a sad day for Mr. Young when his son decided his father could no longer live on his own. His son insisted that his father move in with him. Mr. Young refused and said "This is my way of life and it is in my fields among my crops where I belong, this is the only thing I know and it will keep me going." Mr. Young begged my parents to not let his son take him away. One day his son came with a moving van and forced him to pack up. Mr. Young never got to say goodbye as they hustled him along with his modest belongings into a rented van. He never came back and we never heard from him again. We never knew where in Connecticut his son lived. We did hear that Mr. Young lived for three more months. He was a healthy but aging old man when he left and a broken-hearted idle man when he died. My mother said he died of a broken heart. The property was sold by his son to two sisters. They remodeled the house, putting in a bathroom, running water and a gas boiler for central heat. They built a two-car garage with a room above it that they rented out. The place where vegetables and berries grew became lawn and Happy Valley was no more.

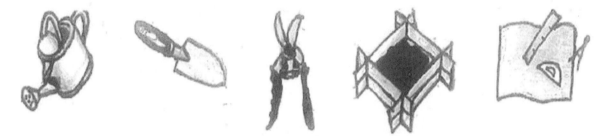

ADD YOUR GARDEN STORY HERE

2. PLANNING (STEP 1)

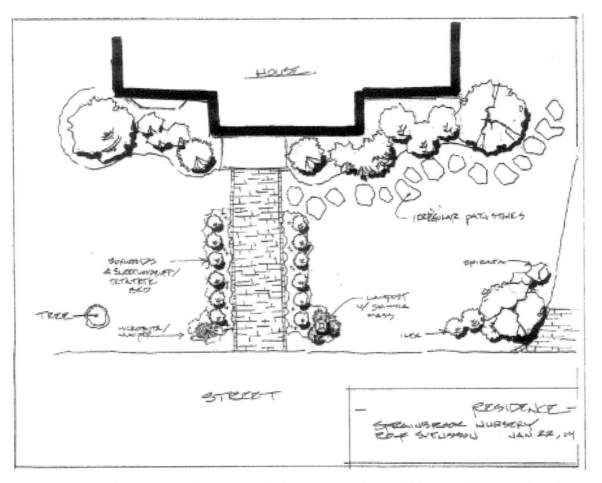

We need to be kind to our earth and work in cooperation with nature in our planning stage. Once we make this decision to side with nature our philosophical point of view will change, bringing with it a greater appreciation of soil, plants and the relationship that we all have with each other. Everything is connected and interdependent, we all have a role to play and a duty to do our part and work with nature, not against her.

Initial planning does not have to be in detail, but general locations and concepts need to be identified. Start by making a master plan of your property that utilizes your land to its fullest. We have desires and needs. When our children are small, we need a grassy area for recreational play. When privacy is desired, we need plants that will provide a screen. To enjoy healthy fresh produce, vegetable gardens need to be planted and located in a sunny area. Beautify your property by developing the front, back and side yards.

Close your eyes and dream of those things you want to be part of your garden and your outdoor living experience. List your needs, wishes and desires. Once this list is completed, discuss it with your family. The family that gardens together stays together. It is important that each member has a chance to be part of this process. If all are on board,

11

the end result will have greater meaning for everyone. Mother Nature will teach us lessons in life that will help us cope in tough times and inspire us in good times. People who learn to love plants develop into loving people.

BASIC LANDSCAPE GOALS

* Curb appeal
* Screening for privacy
* Recreation and entertaining
* Beautification (front yard, back yard, side yards)
* Shade
* Growing vegetables and herbs
* Ground covers
* Cut flowers for the house
* Attracting butterflies, birds and other wildlife
* Low maintenance
* Family bonding

Whatever your goal, each area of the master plan requires its own planning – whether you want to design a terrace, a vegetable garden or other areas around your home. You'll find that different considerations are required for different situations. Curb appeal tells your neighbors and passersby something about you. It's the introduction to your home before anyone steps foot inside. Screening choices are critical to maintain privacy. An organic lawn is important for the health of your children and your pets, and provides a lush carpet for recreation and entertaining. You can increase your children's interest in nature by including shrubs and plants that attract insects and birds.

There are a number of microclimates to be discovered on your property, each with its own requirement for water and some requiring soil correction to grow healthy plants. A beating, hot sun calls for shade trees; bare ground that is susceptible to erosion requires a good ground cover. Destructive insects can be controlled by beneficial insects, such as ladybugs, praying mantis and nematodes—a safe, low-maintenance option to chemicals.

Good drainage is essential in the planning of a garden. Managing your water requires good planning and is essential to the success of your garden. Most plants cannot tolerate wet soils. Develop large grass areas with gentle slopes away from planting areas to avoid washouts. In areas that are naturally wet, the building of a berm is an excellent solution to support good plant growth. Dig holes in your ground 12–24 in. deep to see where your water table is. The building of a landscape berm consists of bringing in rocks and soil so that the good soil for planting is above the wet area, giving plants a well-drained soil to thrive in. A berm can have great aesthetic value as well as functional value. It can create a sound barrier from a noisy road and it can create a great deal of interest and added planting area to a back yard. There is a lot more planting space on a slope than on a flat area.

Planting is an important aspect of gardening. What you plant and how you arrange plants will be your act of creation. The beauty, the interest you create, the magnificence of the look, the extent of the screening, the detail of the design, the layout of your back yard and your foundation design depend on the plants you select. Planting is the most important decision you make in shaping your garden, proper planting and choosing the right plant for the right location are the best ways to ensure that your plants will survive.

Following a thoughtful planting program is important. New plants put new life into your garden. Areas that are dull will be brightened up with new energy. Ugly sights can be screened by placing the proper plants in the foreground. Plant your annuals in the spring to keep your property colorful and cheerful; in the fall add chrysanthemums, ornamental cabbage, kale and fall blooming perennials. Plant your Dutch bulbs for early spring color. Plan your vegetable garden on a yearly basis to supply nutritious foods. Plant ground covers in bare areas and add perennial gardens that will inspire you with their sequence of color.

A good gardener is constantly thinking about adding something new to the garden. That inspiration comes from spending time in the garden. Newly chosen plants become part of your collection—that diverse group of varieties and species that many gardeners consider their friends. Trees will provide shade and shelter, Evergreens will provide privacy. They will house nature's creatures. The birds will serenade you each morning, nestled in shrubs that attract them. The vegetable garden will provide you with healthy organic food and the herb garden will surprise you with many uses. These things all take place when you plan and plant your garden. A diverse collection of plants will attract a large number of beneficial insects. Thoughtful planning is what gives your garden the structure it needs to grow and the mixture it needs to survive.

When you plant, do your research to place the right plant in the right location. The plants you buy need to serve a purpose. An overall design of your property is essential since it will help you to organize your thoughts and develop priorities. If you choose to bring in a landscape designer, work out your goals for the property first. Then convey your and your family's needs and desires for particular areas. A designer needs a lot of input to come up with the right list of plants for your property, so sketch out your rough ideas first.

The initial step in planning is not to over-plan but to HAVE a plan. Take it one step at a time. Then plan each step in detail as it comes up. Your plan will be the first step to Natural Gardening. Once on this path, you will bond with Mother Nature.

The beauty of gardening is that the master plan is a work in progress, and each year there is something you can do to add or to make it better. A garden is not carved in stone and changes can be made as you go along.

MY GARDEN STORY

.....RELATIVES COME FROM GERMANY TO HELP OUT

In the early days of Sprainbrook Nursery, my parents, Hermine and Alfred, did everything on their own. As the business began to grow, they hired extra help. Relatives came to help out in the busy season. My mother's sister, Hattie, would come in the spring to help out with the planting and my Uncle Johnny would come on weekends to join her. Their son, my cousin Al, joined the staff after graduating from high school. He bunked with me for my last school year. I never had a brother and it was cool having him. He played ball with me and my friends and everyone loved cousin Al. This left three guys by the name of Alfred in the house. When my mother called, "Alfred, take out the garbage," we all looked at each other but when she called, "Alfred, I have a piece of lemon meringue pie for you," we all came running.

Through the years my parents sponsored relatives from Germany to work for us. After the war, many wanted to come to America. We were able to get green cards for them. Inge, my cousin, came to this country from my mother's hometown, Battenberg. She grew up in the same house that my mother did. Inge was an incredible worker who worked for us for a long time and became very close to my mother. It was a sad day when she left to go back home.

At that time our staff was made up of European workers and we called ourselves the European Garden Center. Through the years there was lots of hard work but also lots of fun and interesting moments to enjoy with our fellow workers. We lived a simple but pleasant life. We would laugh for weeks about certain mundane things that happened. One story that I still tell was about Inte—a worker who came from the former Czechoslovakia. He spoke very little English. When a customer said he was looking for Peat Moss, Inte said, "I am sorry there is no Pete here." The customer then asked him "What about Leaf Mold?" Inte said, "I am sorry Leif does not work here either." We lost the sale but were filled with laughter for the rest of the week.

The Nursery was strong in organic beliefs from its inception. It was the short course that my father took at Cornell that pushed us toward a chemical approach—the cutting edge of the industry. It had us spraying toxic materials on a weekly basis and using chemical fertilizers to accelerate growth. Chemical fertilizers are not kind to microbes and cause plants to become weakened and susceptible to insects and disease. We were blind to these facts and followed the recommendations of the leading agricultural colleges at the time. We were told these were the programs we had to follow if we wanted to grow good crops. Chemical fertilization coupled with specific spray programs for each crop is still the approach followed to grow most of America's crops. Little did I know at the time that I would be on a crusade to make the change to a natural approach.

ADD YOUR GARDEN STORY HERE

3. PLANTING (STEP 2)

Planting is the act of installing seeds or plants into the ground. Planting is the most important step that we take in developing our property. We plant a beautiful perennial garden, a vegetable garden, a herb garden, a rose garden. We plant a hedge for screening, a foundation planting for curb appeal, a back yard for our own enjoyment, a ground cover to prevent erosion. We plant grass seed to have a lawn area to play on. We place an extra plant here and there to fill a void or to add color. Gardens just don't happen they are planted.

Plants need to be selected, bought, divided, propagated or seeded and this must be done properly if your plants are going to have a chance to survive. We need to plant the right plant in the right location, properly prepare the soil and plant at the right depth. Some people believe in planting by the cycles of the moon—an art followed by many farmers in ancient times. There has been renewed interest in this approach among many organic gardeners. For more information, read "Guided by the Moon" by Johanna Paungger and Thomas Poppe.

Timing is important. Tender annuals need to be planted after the danger of frost is gone; cool-weather crops can be planted earlier than warm-weather crops. Spring and fall are better times to plant than in the heat of summer. Containerized plants allow us to plant year round but watering is critical when planting in the summer.

There are many options as to what you can plant. I am a strong believer in developing as large a mixture of plants as possible. A large mix will attract a greater population of beneficial insects, attract birds, bees and butterflies. The larger the mix, the better the results. Each plant serves a unique function in your garden.

Developing a beautiful garden requires constant tweaking. Though perfection is rarely achieved, it is something we continuously strive toward. Plants sometimes need to be removed or exchanged. Carefully considered planting is the key to a beautiful garden.

You can buy your plants or propagate them. The three most common methods of propagation are seeding, cuttings and division. Each is described below.

SEEDING

As long as you do not apply herbicides, seeding from existing plants, often takes place naturally in many perennial gardens. Most often you will want to remove seedlings so they don't overrun your garden, but you may also want to plant them in a different section. Seeds can be purchased or gathered. They can be started indoors or outdoors.

When starting seeds indoors, use a plug tray with organic soil. Mist seeds daily and cover with a sheet of plastic to hold moisture in. Try to provide bottom heat. Follow the packet's instructions or look up seed germination requirements. Once the seed has germinated, remove the sheet of plastic and give the plants as much light as possible. Light is a growth inhibitor, making seedlings strong but preventing them from becoming leggy and weak. Transplant seedlings that are crowded into larger containers once they have reached the two-leaf stage.

REQUIREMENTS FOR SEEDING

* Good bottom heat using a heating mat, heating cable and/or radiator
* Plug trays
* Organic soil or a sterile peat-like mix
* Specific requirements on the seed packet
* A method to keep seed moist until germination
* A sunny location
* Transplant when plants become crowded and have reached two-leaf stage

HERBACEOUS CUTTINGS

Cuttings will reproduce the plants that they are taken from. Most of my propagation is done through the use of herbaceous stem cuttings. A herbaceous plant is a plant that has leaves and stems that die at the end of the growing season. I use plug trays of appropriate size to fit the cuttings and fill the tray with organic soil. Using a sharp horticultural knife, I make a clean cut at an angle just below where a leaf intersects with a stem and remove the lower leaf. I dip the cutting into a rooting hormone and stick the cutting into the soil, making sure it is not placed too deeply.

The leaf surface needs to be kept constantly moist by misting two to three times a day, and the moisture needs to be contained within an enclosure. Although you can buy special trays for this purpose, you can easily build your own mini greenhouse by creating a plastic enclosure using a sheet of clear plastic and bent coat hangers as a support. You can also create this effect by covering the cutting with newspaper. In the greenhouse, we use a bottom-heat system and a mist system that goes on every 5 minutes for 15 seconds. Once the cuttings are rooted, they should be transplanted into a larger 3- or 4-in. plastic or peat pot.

REQUIREMENTS FOR HERBACEOUS CUTTINGS
* Good bottom heat using a heating mat, heating cable and/or radiator
* Plug trays
* Organic soil or sterile peat-like mix
* A sharp horticultural knife
* A rooting hormone to be applied
* A method to keep moisture on the leaf
* Good filtered light for photosynthesis

METHODS OF PROPAGATION
The four most commonly used methods of propagation are:

* Stem cutting
* Leaf petiole cutting
* Leaf cutting
* Root cutting

DIVISION OF PERENNIALS
A method commonly used to divide perennials is to use a spade with a clean, flat blade to cut down the middle of the root ball, dividing it into two. Leave one portion in place and replant the other section elsewhere. You may want to find a fellow gardener and swap varieties.

OTHER METHODS OF PROPAGATION
* Layering: Layering is a way to get stems to root while they are still attached to the plant.
* Grafting: Grafting is a more advanced method joining a stem piece to a root system.
* Budding: This is a grafting technique using only a single bud from a plant.
* Spores: Spores are the reproductive structures of ferns and mosses and should be sown on a sterile medium and covered to maintain humidity.

PREPARATION OF THE SOIL

It is important that we follow an organic approach to set up the conditions for developing and maintaining a strong food web. Microbes thrive on carbon found in organic products. The preparation of our soils should include at least 1/3 organic matter. The greater the mix of organic amendments, the greater the beneficial results. A mixture of organic amendments, fertilizers and microbes will revitalize our soils and lead to amazing results.

Ever since I switched my greenhouse operation to an organic and natural approach to growing, my quality increased. Our country has ruined many of our soils through the overuse of chemical fertilizers. The heavily advertised liquid chemical fertilizers, which will increase flower blooms, are high in soluble nitrates and phosphates and are not kind to the microbial life that exists in our soils. When planting a new plant, we are particularly concerned with mycorrhizal microbes, which form a symbiotic relationship with the roots of the plants. These fungi help extract nutrients and water from the soil and make it available to plants. They invite the root for a meal and the root system of the plant develops faster and with greater density. Therefore, by using mycorrhizal microbes, transplant failure is greatly reduced and the plant develops a deep root system that can withstand drought and stress.

Microbes in the soil consist of bacteria, fungi, protozoa and mycorrhizal fungi. They, along with nematodes, earthworms and other microorganisms, are all part of the food web. Chemical fertilizers, insecticides, fungicides, herbicides and air pollution all negatively affect our food web. We can grow healthier plants and eliminate these toxic products from our soils if we work to develop and preserve an organic system. Once life is brought back into our soils, the food web will do the work.

PLANTING TREES

When planting a tree or shrub, a hole is dug three times the size of the root ball. Add to existing soil a blended organic fertilizer such as Plant-tone and Myke Tree and Shrub, a product fortified with microbes. Blend the mixture at the bottom of the hole. Fill this mixture to a height where the top of the tree root will sit level with the ground. Backfill this blend around the plant. Bring it up to within 1 in. of the ground level and fill the top inch with compost. Mix into the soil Lobster Compost used for alkaline-loving plants and Penobscot Blend used for acid-loving plants. Add a 2 in. layer of mulch to the planting bed. Make sure there is a mulched bed between your plants and your grass.

Trees are planted either bare-root, balled-and-burlapped or grown in a container. Each of these requires a different approach of handling at planting time.

DEPTH OF PLANTING

Always use proper depth when planting any plant. Proper depth is defined as planting soil level to soil level and never too deeply. In other words, the top of the root ball of any plant should always be even with the existing soil level. Many trees and shrubs die a slow death because they are sunk too deeply into the ground. The trunks of trees and shrubs are meant to be exposed and not smothered with soil. When contractors come in and pile soil around an existing tree, it dies. The trunks of trees and shrubs need air around them, not soil.

If the area you are planting in is wet, plant high and bring in soil to cover the root ball. It is always safer to plant slightly higher and counter that by mulching heavily. When planting large trees with heavy root balls, measure the height of the ball and dig the hole so that the tree will be placed at the proper depth when lowered into the ground. The soil at the base of the hole should be conditioned and tightly tamped so that the height of the ball equals the depth of it. For example, if you want to plant a large-size shade tree, you must first dig a large hole and then you can place a board across the opening of the hole to get the proper measurements. This is important because you want to get it right the first time, so you don't ruin the tree by yanking it up to replant because it was set too deep.

Ericaceous plants, which are broadleaf evergreens that thrive in acid soil, are particularly sensitive to deep planting and require a lot of oxygen in the soil. A common mistake is digging these plants in too deeply. It is important to plant at the proper depth; however, for every rule there are exceptions and some plants such as tomatoes, ornamental cabbage and kale and certain other herbaceous plants thrive when planted deeply. If in doubt plant soil level to soil level and you will never make a mistake.

BARE ROOT

These are planted only in the dormant state. Once unpacked, the roots must be kept moist until planting time. Keeping the roots submerged in a bucket of water prior to planting time is ideal. If you can't accomplish your planting in one day, heel plants into soil or cover with mulch and water well. Leaving them in water for too long a time can rot the roots.

BALLED-AND-BURLAPPED PLANTS

These shrubs and trees can be held for long periods of time before planting, as long as the ball is kept well watered. Several precautions need to be taken when planting. Rope that is tied around the trunk needs to be removed once the plant is set into position, as rope can girdle the trunk and kill the plant as it grows. The burlap should be peeled back below soil level, and wire cages need to be cut away from the trunk and below soil level. Keep burlap and wire cages in place when planting so as not to disturb the root ball.

CONTAINER-GROWN PLANTS

Remove the container carefully or cut the container if necessary. A well-grown shrub or tree usually becomes root-bound. Slice the roots that have circled the plant with a knife and make sure when planting to keep the top of the soil in your container level with your existing soil.

STAKING

Some trees will need staking until the root system becomes strong enough to prevent the plant from blowing over. Stake outside the root area using single stakes for small trees, two stakes for medium trees and triple stakes for very large trees.

I would prefer not staking trees if possible. Trees develop strong root systems by swaying in the wind. This movement sends signals down to the roots which then develop a deeper more massive root system to anchor the tree. Restricting this movement slows root growth. If you were to examine a tree on the side of a windy mountain, it is so firmly anchored it rarely blows down.

THE ORGANIC INSTALLATION PROGRAM

Mine is an organic approach to planting. I use a mixture of organic fertilizers, organic soil and top dress with compost. When the planting is finished, a 2 in. layer of mulch is applied to the surface. The success of this approach is in building the microbial activity in the soil. I build a diverse mixture. I use a blended organic soil, which is a mixture of compost, leaf mold, decayed wood chips and native topsoil.

EVERGREENS AND SHRUBS

Most evergreens and shrubs are now being grown in containers because they can be planted anytime the ground is workable. Proper soil preparation and depth of planting are essential. See chapter 23 on "Trees, Evergreens and Shrubs" for information on maintenance. Vegetable gardens, perennial beds, ground cover areas, annual beds and other bed areas are best dealt with by preparing the whole bed for planting. This initial preparation of the soil should follow my formula for the "Preparation of a New Planting Bed." This fortifies the soil with the organic products that will set up the conditions for the food web to thrive. Once the food web is established, you will want to avoid turning over the soil and will supply nutrients through top dressing, organic fertilizer applications and mulching.

PERENNIALS

When planting perennials, I prepare the whole area before planting. Follow the directions in "Preparation of a Planting Bed." Once the ground is prepared you can arrange your plants and just dig them in. Make sure nothing is planted too deeply. Top dress with a 2 in. layer of mulch. Adding a highly nutritive mulch such as Sweet Peet, Fundy Blend or Dark Harbor Blend can be advantageous.

Follow my formula in "Preparation of a New Planting Bed." This formula transforms the worst possible soil to the best possible soil and builds sustainable gardens.

PREPARATION OF A NEW PLANTING BED

MY FORMULA FOR THE PREPARATION OF A NEW PLANTING BED
Per 100 sq. ft. of area, dig and mix one ft. deep:

* 1 bale Peat Moss (3.8 cu. ft.)
* 1 Coir block
* 2 bags Lobster Compost (40 lb. bags)
* 2 bags Penobscot Blend (40 lb. bags)
* 2 bags Cow manure (20 lb. dehydrated)
* 2 bags Fafard Peat Humus (40lb. bags)
* 1 lb. Mineral rock dust
* 5 lbs. Lime
* 5 lbs. Bone Meal
* 4 lbs. Bio-tone Starter Plus (Organica)
* 5 lbs. Plant-tone (Espoma)

VEGETABLE GARDENS
A similar formula in Chapter 18 VEGTABLE GARDEN, should be followed for the initial preparation of the vegetable garden. Raised beds and fencing are additional considerations when developing an area for your veggies.

In conclusion, plant perennials that add to the beauty of the garden. Plant something new each year. Plant annuals for interesting floral areas. Plant vegetables for home consumption. Plant trees and shrubs to beautify your property and create interest. Planting will help beautify your grounds and develop a diversity of plants to enjoy. Planting is what makes it all happen.

NOTES & OBSERVATIONS

MY GARDEN STORY

.....MY CLASSMATES LEARNED HOW TO CHAIN

Being brought up as a boy in the nursery industry was not always easy. There was a family obligation to help out in the business and, since I was very athletic, there was the obligation to be there for my school team. Our school was small with a grade size of 50 students, but out of the 50 only 20 were boys. This meant that when we tried to field a team, everyone was needed. We happened to have a very athletic class. Every spare moment we had we would spend on the outdoor basketball court. Lunch breaks, recess or after school, we couldn't wait to get on the court.

My family had to work very hard in the early years to get all the work done. They relied on us kids to help with the chores. In the summer this was not a problem—I worked full time as I did during vacation breaks. But during the school year I had my sports and they were very important to me.

One time I had a problem that occurred when we had an unexpected prediction of a heavy freeze on an upcoming Saturday night. My parents had 5,000 non-hardy azaleas that had to be brought in or we would lose the whole crop. "Losing the whole crop would bankrupt us," my mother said, "and we need you to stay home this Saturday and help."

I told my teammates that I would not be able to make the Saturday game. My close friend Kent, a future Rhodes Scholar, said the team would help so I could play the game. He calculated that, allowing for inexperience, we would need to bring in six people to work four hours in the morning. This allowed us some slack if his calculations proved to be wrong. The whole team arrived at eight in the morning.

The method that we use to move plants into or within our greenhouses is called "chaining." An effective chain requires constant walking and no slacking. You walk toward the person in front of you, take the flat away from him, do an about-face and carry the flat to the next person who is walking to meet you. It is similar to the old bucket brigade. This sequence of exchanges takes place until all the plants reach their destinations.

On this particular day, my father and Big John our key worker were at the starting end, lifting the azaleas and placing three in a flat (a shallow box). At the end of this line were two employees who set the plants out onto ground benches. If a chain is working properly, there are no time delays. I knew I had to be in the chain to make sure it kept moving. There were seven teammates in addition to the nursery workers. It is always important to set up the right numbers and keep the chain moving, so when I found a teammate slacking off or walking too slow I would get him to speed up. Walking four hours without a break is a marathon effort; however, we were all very competitive and wanted to make the noon deadline we had set. Miraculously, we got the job done in time. Mother was holding down the fort at the Nursery and taking care of the customers. She switched with Dad and went up to make a big lunch for us. I think she treated us that day to Montauk sandwiches (made of toasted cheese, tomato and bacon on a toasted English muffin) with her famous apple strudel for dessert.

The guys were moaning and groaning about how tired they were and didn't know how they could play ball in the afternoon, but they were very proud of their accomplishment. Whenever I see my friends at a reunion or a visit, they talk about this incident. "I never worked so hard in my life," they would say. They remembered the chain but not that we also won the game. Mother Nature is a tough old lady. Things come up and you are forced to work hard to correct the situation. But when you work hard and overcome adversity, you have been taught a lesson that will stick with you for the rest of your life.

More homeowners should learn the value of a chain. It comes in handy when you need to move products around or within the house. When you get those 40 bags of mulch dropped off as a driveway delivery, get the family together and make a chain. In no time each bag will be where you want it.

Chaining was an important confidence builder for us all. We were sports enthusiasts growing up in Edgemont, New York, in the late forties and we had to win. Life was a game in those days and we gave everything our best shot. We spent a lot of time on the basketball court and being a small school, this was our main sport. We lacked great coaching as the two gym teachers, a man and a woman, coached all sports. Edgemont school went up to the 10th grade in those days and for the last two years we went on to Scarsdale High.

Archie Oldham lived in Edgemont and in college he was part of St. John's famous basketball team with the McGuire brothers. When Archie was working on Wall Street he wanted to get into coaching. He asked if he could coach our 10th grade team. Edgemont was delighted to have him. He saw us play and thought we had potential. To get his foot into coaching he needed to coach a team with an outstanding record. He started practice early in the season and worked on our skills and weaknesses. He taught the defense to be always on the inside, push back with hands up to get the rebound. We had a great rebounding team, got tough and usually got possession of the ball. We developed a fast break with our guards sprinting for the basket as soon as we had possession. We were able to work the ball down and played the corners.

Archie developed forwards with a great shot from the right side and another forward who had a great shot from the left side. The guards would move the ball around quickly, trying to work it into the corner. If the opposition would come out to block the shot, it was passed to the center who, if free, would take the shot, but, if not, would pass off to one of the guards cutting through. The two guards were also excellent outside shooters.

We were a threat from anyplace on the court. To toughen us up, Archie would run scrimmages in preseason twice a week, either in the south Bronx or in Harlem. Our team complained about how rough these guys played. We went undefeated that season and most teams didn't even come close. Archie knew we were going to move up to Scarsdale High the following year. We were outsiders and would have to fight our way into the lineup to make the team. He set up a game against their 10th grade team. It was our big chance to show them what we were made of. We were up for the game big time and badly wanted the win. We beat them 85 to 42. We were ecstatic. When we got to Scarsdale High we all tried out for the team.

In our senior year only two players made the cut and were allowed to play for Scarsdale High. They were not in the starting lineup and ended up leaving the Scarsdale High School team to play basketball with the rest of us as a group in an intramural league. We went undefeated even though we lost Bill Agee, our big center, who went on to a private school at Andover. We won the opportunity to go on to the County Center to play sudden death in the playoffs. Here we were battling rivals for the Westchester County Championships. We rallied and again went undefeated, battling it out for weeks and becoming the Champions.

Meanwhile, our success was creating a lot of controversy at Scarsdale High School. Edgemont writers on "The Maroon," which was the Scarsdale High student newspaper, were writing articles about how Edgemont got shafted and challenged Scarsdale High to a playoff game. The coach, whose coaching career followed the path of the group of boys now playing varsity, refused to be a part of it. We continued to apply pressure. Without the coach's consent, but with the school's consent, we were able to set up a game, which packed the Scarsdale gym. We were playing the great Scarsdale team with an impressive season of wins. We had to once again prove ourselves. It was a tough game with a lot at stake on both sides. We won in the last seconds with a great outside shot. We ended up never losing a single competitive match after Archie Oldham taught us how to play basketball. Archie went on to coach at Columbia and ended up becoming head coach. Unfortunately, his record was never as great as it was with us.

I thought back to the lesson that Mother Nature taught our team when that heavy freeze was coming. The team rallied, set a goal, did the impossible. They didn't know what they were getting themselves into but kept going anyway, accomplished the task and came out of this experience knowing nothing was impossible. We had gained confidence in ourselves and knew we could accomplish anything if we set our minds to it.

ADD YOUR GARDEN STORY HERE

4. WATERING (STEP 3)

Water is a precious commodity we must conserve as the demand for water continues to outpace supply. It is the lifeline to our very existence. It is essential to a plant's survival and to our being. Its value is greater than oil or gold. Fresh water is a product that Mother Nature provides and we often take for granted. As valuable a commodity as it is, we follow gardening practices that cause runoff, leading to erosion and pollution. We install overhead, automated sprinkling systems, which often are run in excess, squandering this valuable resource. Using water wisely and managing rainfalls are good gardening practices.

Filling our properties with plants that will transpire and recycle water sets up an eco-system that is nature friendly. It is nature's way of resupplying us with our much-needed water.

Organic gardening, the addition of mycorrhizal fungi and good soil preparation all work to develop deep root systems, which utilize moisture deep in the ground and require less frequent watering. The trick here is to water less frequently but thoroughly so that water penetrates deeply and roots develop deeply in search of it. Moving water upward from deep within the soil aids in developing a healthy rain cycle. Frequent shallow watering causes surface rooting. In the case of trees, deep root systems are necessary to provide strong anchorage so trees will not blow over in storms.

Preventing runoff water is everyone's responsibility. Water seeks the lowest level and when we allow too much of it to run off rather than to be absorbed, we cause a cumulative effect which causes damage. We make the mistake of filling our small properties with impervious surfaces—the roofs of our houses, blacktop driveways and cement walks and terraces—which lead to greater water runoff.

There are, however, steps that we can take to reduce water runoff. We can have our walks and terraces that are built with hard materials set in stone dust or sand instead of cement to allow water penetration. Driveways built with decorative blocks set on gravel and stone instead of blacktop allow water to penetrate. We can make sure our rain drains are being funneled into dry wells and rain barrels. Rain barrels can store water and supply it to our gardens on sunny dry days. We can trap water through rain gardens which are planted depressions that allow rainwater runoff from impervious surfaces to collect and be absorbed into the soil. A rain garden is located in a position on the property to stop and absorb runoff.

Ground covers and a property rich in vegetation prevent erosion and promote water penetration. Mulches are one of the best ways to trap the flow of water and allow time for water to soak into the ground.

Drainage can be a tricky problem, as you want to make sure that surface water drains away from, not into, your house. Installation of drainage pipes and dry wells may be necessary. In periods of excessive rain, you need to have swales that will lead water away from your home.

Water is the most important factor in tending your plants. Plant cells are made up largely of water, and without water plants can't grow. Virtually all physiological processes in plants take place in the presence of water. In spite of the importance of water, only a small fraction of water is absorbed from the soil and used in plant processes. Most of the water entering a plant escapes from stems and leaves as water vapor. This process is called transpiration.

Certain plants transpire more water than others and therefore require more water. However, waterlogged areas of property exclude oxygen in the soil, causing roots to die from lack of oxygen. In the end, your plants die from lack of water because there are no roots to carry the water to the cells of the plant. There are, of course, plants that flourish in aquatic conditions, just as there are some that thrive in arid conditions. These plants are exceptions. Unfortunately, most of the plants we deal with in the garden are water-stressed by moisture extremes.

As each kind of plant has its own requirements–with some needing well-drained dry soil, others needing moist soil and many requiring something inbetween–it is important to put the right plant in the right location. Research this information and ask questions before you buy a plant. Choosing local garden centers that have trained personnel to help you with this information is a good idea. If you put the right plant in the right location, it is more likely to receive the proper amount of water and will thrive for years.

It is difficult to know where the water goes when it seeps into the soil. But we do know that it may reach underground aquifers and wells, eventually working its way to streams, ponds, lakes and rivers. As gardeners, we must be careful what we put into our soil since water can carry soluble substances to unwanted places. We not only want a beautiful garden but we also want a safe environment. This can all be accomplished through good gardening practices. Since organic fertilizers break down slowly, they are readily absorbed by the plants, thereby reducing the amount of nitrates and phosphates leached into the soil.

Counties and states across the nation are passing zero phosphate laws for lawns without making a distinction between chemical fertilizers and organic fertilizers. Organic fertilizers are the good guys, while chemical fertilizers–which are water soluble–cause problems. All organic fertilizers contain phosphates, but organic phosphates get tied up in the ground and do not run off into our water system and organic nitrogen does not leach into our water systems. Zero phosphate laws that do not distinguish between organic and chemical fertilizers are poorly crafted laws that in the long run will cause more problems than they solve.

Newly planted material requires special treatment in your watering schedule. Most plants are now grown in containers. Container plants allow you to plant at any time of the year without transplant shock and they are easy to transport. They have a very confined root system, which grows in a circular fashion and should be scarred by using a knife to slice down the side of the ball before planting to encourage wider root development. Hand watering or drip irrigation at the root ball is essential for the survival and development of the plant. Overhead methods of watering often do not work in the initial watering stages because the plant can act as an umbrella, preventing the water from reaching the compact root ball developed in a container. A good root system will go deeper and wider and will be able to fend on its own in more difficult situations. The strength of a plant is its roots and to develop a good root system adequate water is necessary to all of the existing roots.

Water pouches are used when planting large trees. The pouch is filled with water and the water slowly drips into the soil. Soaker hoses are another option and can be hooked up to a hose to supply a low volume of steady water. Drip irrigation is a more permanent solution.

Watering is an art. Long days, hot days, clear days and windy days require more water than short, cool, calm, rainy and cloudy days. Judgment calls need to be made by observing and feeling the soil. Problems occur when we are not diligent in making these observations. Too much water displaces necessary oxygen from the pore spaces. Without enough oxygen, roots suffocate and die. Without roots, the plant can't absorb water or nutrients. Top growth exhibits symptoms of stress, wilting, leaf drop, die-back, shriveling and eventual death because not enough water is reaching these tissues. Too little watering causes wilting, drying out of plant parts and eventual death. What happens here is that transpiration exceeds absorption and roots dry up. The root growth is no longer able to support the top growth and if nothing is done to correct this, the plant eventually dies.

We can often save a stressed plant by reducing top growth through pruning and increasing root growth by increasing microbial activity. It is interesting to note that both overwatered plants and underwatered plants die from the same lack of water and show the same set of symptoms—which oftentimes don't show up until the plant is further stressed by summer heat. We are amazed at how a plant suddenly dies. Correct watering is the most critical task for the healthy growth of our plants.

Proper management can often bring a plant back. During the winter, top growth is dormant but roots continue to grow. By feeding them with organic products we help develop a better root system.

Types of soils affect watering practices. Heavy clay soils hold too much water and sandy soils hold too little. I have found the best practice in gardening is to properly prepare your soils, adding at least 1/3 organic matter. Topography also affects your watering practices. Steep, windy slopes require a lot more water than level, protected slopes. Even on a small piece of property there are many different watering situations that occur. Identify these areas and compensate for them accordingly. More mature plants develop a deeper root system and are more able to fend on their own. However, some plants, such as ericaceous plants, develop a shallow root system and need extra care throughout their lives. They are plants that need lots of oxygen in the soil and will not tolerate wet feet. But in dry weather they need lots of water. Even the big trees need a deep root soaking for optimal plant growth and survival during dry spells.

Container plants, hanging baskets, window boxes and raised planter beds require special attention. Seasons and days within the season require adjustments. On a hot, sunny, dry or windy day you may have to double and triple water, especially if the container size is small. Large containers will require less frequent watering than small containers and an impermeable container will need less watering than a porous container. During cool, moist weather, you may have to hold off on water. Plants that run too dry have no capillary-holding ability and water may run through them like a sieve. These plants need to be soaked before they are able to absorb water again.

There is one rule I always try to advocate and it is particularly true with container plants: You never overwater by watering too much at one time; you overwater by watering too frequently. Always fill the container up to the rim with water. Wet the full root system so that all of the roots get moisture. Allow enough oxygen back into the soil by letting the soil partially dry before you water again.

Frequent watering causes leaching, which will later require additional fertilizer. Old-time greenhouse growers would grow their poinsettia crop in clay pots. The roots of poinsettias are very sensitive to overwatering. They would tap each pot with the tip of the water wand and by the sound of the ring they would decide if the plant needed water or not. Growers will often knock out pots to see what their root system looks like. There are plant probes on the market that measure moisture in the soil—they are good tools to help you develop a watering schedule. Visual examination or sticking your finger into the soil is an old-fashioned way of making decisions of when to water. Routines must be scheduled and adhered to, then changed according to the weather, the feel of the soil, the size of the pot, the size of the plant in relation to the pot and the variety that is planted in it.

There are many tools that can help with watering tasks. I am a strong advocate that only grass and ground covers should be overhead watered and that everything else should be watered at the root zone. Overhead watering is detrimental to opened flowers and causes numerous fungus problems on leaves. Choose tools that will allow you to water the roots, not the foliage or flowers. If you are hand watering, a wand with a long handle and a water breaker at its end allows you to gently water your plants. With a long extension, water can easily be brought down to the soil level. There are extensions with a larger angle specifically made for reaching and watering high containers. Hand watering can be a very pleasant and relaxing task, but it can also become very time consuming.

If the amount of watering you do is extensive, you may want to rely on an automated system for some watering. When you choose to have an automated watering system put in, choose a company that will integrate both drip irrigation and overhead watering. Choose the watering system best for your plants. If you are handy, you may want the contractor to do the overhead watering systems for you and then install the drip system on your own. Make sure he provides you with enough extra zones to attach your drip systems to. Confine overhead watering to grass and ground cover areas. Avoid overhead watering of flowering shrubs, perennials, roses, broadleaf evergreens, vegetable gardens and annual beds as this causes fungus problems and produces poor-quality plants. Keeping leaves, flowers and upper plant parts dry but roots moist is the goal when designing an automatic system.

Hanging plants, hard-to-reach window boxes, terrace boxes and other container boxes can also be watered with drip-type systems. Many greenhouse operations water all their hanging plants through a spaghetti-type drip watering system. To conserve on water, use water sensors, which will turn water off during periods of rain.

I once sent out an e-mail to my customers which I feel will help you understand the importance of adjusting your watering practices to the weather conditions. It was summertime and the temperatures were hovering close to 100 degrees. We were in the middle of a heat wave. It had not rained in a week and there was no rain in the forecast. I told my landscape crews to stop work and visit all the plant installations we had done. Their job was to water plants that were too dry, speak to the homeowners if they were home and leave watering instructions if they were not.

Plants will tell you when they are suffering. That is why it is important to be observant during heat spells. The first indications are tip burns at the edges of the leaves. This is caused by a plant losing more water than it is able to absorb. It occurs when there is not enough moisture in the soil; but it can also occur in windy and sunny locations where transpiration exceeds the ability to absorb. As a plant suffers stress, it will lose lower leaves and show damage to its outer leaves. In extreme cases the plant will wilt as the soft tissue becomes limp. A good drink of water if caught in time can bring the plant back to life but if left for too long, the plant will collapse and die. Summertime is a critical time for watering.

Let us assume a plant is dying. What can we do to save it? Revival odds depend on how badly the root system has been damaged. Here are some things that you can try which have a chance of working.

If 1/3 of the root system has been damaged, then 1/3 of the top growth needs to be removed. Remove all dead wood. Regrowth takes place in green healthy tissue. Rebuilding the root system is done by stimulating the formation of new roots. Develop a root system large enough to support top growth. Below are steps that can be taken to reach this goal.

1. Inject or dig into the existing root area mycorrhizal fungi to help increase root mass. MYKE is a product I have used with great success.

2. Apply compost tea to the surface, watering it in thoroughly so it reaches the root system.

3. Remove existing mulch and top dress with a ¼ in. layer of compost over the existing root system. Use a fungal-dominated compost for acid-loving plants (Penobscot Blend) and a bacterial-dominated compost for alkaline-loving plants (Lobster Compost).

4. Feed weekly with Daniels or another organic liquid fertilizer.

5. Make sure the plant is mulched to a 2 in. depth.

6. Keep the plant watered. Watering will be critical here. We often neglect to water and then compensate by overwatering. The root system is not as large as it once was and its ability to absorb moisture is reduced.

Good luck, as this is worth a try and has worked for many, but not all.

In conclusion, water is the most important element you can supply to your plants. Managing and conserving your natural rainfall and supplying your plants with additional water when they need it, are essential tasks in growing beautiful plants. Many of us will find that the most enjoyable time in our garden is the quiet time we spend watering. My father would sing or whistle the whole time he was watering the flowers in his greenhouse. We always marveled at how happy he was in this atmosphere.

MY GARDEN STORY

.....MY MOTHER WAS AN INTEGRAL PART OF THE BUSINESS

Mother was always an integral part of the business. In the early days she did everything–bookkeeping, waiting on customers, delivering, watering, planting, supervising and cooking. At lunch time she would always put out a big spread. Most of our workers in the early days were relatives or close friends and would come up to a big table for lunch. She was known for her shrill whistle that would call everyone to eat. She opened up the window from her kitchen facing the Nursery and blew as hard as she could. The shrill call for lunch was heard throughout the Nursery and everyone came running. Lunch was always filled with laughter, funny stories and good food. We had German cold cuts, fresh rye bread and soft butter. I loved it when she brought out the Landjager, a type of hard salami which was one of my favorites. Sometimes she would make Montauk sandwiches for us as a treat.

In the early days we grew a lot of cut flowers and once or twice a week my mother would drive to the New York wholesale flower market. She would get up early in the morning and make the drive from Scarsdale, New York, to Manhattan and be back by seven to get us up, make our breakfast and send us off to school.

In the fifties and sixties we had found a niche market in African violets. We were one of the few greenhouse operations growing them. They became a fad. Dad put in a sub-irrigation system to water them. The plants were beautiful. We propagated our own plants and could not keep up with demand. We knocked each of the plants over from their clay pots into white clay pots, which gave them a unique look, and we seemed to have cornered the market by creating a superior product. My mother would go out daily to all the flower shops in Westchester County and the New York Metropolitan area. She had our station wagon that was double- and triple-layered in African violets.

In the later years, after my father passed away, she would spend her time watering and working in the greenhouse, but mostly she was at the potting bench planting and making cuttings. Her potting bench faced the cash register and the front door; she was the first person a customer would see when they walked in. Customers would talk to my mother and she gave lots of advice on plant care. Through the years they became her friends. They constantly tell me how they still follow her advice. When you bond with plants, you know what the plant wants and needs. She took the suffering of a plant very personally and always took the side of the plant. Mother would relate what was needed to bring the plant back to health. Proper growing techniques are essential to growing good plants. I think she as much as anyone taught me the 12 Steps to Natural Gardening.

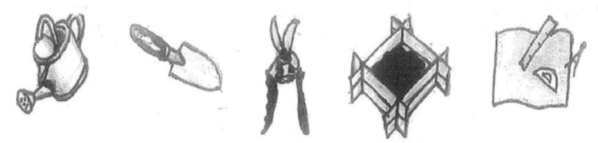

ADD YOUR GARDEN STORY HERE

5. WEEDING (STEP 4)

"C'MON LET'S GO!"

    Weeding is a term that refers to the removal of unwanted growth from an area. A weed is any plant growing in the wrong place. It competes for sun, water, food and space. It can shade out, choke out or outgrow the plant chosen for the location. If prone to insects and disease, it can spread them to the desired plants. It can create an ugly look in a beautiful garden. Just like chosen plants, weeds can be biennials, perennials or annuals. Summer annuals germinate each spring and go to seed in the fall. Cool-weather annuals will germinate in the fall and go to seed when the hot weather hits in the summer. Seeds can lay dormant in the soil for many years. Biennials will flower and produce seed only in the second year. Perennial weeds are hardy and live throughout the year. The control approach for each of these categories is different.

    Many weeds can be beautiful in their own right. In the 1950s, a professor at Cornell University went on a sabbatical and brought back a very beautiful, blue, low-growing perennial called Veronica filiformis. It escaped into the lawn and took over the Cornell campus. It has now taken over New York State and beyond. This was a beautiful native plant somewhere and a terrible weed to control for lawn lovers ever since. Many unwanted plants have invaded our areas. We need to know something about them in order to control them.

In the organic world, we do not use toxic weed killers that affect the health of our soil. In a lawn, our objective is to grow grass so thick that it will crowd out all weeds. We do everything that will favor growing thick, strong grass; we add extra seed regularly, keep our cut high, the pH up around 7, the lawn well fertilized and we water less frequently but deeper. We use corn gluten as a pre-emergent herbicide in early spring and we do hand weeding on a regular basis. Organic weed killers derived from iron kill many common weeds and are now available for homeowner use. Iron is a natural product and is safe to use on lawns.

Mulching is the most widely used practice to reduce weeding in other areas of the garden. A 2 in. layer of mulch is recommended with a caution not to exceed 3 in. Building mulches too high can injure the health of your plants. Most mulches will eventually break down and add organic matter. They need to be replenished in time. Mulches keep the soil covered, keep seeds dark, prevent germination and eliminate cultivating which would bring new weed seeds to the surface. Occasionally, weeds will find rays of light, germinate and grow. Hand weeding must be done on a regular basis.

GROUND COVERS

We employ the same principle for ground covers as we do for grass. We strive to help a plant become so strong and dominant that it will crowd out everything else. Planting a new ground cover is usually a three-year project.

Remove all weeds and vegetation before planting. Make sure the roots of perennial weeds are dug out and removed. Difficult sites might require several applications of an organic weed control, such as a product that contains Citric Acid, Clove Oil or Ammoniated soap of fatty acids which will kill weeds by foliar burns. Prepare the soil with a proper organic amendment. Plant your ground cover, mulch the soil and keep well watered. Corn gluten is a pre-emergent organic weed preventer that can be applied prior to mulching. It is very important to remove weeds on a weekly basis for the first three years. Once the ground cover takes over the area, only occasional weeding will be necessary.

VEGETABLE GARDENS

The vegetable garden can present some serious weed problems once the main harvest has taken place because the area is open. Vegetable plants compete with the weeds in the growing season, but once the ground is bare, weeds will find a home. Bare ground is always a big weed problem.

One of several methods gardeners use to reduce weed populations is to use a cover crop, such as winter rye. The seeded areas crowd out weeds and the cover crop is turned under in the spring, adding organic matter to the soil. Some gardeners like to top dress organic matter in the fall, raking it lightly into the soil and letting weed seeds germinate to be hoed out before they go to seed—the theory being if they germinate now, they will not be there to germinate during the season. Many organic vegetable gardeners do not like to disturb the ground by digging deeply. They feel this brings weed seeds to the surface and damages the food web that exists below the surface in an organic soil.

Adding 2 in. of properly composted material as a mulch not only prevents weed seeds from germinating but also adds nutritive value to the soil. The point here is that vegetable gardens should not be abandoned and weeds that germinate must be removed and not be allowed to go to seed.

PERENNIAL GARDENS

A heavily mulched perennial garden should not present a severe weed problem as long as you follow a weekly weeding program. Densely planted areas shade out and crowd out many of the potential weeds. Spend some time in your garden and pull those few weeds that come up when they are small and easy to pull. Remember, a small weed will become a large one. Don't let weeds go to seed and don't let weeds become large and overpowering.

For annuals planted in window boxes, hanging baskets and other containers, use sterile organic potting soil for planting. Plant by squeezing in as many plants as you can to see an explosion of color as your plants fight for the light on the perimeter. Heavy planting will crowd out most weeds. Monitor your containers for the emergence of any potential weeds and hand pull as they appear.

Foundation beds, borders, irregularly-shaped beds, herb gardens, rock gardens will benefit from dense planting as they will shade out and effectively compete against weeds. Mulching and hand weeding are important in keeping the weeding chore to a minimum.

Permeable surfaces, such as walkways, terraces and driveways can also develop weeds and are best taken care of by applying an organic weed killer. Keep in mind that permeable surfaces are a better solution than solid surfaces which cause water runoff, erosion and water contamination issues for our environment.

Annual weeds, like any other annual plant, will come back each year. If it's a cool-weather weed such as chickweed, apply controls in the fall; if it's a warm-weather weed such as crabgrass, apply controls in the spring. Annual weeds can be controlled through heavy mulching and the application of corn gluten, or through frequent cultivation of the soil. For perennial weeds, a weekly inspection is your best road to offensive action. Weed frequently. Once you have your weeds under control, everything else in the garden becomes easy. When your garden is weed free, you enjoy it twice as much.

IN CONCLUSION

Weeding can become the worst and most discouraging job in a garden if you let the weeds get ahead of you. They will make your beautiful garden look terrible. If weeds become established, they can become a war zone. But if you keep up with them, they are an interesting battle which you can win. Keeping your beds clean is like keeping your house clean—you will feel good about it! Weeding will let you spend some time with your plants, soak up some sunshine and breathe in some fresh air. Weeding can be relaxing, therapeutic and provide you with some great stretching exercise. We all love to be in our garden and what better excuse to be there than to pull out weeds.

Weeds exist only in the eyes of the beholder. Wildflower gardens are considered beautiful by many, but they can easily be considered a mixture of beautiful weeds. Weeds are nature's greatest and most diverse group of plants. They play a very important role with different weeds having different jobs to do. Without them, the topsoil of our earth would have eroded years ago.

Weeds form a green blanket that keeps our soils cool and damp and prevents the soil from crusting. They help remineralize the soil by pulling trace elements, minerals and other nutrients up from deep within our soil. They add organic matter back into the soil as they complete their life cycle. Weeds are tough and in their diverse mixture often complement each other. Some weeds repel insects, some go deep into the ground and pull water to the surface and others loosen hard-packed soil. Weeds do not rob the soil; whatever they take they give back.

Nature provided us with a system. When the ground is left vacant, weeds come back to do their job. It is up to you to control the biodiversity of your own back yard. If you leave your ground bare, the weeds will be back playing their very important role in nature.

NOTES & OBSERVATIONS

MY GARDEN STORY

.....MEETING MY WIFE

I met my wife, Heidi, on a landscape job. In the early days when I was trying to build up the Landscape Department, I would go out in the evening, visit a customer and draw up a plan. My cousin worked for us part-time, while working nights in the post office. He did my installations during the day with a crew of his post office co-workers. He ran out of time one day and I went over to finish the job. Heidi was trained in business, had finished her schooling in Germany and came to live with an American family to improve her English. She lived with a loving family about a mile from the Nursery. The landscape job I finished installing because my cousin had to leave was next door to where she lived.

The customer knew I was of German descent and introduced us to each other. We became friends and later fell in love. Heidi is still very close to her American family. In 1967 we were married. We built an apartment above the garden center and lived there.

Being a designer, I decided to create all interior walls of our home at angles. Our interior walls were Texture 111, an item usually used for exterior wood siding. We stained all walls a dark color, added beams to the ceilings and built heavy bookshelves 2 in. thick and 8 in. deep. I hand hewed all of the wood as well as the upright door frames. We built a brick counter with a butcher-block top, located at an angle in the middle of the room. We had one of the first great rooms of our times, with kitchen, dining area and living room all built into one big room. Rustic pots and pans hung above the counter on a suspended wooden beam. The counter acted as a divide between the kitchen and the living room, seating six. All of our bedrooms had closets built in and required no dressers.

The floors were pegged, wide oak boards stained a dark color. Our bedroom came off the main room at an angle with no door. Our home served us well through the years, since the more we beat it up, the better it looked. Soon we had two children and built an extension, adding two bedrooms, a bathroom, a large rec room with a fireplace and a loft upstairs. The large supporting beam on top of this extension was held up by four large beams angling up to the top. It was an impressive and interesting structure and became our architect's favorite—although it drove our carpenter crazy getting the right angle.

We always ate breakfast and dinner together and lunch whenever the kids were home. This was a must for my family when I was growing up and Heidi and I made it important for our family as well. At the front door was a braided rug and no one was allowed beyond this point without taking their shoes off. Heidi was protective of her wood floors. Our house was always full of children and you could tell how many were inside by counting the shoes.

When the children were small and I would have to go out on landscape appointments after work, we would eat dinner, put the kids in their pajamas and their little wooden clogs, pack up the whole family and take a ride with daddy. When we came back home, my job was to put them to bed. I would start with Tonja the youngest, scratch her back, tell a story or read to her until she fell asleep. I then went to Torsten and did the same.

One of their favorite stories was about Babe our bull terrier. I was about 15 years old at the time and was visiting a friend who lived near the Catskill Aqueduct. The Aqueduct is a dirt road covering huge pipes that still bring water from the Catskills down to New York City. The road was closed to the public, but it was used as a terrific shortcut for those of us who lived adjacent to it. One day I took this shortcut and was riding my bike when I was attacked by three Doberman pinschers that lived on a nearby estate. I kept riding, kicking them, but they kept attacking. When I reached the road above the Nursery, I yelled as loud as I could. My mother ran out and looked up, my father came out and looked up and Big John, our main worker, came out and looked up. But Babe tore up the hill like she was the Stamford Express and took each of the Dobermans by the neck and shook them until they ran home. She then stuck by my side until my parents arrived on the scene. I was rushed to the hospital and needed 29 stitches. My dog saved me and I would always reward her by sneaking her bits of my food under the table.

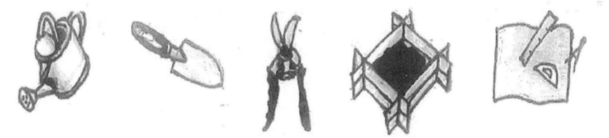

ADD YOUR GARDEN STORY HERE

6. FEEDING (STEP 5)

Feed the soil and the soil will feed the plants. Organic fertilizers supply nutrients from dead organic matter. One book I read said organic fertilizer might be better called microbe food. I like that description. It is organic matter which feeds the microbes and the microbes feed the roots in the soil. There are many forms of organic matter that can supply important nutrients. The natural approach to gardening relies on carbon, microorganisms and remineralization. We need to build a self-sustaining system in the soil that is called the food web. Fertilizing involves more than NPK=Nitrogen, Phosphorus and Potassium; it is all the macro- and micro-nutrients that a mixture of organic matter can provide which leads to the development of healthy and strong plants. The greater the mix of organic products, the greater the mixture of nutrients available to the plant. The organic way is nature's way. We need to work with nature not against her. The blueprint for a rich organic soil has been worked out for us and all we need to do is follow and enhance it.

The food web is a biological process that breaks down organic matter, paving the way for nutrient uptake into the plant. I will discuss the role of microbes in greater detail, but for now I'd like to stress that microorganisms turn organic matter into the best possible meal for plants to feast on. One of the advantages of organic foods is their increased nutrient value. The subsoil drama is quite amazing and, if magnified and amplified, would make a great feature-length film filled with the microbe activity of bacteria, fungi and protozoa and balanced with plant hormone and enzyme systems all working together for the benefit of the plant.

Chemical fertilizers supply plants with the three essential nutrients for plant growth—nitrogen, phosphate and potassium. When applied to plants, they produce a spike in growth and farmers learned they could greatly increase crop production with NKP. Relying heavily on salt-based chemical fertilizers kills microbes. When we substitute chemicals for the organic matter in the soil, microbes have a reduced food supply to live on. Without microbial activity, the many beneficial micronutrients necessary for plant growth are missing. Plant growth is weakened and plants become more vulnerable to insects and disease. Toxic cures kill more of the microbes. Consequently, many farmers are now ending up with fields of dead soil.

As home owners, we face serious concerns in the responsibility we bear for the health of our families and pets. Most people follow a popular chemical approach in their lawn programs that should be reconsidered with good health in mind. Chemical companies have brainwashed us through television advertising into believing that a four-step program will produce a beautiful lawn. We end up pouring on our lawn four applications of chemical fertilizers, preemergent crabgrass control, toxic weed controls, toxic insecticides and fungicides. To produce a beautiful lawn, we are always fighting to provide a cure for the next possible problem. We are stuck with high maintenance and never win the battle.

Chemical companies advertise miracle-type chemical fertilizers to increase the deep green color of foliage and beauty of our flowers. But without microbes in the soil, weakened plants become more susceptible to insect and disease problems, which we then combat by adding more toxic controls. Weeds take over and again we add more toxins which further reduce the microbial activity. Along with weakened plant growth, we are creating other environmental problems. Water-soluble nitrates and phosphates, along with toxic insecticides, herbicides and fungicides, are being leached or washed into our water systems, causing environmental havoc. The chemicals that remain in our lawns are causing health problems for us, our children and our pets.

To understand feeding the natural way, you have to understand the organic soil. Healthy soil is the key to any gardening program. Microbes are the one-celled, unseen workers that are essential to an organic soil–the decomposers. These beneficials fall into three major categories: fungi, bacteria and protozoa and they require organic material to survive. When they have the right amount of air and moisture, they reincorporate organic material into the soil and facilitate nutrient uptake into the roots of the plants. This is a function of the food web called nutrient recycling. Plant protection is afforded by hormone and enzyme systems against viral, bacterial, fungal and insect attacks. Plant signals are transmitted to them by hormones and enzymes which invite roots for a meal. These signals, produced by microbes, come from outside the plant. The plant finds these signals and accepts the meal.

There is a lot of drama that takes place within the soil. Without organic material in the soil, the microbes die of starvation; but when it is present, they fight for this food supply. Bacteria tend to construct alkaline byproducts and fungi construct acid byproducts. Nitrogen-fixing bacteria convert nitrates from the air into ammonium nitrate, making nitrogen available to the plant. Nutrient mineralization occurs when protozoa consume soil bacteria in order to satiate their nitrogen and carbon requirements. They spit nitrogen back into the soil where it is absorbed by the plant. Beneficial microorganisms have the ability to suppress disease. Micorrhizal fungi are of special concern to us as they affect the root's ability to survive. They attract roots to the food, thus building a larger root system. This, in turn, reduces transplant shock and ensures the plant's ability to acclimate. In addition, beneficial microorganisms facilitate and expedite nutrient uptake and provide nutrients to plants over an extended period.

Microbes affect plant nutrition, soil structure and plant growth; suppress disease; stabilize soil pH; increase humus levels; improve exchange capacity; increase photosynthetic capacity of plants; enhance root architecture and provide plants with increased resistance to environmental stress such as heat, cold, drought and foot traffic.

It may be difficult for most of us to understand the food web. But we know that it works because we see the results. We need to provide conditions that will facilitate this process. My organic programs are designed to accomplish this with monthly recommendations of what to do. Chemical fertilizers have been developed with formulations manipulated for different plants and for creating different spikes. Tailored for a specific crop or plant, they feed the plant but have no carbon and their high-salt content repels and kills the microorganisms and earthworms in the soil. They provide no benefits for the soil. Resistance is lost, our soil is dead devoid of microbial activity and we face the battle of cures resulting from a weakened plant. Insects and diseases plague our plants and the race for controls is on.

The organic feeding program has a totally different philosophical outlook. It focuses on prevention rather than cures. We do this by building a rich organic soil, feeding the microbes, building upon fertility derived from carbon that will build a strong food web and living by the principle that a strong healthy plant will not be as prone to insect or disease problems. If we fill our soil with a diverse mixture of organic matter, it will grow stronger and healthier plants. If we have a biodiverse planting, we will attract enough beneficial insects to control most harmful insect problems. In the organic world there are lots of ways to feed our plants. Biodiversity and sustainability is what we all must strive for.

When possible, it is best to start off with a soil that is rich in organic matter. In most cases this means conditioning the soil. My formula in "The Preparation of a Planting Bed" has provided great success for many of my customers throughout the years. When this diverse mixture of organic ingredients becomes part of the soil, it sets up the environment for microbial buildup. The food web will become established and plants will thrive. Once this takes place, do not disturb or invade the bed's area. Supply food through surface means. Organic fertilizers, composts and mulches will all add food to the soil as they break down. The carbon in organic matter is essential to microbial survival. Nature has built us a system where plants can flourish.

Organic fertilizers are processed from many different organic materials. It bears repeating: the greater the mix, the greater the results. Among the ingredients to look for in a good organic fertilizer are alfalfa meal, blood meal, bone meal, cottonseed meal, feather meal, fish meal, kelp meal, manure, seaweed extract, iron, humates, crab meal, cocoa meal, corn gluten, green sand, rock phosphate, sulfate of potash, sulfate of potash magnesia, wheat shorts, amino acids, humic acids and soybean meal. Blended fertilizers are your most practical means of getting these products into your soil. You will not find them in one blended mix, so it is important to mix your brands to come up with the largest and most diverse mix possible. Liquid fertilizers can also add to the mix and I particularly like Daniels, a seed-based fertilizer; but fish emulsions, seaweed extracts and other organic liquids all are beneficial to an organic soil. Other ways of getting nutrients into the soil are through mulching and top dressing with compost.

In conclusion, soil is not an inert material that we walk on and that many people call dirt. A rich organic soil is an ever-changing complex of living systems, working day and night for our plants' benefit. It is a mix of fine rock particles, water, air, minerals and other creatures. It is a dynamic area filled with energy as microbes decompose the food and offer it to the roots of our plants as a meal and as earthworms feed on organic matter aerating soil and decomposing organic matter. Good soils are teeming with life and every organism needs energy to survive. Feeding the soil with organic matter provides the energy that builds a great natural soil.

Not all soils support plant life equally. We can't see what is in our soil, but we can see what it produces. Building a rich natural soil pays dividends. Great soils produce great gardens. Feeding our soils with organic matter is a vital part of any organic program. All of life as we know it comes from plants. All plants come from the earth. We need to preserve and enrich our soils.

......MAKING THE CHANGE TO NATURAL GARDENING

I was brought up in the nursery industry. My youth was spent with my sister on a property that had 17 greenhouses where my parents grew the most beautiful plants. My father was trained as a grower in Germany and started Sprainbrook Nursery in 1944; he, along with my mother, worked hard and built the business. I went to school in Scarsdale, New York and got a good education going through the Edgemont School District. I graduated from Cornell University, majoring in Floriculture and Landscape Design, and joined the family business after graduation. I diversified the business by adding a garden center and a landscape design and installation division.

I married Heidi and had two wonderful children. My daughter, Tonja, went to college in California, got married and became a psychologist. She has written four books, has two wonderful boys Tyler and Brody and lives in Silicon Valley. My son Torsten studied at Musicians Institute in California, writes his own music, has produced seven CDS of original music, heads his own band and is well known in the Berkshire music circuit in Massachusetts. To satisfy our plant needs we put up three greenhouses on a ten-acre piece of property in Stephentown, New York. Tor lived on this range and ran this operation for us for many years. On a weekly basis we would truck down a load of beautiful 4½ in. bedding plants to be sold at the Nursery.

When Tor wouldn't follow my rigid chemical programs by refusing to use chemical fertilizers and pesticides, I was beside myself. "You can't send me back plants with insects and disease," I said, "how will I be able to sell them?" His reply was, "I just won't use toxic sprays. I believe in a natural approach to growing plants." Tor is a person who is into organic living and, for him, the preservation of the earth comes first; it is in his DNA. He holds strong beliefs and has written these beliefs into his songs. In desperation, I needed to come up with a plan. I had heard of several growers that started using beneficial insects instead of insecticides, so we decided to give it a try in our Stephentown operation. Tor did everything organically and brought in and released beneficial insects among the plants.

That year I was fighting whitefly in our Westchester operation. Every Friday I would suit up in my bright yellow protective gear, wearing long black rubber gloves and a respirator, to spray all the plants in our range. As a grower, you have to rotate insecticides during the weekly spray program. If this is not done, a new resistant strain will build up. You never win the battle.

When Tor's plants arrived with our weekly spring deliveries, they were beautiful and insect free. By summer our whitefly problem had vanished. I asked my greenhouse supplier if whiteflies were on the decline? He said, "No, they are worse than ever, but I have a new product you should try." I said, "You don't understand, they're gone." I suddenly realized what had happened. Beneficial insects piggybacked their way along with the plants that Tor sent down. The results were an awakening for me. From that point on the idea of organic gardening intrigued me. When I got a letter from the Nature Lyceum in Long Island, New York, I enrolled in the Organic Course that Jeff Frank taught. The rest is history.

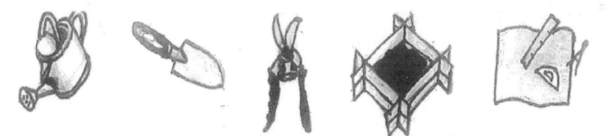

ADD YOUR GARDEN STORY HERE

7. MULCHING (STEP 6)

Mulches shut out light and thus prevent germination of weeds. Relatively few weeds penetrate a thickly mulched area and the few that do can easily be pulled. Mulches are easy to spread and weeds are difficult to pull. Controlling weed problems is a major task in any garden. A tremendous amount of time spent on weeding can be saved by applying mulches.

Mulches gained popularity in our area in the eighties when drought conditions forced us to come up with measures to conserve water. Garden supply outlets offered many choices and home gardeners quickly realized the many benefits mulches offered. Mulch is a layer of organic or inorganic material added to the surface of the soil. Most garden experts claim that the best thing you can do for your garden is to apply a 2–3 in. layer of mulch on all beds. Mulches conserve moisture, increase water penetration when it rains, prevent erosion, reduce weeding, prevent alternating freezing and thawing in the winter, keep soil from getting too hot in the summer and protect it from the cold in the winter, prevent soil compaction from heavy rains, keep the surface from crusting, prevent splashing water and the diseases that come from the soil. Organic mulches return nutrients to the soil and all mulches provide a neat aesthetic look. Mulching is the greatest time-saver that you can employ.

However, there are cautions to be observed when we mulch. Too much of a good thing does not make it better; it makes it worse. Overzealous gardeners and homeowners have been known to pile up huge cones of mulch around their trees, killing them in the process. Mulches should not suffocate plants. Keep mulches shallow and 1 in. away from the bark of trees and keep mulch beds 2 in. deep. Excessive mulching will cause a slow death for many of your plants.

Organic mulches, as they break down, add nutrients and become part of the soil. Mulches that are not aged can rob nutrients from the soil when bacteria rush to break them down. In a well-balanced soil, roots will be able to pick up nutrients at a deeper soil levels. In the end, these nutrients will come back to nourish the soil. Adding a layer of compost prior to applying mulch can do wonders for your soil and will aid in the breakdown of the mulch. Add mulch when your soil is bare, keeping it to a depth of 2–3 in.

Mulches come in both organic and inorganic types. As organic gardeners, we favor the former. Synthetic mulches are being used heavily in playgrounds but have been reported to cause problems to the health of children. Stone mulches have aesthetic appeal in certain situations, such as driveways or gravel walks, where they benefit the area by allowing water to penetrate instead of running off. But they can be a problem when used among plants. The stones become dirty and messy with age. Weeds seem to grow more rapidly between them, making the mulch more difficult to control unless landscape fabric is used in conjunction with its application. But even here a problem occurs when weeds root through the fabric into the soil and can't be removed. If you want to remove a stone mulch, picking the stones out of the soil is difficult and time consuming. In contrast to these issues, organic mulches add nutrients to the soil and can easily be incorporated into the soil.

I am not a great believer in landscape fabric or plastic as a mulch. Other mulches need to be added to weigh them down. Plastic pockets and water holes need to be poked into it. One never gets this procedure right and the plastic becomes noticeable and ugly. Plastic is difficult to dispose of because it degrades poorly in landfills. Landscape fabric allows water in and keeps light out. But it still needs to be covered with mulch and it is a problem when weeds begin to root into it. Stick to organic mulches that can break down, eventually adding rich organic matter back into the soil. The few weeds that grow through them are easy to remove.

Mulches add aesthetic appeal to any garden. They accentuate the contrast between green grass, garden and curving lines. They can create a contrast in color tones for different areas They feature flower beds and perennial gardens. They show off your foundation plants and your border planting. They make your property look neat and clean and tie your landscape together. They provide a needed barrier between grass and trees. The finished look of a well-mulched yard reflects on the person tending it.

Mulches are very porous and trap water, giving it a chance to soak into the soil. Evaporation, caused by the baking rays of the sun, takes place on bare soil. Mulches shade the soil and reduce evaporation from the soil's surface. They keep the soil cool and moist. Mulches also keep the soil more permeable by preventing the soil from crusting. Providing a mulch for your plants can reduce water consumption during the hottest months.

One of the biggest problems that we face is erosion. Not only does erosion wash valuable soil away from our property but also it brings contaminants into our water system. Mulches can reduce or prevent erosion when using types with long strands that knit together, such as cedar mulch. Choosing these types of mulches for newly planted ground covers or evergreens located on a slope is an effective method of reducing erosion.

Alternating freeze and thaw cycles can be very damaging to plants in your garden, especially to young plants that have been recently planted. A 3 in. layer of mulch insulates the soil, keeping it warmer. Shading soil from the rays of the sun prevents rapid thawing. Rapid fluctuations in temperature within the soil cause heaving, which causes the roots of plants to be exposed and results in winter damage. When heavy snow coverings are not present, mulches need to cover the bare ground.

Fungus spores in the soil can become activated with warm weather and rain. Mechanical watering can spread fungus, which enters through the tissue of the plant. A good thick mulch keeps the spores confined and prevents splashing water. Mulches play an important role in suppressing soil-born diseases.

I love organic mulches because they return organic matter to the soil. Mulching is a natural process that takes place in nature–it's the process which we have adopted in our gardens. Everything from the earth should be put back into the earth. Many of today's mulches are byproducts of nature, such as a tree supplying us with wood for building and the bark becoming a mulch. They have become a valuable product recycled back into our ecosystem rather than ending up in a landfill. Some mulches have been composted and even blended, making them very high in nutritive value. They are used as both a top dressing and a mulch.

Different organic mulches serve different purposes and come in different shades of color. Most garden centers carry many choices. Buying in bags makes for easy spreading. Slit the end of the bag and pour it around, covering the soil between your plants. You can then easily even out the mulch to a 2–3 in. depth. Bulk mulches require a place to store and more labor to spread but often cost less. The selection is smaller as they are locally processed from area waste. They are often of inferior quality. Finer, darker and more composted mulches will usually break down with a higher bacteria count and will greatly benefit alkaline-loving plants. Larger chunks, particularly of bark or wood, will favor a fungal soil and are of great value to acid-loving plants.

The variety is huge and mulches can vary from area to area. Shipping costs often determine the market price, so mulches coming from close to your area are usually the best buys. If you can match up the mulches with the types of plants that you are growing, you can set up a great environment in which to grow your plants. A fungi-dominated mulch will support acid-loving plants that include most of the evergreens and many of the shrubs. Dryer bark-type mulches of larger sizes are excellent fungi mediums. Bacteria-promoting mulches are ideal for alkaline-loving plants. Well-composted mulches or those from green plants are bacteria dominated. These mulches are ideal for vegetable gardens, perennial gardens, annuals and other alkaline-loving plants. Applying a light layer of compost prior to adding mulch can do wonders for plants. Mulches are great whenever used. But they are incredible when used in conjunction with building the right food web for your plants.

Below are mulches that I have used with great success. I am using them only as examples as there are many more to choose from.

PINE BARK MULCH

A popular mulch providing a neat dark-brown appearance. Pine bark mulch comes in three grades—mulch, mini nuggets and nuggets. Mulch has greater bacterial dominance and mini nuggets and nuggets have greater fungal dominance.

SWEET PEET MULCH

A popular mulch providing a neat very dark-brown appearance. It is a 100% organic, made up of virgin wood, manure and plant fibers. Highly nutritious and filled with beneficial soil organisms.

CEDAR MULCH

Brown in color and with an aroma that repels insects, it is my favorite mulch for banks and erosion control. It is shredded into long strands that lock together and form a dense mat, allowing it to stay in place when exposed to heavy rains.

DARK HARBOR BLEND

A rich, dark color with an exceptionally rich mixture of finely textured and naturally composted barks.

HEMLOCK MULCH

A natural reddish-brown color that lightens with age, it is a ½ to 2 in. grounded material made from hemlock wood. Provides nutritious value once it decomposes.

FUNDY BLEND (ENRICHING MULCH WITH SEAWEED)

A dark mulch with great nutritive value, it is an ideal top dressing for perennials. It is made from very old humified birch, maple and hemlock bark mixed with a very rich compost made of kelp solids and sphagnum peat.

BUCKWHEAT HULLS

The husks of the seed, rich brown to nearly black, provide a neat, dark look that is highly popular. They are not stable on slopes.

COCOA SHELLS

They are the pulverized brown hulls of cocoa from which chocolate is made and make a neat appearance. They release potash into the soil; with excessive use it can cause injury to surface roots. They will often develop a white mycelium on the surface when first applied. Aerate with a rake and the white mycelium will go away.

SALT HAY OR WEED-FREE HAYS

Not very attractive but a favorite among many vegetable gardeners. To be effective, 3–4 in. are needed.

COMPOST

Compost can be an effective mulch, but blown-in weed seeds will germinate easily. Partially composted materials are more effective. Applying a thin layer of compost and then a layer of a bark or leaf mulch can be very effective.

OTHER MULCHES

There are many other mulches that you can develop on your own property. Leaf mulch, if pulverized and partially composted, is an excellent mulch. Leaves can be chopped up by going over them several times with a lawn mower, bagged on the third pass and put into a pile to partially compost. Grass clippings are tricky as carbon is limiting and anaerobic-buildup can become a problem. If mixed with leaves, they will be more effective. Root mulches are common as this is an available product of great value.

In conclusion, mulching, when used properly, is the greatest tool a gardener has to save time on both watering and weeding and on improving the health of one's plants. Nature does not allow bare soil and neither should we. Mulching mimics what is done in nature. When we follow the lead of Mother Nature, we are working with her. We are doing what is right for our soil.

NOTES & OBSERVATIONS

.....BEING FIRST DOESN'T MATTER ANYMORE

Sprainbrook Nursery was here before houses were built around it. As kids we would roam the woods and pick bayberries to decorate our Christmas wreaths. The property behind the Nursery was woods. People would come to picnic in this lovely wooded area. The Sprain Brook was stocked with trout each year and ran through this property. A natural spring was fed through a pipe and people came to fill their containers with spring water.

Dad built a brook-fed pool using 1 in. thick x 12 in. wide redwood boards that he bought to build greenhouse plant benches. After leaving Stamford and living on a big estate with two beaches, we longed for our own swimming hole. Big John dug out the area on his own time, coming in one hour early each day. He removed large boulders from this spot and lined a beautiful brook with them. He never would accept money for the time he put in. Once the pool area was dug out, we built the forms. We braced the sides well, but when the cement trucks arrived, the sides buckled and Big John ran into the woods and cut down locust trees to re-brace them. As the cement was poured from the shoot, we pulled it around with hoes. The pool had a mud floor the first year, so every time we walked on the floor we would stir up mud. So the next year we poured a cement floor. Being spring fed, the water was very cold but very pure. After spending the day working in a hot greenhouse, jumping into the pool was the most refreshing thing you could do. We didn't have air conditioning in our house, but if you took a plunge before bedtime, you would sleep like a log. Big John never went into the water because he didn't know how to swim.

After we dismantled the forms, we used the wood for what they were intended—to build Dad's benches. We built V-pattern benches, poured hot tar over them to form a watertight seal, filled the benches with gravel and then with sand. Dad flooded the African violet benches with water once a week and grew the most beautiful crop by sub-irrigation. This crop is what brought Sprainbrook Nursery fame.

Our upstream neighbor liked our idea of a spring-fed pool and copied it. He built a pool just like ours, which caused problems for us when he emptied it because we ended up with his dirty water. At a later date he bought the property behind the Nursery as an investment. This was the area where Dad had us gather leaf mold for use in our potting soil. Our neighbor then sold the land to a builder at a nice profit. The builder put up 14 houses, removed many of the beautiful trees and moved soil around to develop level areas. He changed the course of the brook onto our property and bulldozed soil onto our land. He claimed our property was his and started building a house on it. Each day I would put up a rope to define our property line and each day he would have his workers take it down.

We called the police to have them stop work until this dispute was settled. The builder said he had a permit to build. The Town Building Department told us to get it surveyed to prove it was ours. We were unable to stop the builder's work. We called the surveyor daily, stressing the need to get this done quickly, but something always stalled the project and it took 2½ months to get the survey done. Meanwhile, the house was built. Our lawyer considered this an outrage. The survey, when it was finally done, proved we were right and the builder was in error. The house was built 4 ft. from our property line and the brook was moved over onto our land. The builder denied moving the path of the brook. The builder was granted a variance if he built a wall to retain the soil. They built a 2' drywall from some leftover stone, which did nothing. The soil that was pushed onto our property was never removed. The bulldozer driver did some work for me years later and said "I remember you. You were standing on your boundary line holding a rope in your hand. I asked the builder what should I do, and he said 'run him over, he will jump out of the way.'" Which is exactly what I did. We ended up being right but ended up a loser.

With the woods gone, we were forced to find our own leaf mold. Town trucks and gardeners brought us lots of leaves in the fall. We heeled our nursery stock into them. The roots of the nursery stock were kept warm through the winter as the leaves decomposed and produced rich leaf mold for us to harvest. My father called leaf mold black gold and we have used it ever since as the main ingredient in our potting soil.

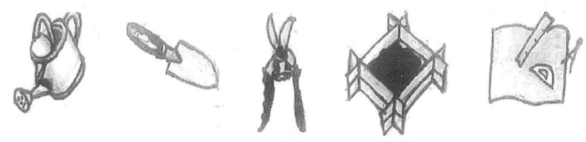

ADD YOUR GARDEN STORY HERE

8. PRUNING (STEP 7)

YOU CAN'T PRUNE A PLANT UNTIL YOU DETERMINE WHAT FUNCTION YOU WANT THE PLANT TO FULFILL.

To become good at pruning you need to first define what it is that you want to accomplish. A hedge between you and your neighbor that provides screening requires a different type of pruning than a plant located in your foundation bed. Trees, shrubs, foreground planting, island planting and ground cover all have different functions in your garden. In order to do a good job of pruning, you first need to understand the reason these plants have been placed there. Pruning is manipulating the size and shape of a plant to have it achieve a specific look or function. Pruning can be done to develop a strong, healthy plant, to increase its flower potential, to develop its stature, to create a barrier you can't see through, to open up views, to provide you with shade, to create a noise barrier or to make your yard more beautiful.

KNOW YOUR PLANTS' HABITS AND GROWING PATTERNS BEFORE YOU DETERMINE WHEN TO PRUNE.

We can group plants into general categories but there is always the exception to the rule. You need to know the growth pattern of your plant and what you want the plant to do for you. Lots of people say pruning is an art. I say it is an educated decision of what, when and where to cut. Each cut is made as a thoughtful decision. I will go through these decisions with you and show you how to become great at pruning.

Flowering plants are treated differently than evergreens. Ericaceous plants such as Azalea, Rhododendron, Andromeda and Mountain Laurel are pruned after flowering. An Azalea flowers in early spring, puts on its spring growth, initiates its flower buds during the summer months and develops its buds during the cool temperatures of winter. It blooms when the weather gets warm in the spring. In knowing this, we realize the only time we can prune an Azalea or a Rhododendron without reducing its flower buds is after it flowers in late spring or early summer.

This, however, does not prevent us from pruning out that one aggressive shoot that grows up above all the rest. We can prune it out to maintain height control and still have lots of flower buds available for bloom in the spring. Evergreen hedges, on the other hand, require yearly pruning and many can benefit from several light prunings throughout the year to maintain a thick hedge that stays full to the ground. If we analyze the growing habits of each of our plants, then we will know when to prune.

THE PROPER TOOLS ARE VERY IMPORTANT.

Before you get started, having good tools is a necessity. The most important investment you can make is to own high-quality tools. The following tools are a must for any gardener who is committed to pruning:

* **BYPASS PRUNER:** This is by far the most important tool that you should never be without. Have a sharpening tool in your pocket and a holster to make it a part of you whenever you enter the garden.
* **SAW:** A simple folding saw is my favorite. Larger saws can cut heavier branches and can be added as you develop a greater appetite for pruning.
* **PRUNING KNIFE:** I always have a high-quality knife in my pocket. As a grower, I would never be without my knife. It plays a part in most of my daily activities.
* **SHEARS:** Hand shears operate with a bypass cutting action. When pruning a hedge, start from the bottom and work your way up.
* **A LONG-HANDLED BYPASS LOPPER:** This kind of pruner can handle larger branches than what your hand-held pruner can cut.
* **POLE PRUNERS AND POLE SAWS:** These are used to prune high branches without a ladder.

THE EFFECT OF PRUNING CUTS ON PLANTS

HEADING CUTS

This cut stops the terminal growth and forces lateral growth. It is used to reduce height and as a growing tool to develop a full and bushy plant, making it more dense.

* **NONELECTIVE HEADING:** This refers to cutting everything back evenly without any regard for the growing needs of the plant. It is effectively used to trim formal hedges

and create topiary plants and shapes. It is indiscriminately used to shorten foundation plants. This type of pruning weakens plants and leaves them with an unnatural look. It is referred to by many as butchering a plant. It is a technique that is often used by gardeners who don't understand the decision-making process that is required of the pruner. An uninformed pruner will zip through your property with a pruning tool doing more damage than good.

* **SELECTIVE HEADING:** This cut is directed at reducing the overall height of the plant without changing its natural shape. A hand-held bypass pruner is your best tool to accomplish this task. The best pruning is done by doing a little bit here and there on a weekly basis. If one branch shoots up too high or out too wide, cut it back. This technique will control your plant, leave it with a natural look and, on flowering plants, still leaves you with most of the flowers. This type of soft pruning maintains your desired forms without stressing the plants.

THINNING CUTS

Thinning cuts remove branches completely. They can be used to redirect growth, reduce the width of a plant, eliminate crisscrossing branches, open up a plant and increase flowering. They can also redirect a plant to grow away from a building or in a different direction or to open a view. Thinning can be used to help with disease control, the overall health of a plant and to develop a better plant structure. Thinning cuts are of particular value when a plant is young and can be done on lower branches to raise the height of a shade tree so that you can see beneath the branches or play ball under it. Thinning cuts are also used to cut overgrown branches that could be prone to breakage in heavy snows and to increase light to the plant, thus promoting better flowering. Thinning reduces crisscrossing branches, which cause thick, uncontrolled, cluttered growth. All dead wood should be cut out of plants.

STYLES OF PRUNING

* **THE NATURAL LOOK:** This is the look that most home owners try to achieve. It allows plants to look in their natural state, providing their natural beauty and interest. The best way to achieve a natural look is to use your hand-held bypass pruner for most of your pruning chores. The flat tops and formal shapes obtained by power tools look anything but natural. They are the result of quick jobs that leave you with an undesirable look for a great part of the year.
* **THE FORMAL LOOK:** Formal gardens will usually require heavy pruning to maintain the desired shape of designed areas.
* **TOPIARIES:** To maintain these intricate shapes, frequent pruning needs to take place during the year. Weekly or bimonthly pruning is advised.

PRUNING TECHNIQUES AND MISTAKES

PROPER TECHNIQUES

* Prune out all dead wood first.
* Prune from the bottom up, from the base of the plant tapering inward to the tip.
* Prune large plants from the inside out.
* Look for crisscrossing branches that cause cluttered growth to see if they can be eliminated.
* Prune to open up the center areas to allow in more light and air.
* Prune back overextended branches, those that are touching the ground and those that are encroaching on other plants or structures.
* Prune weak growth back hard to stimulate more growth and to shape a plant; prune strong growth back lightly.
* Prune at an angle with a sharp cut just above a node.

PRUNING MISTAKES: MORE PLANTS ARE KILLED BY IMPROPER PRUNING THAN BY PESTS.

* Indiscriminate shearing: Cutting back all the plants evenly to make them shorter again. This stimulates an upsurge of messy regrowth.
* Overthinning. Prune out only what causes growth problems.
* Cutting evergreen branches back into the hard wood. New breaks will not form. Always leave enough needles on the branches for them to grow back.
* Late-summer pruning: It will stimulate new plant growth that doesn't have enough time to harden before winter. In the spring, allow new growth to harden before pruning.
* Removing limbs too close to the main branch or trunk or too far from the trunk. Pruning too close causes large wounds which don't heal. Pruning too far results in die-back. Leaving a collar encourages healing.
* Pruning deciduous trees while leaves are falling: Wait until they are gone.
* Infected pruners: When pruning out diseased branches, dip your pruners in alcohol before making another cut.
* Delayed pruning: Waiting too long in a plant's life to prune is one of the biggest mistakes we make.

RENOVATION PRUNING

Overgrown shrubs with crisscrossed, out of control, tangled branches are candidates for renovation pruning. Severe pruning can be employed on many species but a safer method is to work out a 3-year plan to reduce the plant's height and width by 1/3 each year. Reducing its height should be done at the same time as reducing its width. Thinning out branches that cross each other is important in developing plant structure. This procedure should be followed for three years until the plant has developed its proper shape.

ROOT PRUNING: THREE MAJOR PURPOSES

1. Root pruning should take place each time you transplant a pot-bound plant into a larger container. Simply cut the roots by using a pruning knife to slice down the side several times around the tightly knit root system. This prevents roots from choking and encourages new roots to develop into the surrounding soils.
2. Root prune larger trees that have been in their location for a long time and you want to transplant. By cutting off larger roots through trenching or slicing, a new, tighter, compact root system develops. This procedure should be done one year prior to transplanting.
3. Prune roots in order to slow growth and promote fruiting or flowering. Follow the same procedure as above.

GENERAL CATEGORIES AND PRUNING PROCEDURES

These are general principles to follow with the understanding that there are exceptions to every rule.

❋ Hedges: A well-shaped hedge remaining full to the base is no accident and requires pruning from the start. Hedges should be pruned at least once a year and formal hedges frequently to maintain their shape. Hedges should be pruned from the bottom up and taper to the top. Do not prune conifers too severely. Pruning into hardwood will prevent regrowth. Most evergreen hedges prefer fall pruning as they go into their dormant state. Prune off any branches that might break or pull apart in heavy snows. Do not cut back the growing tip until you decide on the height of your hedge. Cut back candles on pine trees. Leyland Cypress should be pruned in the summer not the fall. Rejuvenate overgrown deciduous hedges by severely pruning them back and selectively pruning for the next three years. However, most evergreen hedges will not grow back following this method. Taxus hedges are an exception.

❋ Foundation plants: A group of plants that are arranged in a pleasing manner to complement your house and create a transition from a man-made building to nature. Each plant is arranged to perform a function in a landscape. Upright plants may be used to soften harsh corners or to frame an entrance. Their shapes need to be maintained through pruning. Plants need to be kept short so that they do not become overgrown. Pruning here and there throughout the season, cutting out one or two shoots that grow too high preserves the natural look of the plant and keeps them in proportion. Individual plants have individual requirements for successful flowering the following year. Each cut is an educated decision. The worst thing that can happen to your foundation plants is the use of a powered pruner to uniformly lower all your plants. This not only looks very unnatural but creates health problems for the plant during the next growing period.

❀ Trees: Determine if you want your trees to be full to the bottom or just thinned, so that your view or your recreational activities are unimpaired. Trees need to be trained to do what you want them to do for you. In most instances, shade trees should have the lower branches removed as they grow. High shade is preferable for growing plants and grass underneath. Leave the main leader intact and cut out crossing branches. Don't prune birches in the winter. After storm damage, remove all broken branches and reshape the tree. Clean all wounds with a sharp cut removing jagged edges. Allow the plant to heal on its own.

❀ Shrubs: In general, prune shrubs to thin out crossing branches and head back tall shoots. This will maintain a healthy controlled plant. Spring flowering shrubs should be pruned shortly after blooming. Summer flowering shrubs can be pruned after their leaves have fallen off and prior to new spring growth. To rejuvenate overgrown shrubs, cut back one third every year until the proper height is reached. Do lateral pruning to remove unwanted branching.

❀ Ground covers: Ground covers require very little pruning and the main purpose of pruning is to confine the ground cover to the area you want. Contain them by cutting back as they go beyond the desired area. Occasional pruning of plants where the shoots are too high is advisable.

❀ Vines: If left unattended for many years, vines become unattractive. Cut back dead tissue or wild growth. Fast-growing vines such as honeysuckle may need considerable pruning while others may need minimal. Wisterias should not be pruned in the winter but during the growing season to promote flowering.

❀ Espaliered plants: These plants are trained to grow against a wall or trellis. Prune out new growth to the front and any growth which destroys the pattern. Keep growth flat against its structure.

❀ Perennials: Most herbaceous perennials should be cut down to 4-6 in. each fall. New growth in spring can be headed back by 1/3 in June to encourage shorter, bushier and later blooming plants. Chrysanthemums should be pinched every two weeks until July 4th and Asters should be cut back 1/3 in early July. Grasses should be left alone so you may enjoy their plumes as winter interest. Prune grasses back to within 6 in. in the spring.

SEASONAL PRUNING: TIMING IS EVERYTHING. PRUNING IS A YEAR-LONG COMMITMENT.

❀ SPRING: Prune shrubs that flower on new wood. Prune spring-flowering shrubs after they have bloomed. Prune Roses. Prune deciduous climbers that flower on new wood and, after flowering, those that flower on old wood. In the rock garden, prune shrubs, woody perennials and shrubby herbs to keep short. Cut down grasses.

* ❊ **SUMMER:** In early summer prune spring-flowering trees that need shaping. In mid summer prune trees that bleed heavily, like Birch. Prune shrubs that flower on old wood. Prune Wisteria back severely. Prune back Roses after flowering to initiate new blooms. After the first heavy flush of bloom, many varieties will benefit from a haircut to stimulate a greater set of blooms in September. Cut back herbaceous herbs after flowering and cut back shrubby herbs.

* ❊ **FALL:** Prune evergreen hedges as they go dormant. Do not prune Leyland Cypress in the fall. Prune deciduous hedges when the leaves have fallen off. Prune shrubs and trees after leaves have fallen. Prune branches that may break from snow loads. Prune out dead and diseased branches. Remove old canes from blackberries.

* ❊ **WINTER:** Prune deciduous trees and shrubs while dormant. Prune flowering shrubs that bloom in late spring or early summer on new wood. Prune out dead and diseased branches. Study plant structure and prune out crossing branches to develop strong structural plants. Prune evergreen branches that may break in the snow.

PRUNING EXAMPLES OF COMMONLY GROWN PLANTS

* ❊ **AZALEA RHODODENDRON HYBRID (AZALEA):** Prune immediately after flowering to maintain their shape. Remedial pruning: Work height down by heavy pruning over a 3-year period.

* ❊ **BUDDLEIA DAVIDII (BUTTERFLY BUSH):** These shrubs should be cut down to within 12 in. of the soil. Do this early each spring before new growth starts. Cut out any weak or crossing stems to the ground. Left alone, these shrubs become overgrown and leggy. Remedial pruning: Cut back to the base in early spring or winter. Thin out weak and overcrowded branches.

* ❊ **CAMPSIS RADICANS (TRUMPET VINE):** These are vigorous deciduous climbers. Create a framework and keep within their allotted spaces. Cut main growth back by 2/3 of original growth in early spring. Cut lateral shoots to 2 or 3 buds. Cut out damaged or weak shoots. Remedial pruning: Cut back to 12 inches in early spring.

* ❊ **CLEMATIS SPECIES (CLEMATIS):** For early flowering Clematis, cut back the old flowering stems in early summer to a strong pair of buds. Remedial pruning: Cut back to 2–3 in. of soil and remove any dead shoots. For mid-season flowering Clematis, remove any dead or weak stems in late winter or early sring. Shorten half of the stems by 12 in. and the other half by 18 in. to develop staggered flowering. Late-flowering Clematis blooms occur on current year's growth. Cut back in early spring to 6–12 in. from the ground. Remove old wood. Remedial pruning: Cut back plants to within 6 in. of the soil.

* **CYTISUS SCOPARIUS (SCOTCH BROOM):** After flowering, cut back branches by 1/3. Does not respond to remedial pruning.

* **FORSYTHIA X INTERMEDIA (FORSYTHIA):** Prune heavily after flowering. Cut back branches to half the length just above a bud. Cut out overcrowded branches to encourage new flowering shoots and a natural look. Cutting back in the fall leaves a clipped look in the spring. Remedial pruning: Cut back severely for 2–3 years. Cut out stems to the ground to stimulate new growth from the base. Keep plants in shape.

* **HYDRANGEA SPECIES (HYDRANGEA):** Hydrangeas need regular pruning if they are going to flower well. Dead wood needs to be cut out each year. Thinning by lateral pruning needs to take place to develop a well-rounded bush. Prune out thin scraggly branches and any branches that are crossing or touching each other. Prune Hydrangea arborescens (Annabelle), paniculata 'Grandiflora' PG, and quercifolia 'Oakleaf' in spring using terminal cuts as new growth starts. Prune Hydrangea macrophylla 'Hortensis' (Niko Blue) (Endless Summer) and 'Lacecaps' and seratta (Blue Wave) in late summer after flowering. Dead branches are removed and new growth is left for next year's blooms. Do not cut back too hard; protect next year's blooms. Prune climbing hydrangea (hydrangea anomala and petiolaris) to train plants.

* **ILEX CRENATA 'CHESAPEAKE' (JAPANESE HOLLY):** Maintain the desired shape by frequent pruning throughout the year. For hedges, trim to a hedge shape. For foundations, trim to a pyramidal upright shape. Use hand shears to maintain natural look and to have a wider base that tapers to the top. Prune at any time of the year except in early fall, as new growth could be subject to winter injury. Remedial pruning: Prune back heavily to maintain desired shape and form. Lower height gradually over a 3-year period.

* **ILEX X MESERVEAE HOLLY (MESERVE HYBRID HOLLY):** These flower in the spring and females bear berries in the fall. They can be pruned through the year except in late summer to early fall, when new growth may occur, which could become susceptible to winter injury. Use hand shears and control only those branches that grow out of bounds. Do not prune back all branches at the same time if you want to enjoy a heavy berry set. This plant can be pruned to many heights and made to conform to certain widths. If a tall tree is desired, maintain a central leader. Shape should be wider at bottom tapering to the top. Remedial Pruning: Lower height and width through drastic pruning over a 3-year period.

* **LONICERA JAPONICA (CLIMBING HONEYSUCKLE):** A vigorous grower that needs containment pruning. After summer flowering, cut back overgrown shoots and prune back lateral shoots to 2 or 3 buds from the main stem. These will bear next year's flowering. Remedial pruning: Leave 3 or 4 branches 2 ft. long. This will encourage development of new shoots.

❋ **PRUNUSLAUROCERASUS 'OTTO LUYKEN'** (English Laurel): Pruning is done in late winter or early spring before new growth takes place. Use hand pruners and cut back overgrown branches to maintain the plant's natural shape. Cut back old flower spikes. Remedial pruning: Cut down the oldest stems to within 6–8 in. of the soil.

❋ **PYRACANTHA ANGUSTIFOLIA (FIRETHORN):** This is a rapid-growing shrub that needs frequent but not severe pruning throughout the season. It is grown as a freestanding shrub or trained against a wall and has a red berry display in fall and into winter. When free-standing, keep them full and bushy. To use as a hedge, keep within desired bounds; and when trained against a wall, keep the shrub flat by pruning back outward shoots to within 3 in. of the wall. Remedial pruning: Cut plants down to 12 in. and start over again.

❋ **RHODODENDRON HYBRID (RHODODENDRON):** Remove dead flowers to prevent the formation of seed heads. In mid summer, immediately after flowering, cut off old flower-bearing spikes to a strong healthy bud or down to lower, stronger shoots. Keep growth controlled and plant in check. Remove suckers. Remedial pruning: Cut back just the older stems to 12–18 in.

❋ **ROSA SPECIES (ROSE):** Prune Roses in early spring.

Hybrid Tea, Grandiflora and Floribunda: Prune out dead wood and weak or crossing branches. Reduce height 8–12 in. or 7–9 buds. Last bud cut should face outward. Summer pruning: After the first heavy flush of bloom, many varieties will benefit from a haircut to stimulate a greater set of blooms in September. In late fall: Prune only those branches that may break from heavy snow loads.

English Roses, Landscape Roses, Knock Out Roses, Ground Cover Roses and Miniature Roses: Prune back about 1/3 and shape. Cut out dead, weak wood and crossing branches

Standard Roses: Cut back crown 12 in. from main unbranched stem. Shape evenly to form and achieve a balanced head.

Climbing Roses: They flower on second-year wood. Train main shoots to form a cover. Train them horizontally and remove any shoots coming forward. Keep plants flat. Once you have a canopy, prune yearly by shortening lateral shoots to 2–3 buds. Always remove dead, diseased or twiggy growth. Shorten main shoots when they exceed their allotted space.

❋ **SYRINGA VULGARIS (LILAC):** Prune young shrubs to form a bushy habit. Prune tips of main shoots by removing 1/3. Avoid long straggly stems with bare wood which will not produce flowers. Immediately after flowering, cut the old flower-bearing stems back to a strong pair of buds. This will increase flowering for the following year. Cut out any weak or crowded branches. Remedial pruning: If left unpruned, Lilacs may end up with lots of bare wood which will not produce flowers. In the winter, cut back ½ of the old stems to 18 in. from the ground. In the second year, cut back the remaining branches as well to avoid spindly growth. Suckers can be used to rejuvenate a plant.

❋ **TAXUS SPECIES (YEW):** Yews come in different heights and shapes. They are used as hedges, upright accents or spreaders. Unlike other conifers, they can take hard pruning into the hard wood. They require regular pruning throughout the year to confine them within their boundaries. Prune with hand shears to maintain a natural look and the health of the plant. Remove selective vigorous shoots to maintain its balance. As they age, Taxus develop less growth at the tips, increase in size and become bare at the base. Remedial pruning: In late spring, cut back to 18–24 in. from the ground. In summer, remove thin or overcrowded shoots.

❋ **VACCINIUM CORYMBOSUM (BLUEBERRY):** Prune young plants back heavily by half to encourage bushy growth in early spring. Remove weak or dead branches. Try to develop a compact bushy framework. In winter, remove any long vigorous shoots and crowded growth. Remedial pruning: They become overcrowded with age and produce smaller flowers. In winter or early spring, sacrifice this year's fruit and prune to 4–6 in. above ground level. Cut out thin and weak growth to encourage new growth.

❋ **VIBURNUM SPECIES (VIBURNUM):** Viburnum need little pruning other than controlling direction and size. After flowering, most will develop berries. Do not prune off the berries. Selectively prune branches that grow out of bounds, that crisscross or that are too weak. Remedial pruning: If never pruned, they can develop a thick mass of weak, scraggly stems that makes them susceptible to pests and diseases. To remedy this, cut down all stems to the ground in late spring, leaving a 2 in. stub from which new stems will develop. Cut out weak stems in summer and thin out crisscrossing and crowding branches.

❋ **WEIGELA FLORIDA (WEIGELA):** When young, shape the plant to grow bushy and strong stems. Remove weak stems. To flower well, this plant needs regular pruning. Cut back old flowering stems at least half way. Remove one quarter of old stems each year and shorten below vigorous new growth. Remedial pruning: Weigela can become thick, congested and weak with age. In early spring, cut the plant down to the ground, leaving 2–3 in. for new shoots to break from. In mid summer, remove any weak stems and prune back any old ones.

❋ **WISTERIA FLORIBUNDA (WISTERIA):** Prune leaders back to form lateral branches. Create a framework from this branching. Wisteria flowers develop off main stems and flower on shoots called spurs. These spurs form on old wood and the object is to develop well-spaced spurs on a main stem. In summer, cut back new side shoots 6 in. to foster the formation of spurs. As they grow, prune side shoots to 3–4 buds. Create more lateral branching as needed. In winter, cut back leaders to about 3 ft. above laterals. As they grow, cut back leaders and tie in laterals. Prune back laterals by 1/3 and keep following this process until the space is covered.

NOTES & OBSERVATIONS

MY GARDEN STORY

.....MY SENIOR YEAR AT CORNELL

In my senior year, Cornell had just built the new Veterinarian College. The landscaping was designed by a professor from the department and they needed a student from the Landscape Department to supervise the 30 untrained, part-time workers who did the installation. I was finished with sports for the season, needed money, applied and was chosen. The Cornell Plantations, which oversaw the project, hired me to work on Saturdays. This was a nerve-racking assignment to supervise 30 untrained workers and execute a large project like this. But I was brought up in the nursery industry and my father taught me that you need to keep everyone busy, productive and following directions. Proper installation procedures were essential to the survival of the plants. I am not sure how I made it through those six Saturdays and got so much work done with an inexperienced crew.

We worked with bare-root plants that were shipped in weekly. We had them soaking in water in large tubs. On planting day they were trucked for us to the site. I divided my work force into groups and had each group learn just one skill. One group dug the holes, another added the soil amendments and another group placed the right plant into the hole and held it at the at the right height so that the roots would not be planted too deeply, while another group backfilled the holes. I was responsible for executing the plan. I also took care of the watering afterwards. Everyone was happy with the outcome.

One day I was shocked when I was pulled out of class during an exam. A large truck carrying a huge shade tree arrived on campus during the week and they needed to know where it was to be planted. No one had a clue as to where it should go, so they ended up searching for me. After the project was completed, I was allowed to stay on for an extra month and work in the Plantation gardens.

I fell in love with the Cornell Plantations. It was such an amazing place to be. I will never forget how they were able to keep a White Pine Hedge 8 ft. tall and narrow but so thick you could not see through it. This left me with the lifelong impression that by pruning regularly you can shape a plant to your needs. Many years later, on the corner of my mother's red brick house, adjacent to the Nursery parking lot, we planted a 'Fat Albert' Blue Spruce. It was a beautiful color. Thirty years later it should have taken over the parking lot. But, each December we would cut all the blue tips and place them in our Christmas wreaths for color. This yearly pruning of every tip kept the tree very narrow. Hardly a week goes by that a customer does not ask me about this plant. Even professionals are stumped, saying they have never seen a variety like this that remains so narrow, so blue and so tall.

ADD YOUR GARDEN STORY HERE

9. COMPOSTING (STEP 8)

The strength of any soil is in the diversity of the organic products put into it and the activity of the microorganisms that work and develop the food web. Composting plays a vital role in developing heterogeneous mixtures within soils. The greater the mix, the greater the success. All things organic should go back into our soils to enrich them.

In the middle of a compost pile billions of microbes and other organisms digest, shred and break down wastes and turn them into a nutritive, beneficial soil conditioner. In the process, they are developing porous nutrient-rich soil. Compost is one of the best things you can incorporate into your soil or top dress your soil with. Chemical fertilizers do not add carbon to your soil and, without carbon, microbial activity cannot exist. The high salt levels are detrimental to microbial populations. They are like junk food for the plant and do nothing for the soil.

The organic philosophy is to work with Mother Nature and to preserve and nourish our soils. Everything that comes from the earth should be returned. Organic matter has carbon and carbon feeds the microbes, which are part of the soil and soil feeds the plants. Healthy soils produce healthy vegetables and fruits; beautiful flowers; and healthy and strong trees, shrubs, turf and ground covers.

Composting is one of the best methods we have to add a diversity of carbon-rich products to the soil. Anything organic can be composted. Three quarters of household wastes are compostable. Composting is good for your garden, good for your pocketbook and good for our landfills. Composting bins can be built or purchased and the process is easy once you understand a few basic facts.

Composting requires adequate moisture, lots of aeration in the pile and the addition of microbes to help in the breakdown process. CN ratio is important. C stands for carbon, which is usually made up of organic products that are brown or yellow, dry or bulky, or parts of stems with more cellulose fiber. N stands for Nitrogen. Nitrogen products are usually green or fleshy. Add alternate layers as you build your pile. You will want roughly 2/3 carbon organic to 1/3 nitrogen organic. Build composting sites on a well-drained surface.

The greater the mix of materials in your pile the more varied the nutrients that will be available to your plants. All composts are not the same. What are constant are the bacteria and fungi and other microorganisms that break down the organic matter into rich, useable nutritive soil conditioners. When this rich mix is fed to your soil, you are inoculating it with a large population of microbes. Once they become part of your soil they will work for you day and night. They are the unpaid workers that develop a remarkable system called the food web.

THE ELEMENTS OF COMPOSTING

AIR

The beneficial microbes and other microorganisms that break down organic matter need oxygen to breathe. These are the guys who do all the work of shredding and breaking down the material; and without air they cannot perform their job and reproduce. As composting slows down, air needs to be added to induce bacterial activity and get the process going again. If the pile becomes too hot (more than 155 degrees) activity once again slows down. Mixing in air will cool down the process. We like to get the heat up to 140–150 degrees for three days to kill the weed seeds and the pathogenic microbes. The warm temperatures also help in speeding the breakdown of complex carbohydrates. Above 155, carbon starts to burn off. Cool the compost by turning it to aerate or, as a last resort, add water. After 3 days of 150 degrees, the pile usually cools. Ideal temperatures to maintain until maturation are 104–135 degrees. It is good to monitor the heat in a compost pile by using a thermometer.

Adequate air circulation is the key to good composting. Adding air will speed up bacterial activity, thereby increasing heat. It will also cool the pile when it attains excessive heat. Turning a pile will add air; tumbling a pile in a composter will add air. Some composters are built small with lots of air holes. Try to achieve good air levels within the mixture. Too little oxygen will produce a sour smell. Turn the compost pile to bring the oxygen level up.

WATER

Water is essential for all life functions including microbes and other microorganisms. Too much water cuts out the oxygen in the soil; too little water cuts out one of the essential needs of all living things. Both overwatering and underwatering will cause death to living organisms. If the compost is very dry, add water; if it's too wet, cover it to prevent the area from becoming saturated by rain. If it does become saturated, turn it to mix it in and dry it out. Adding greens to your compost adds moisture to the mix. The proper amount of moisture in your compost blend is essential to developing an ideal environment for composting to take place.

ORGANIC MATERIAL

Any organic material will decompose and can be composted. Kitchen scraps collected in kitchen caddies, weeds, dead plants or plant parts, grass clippings or anything else green will add great nitrogen to the mix. Leaves, woody material such as wood chips, branches, straw and sawdust will add lots of carbon. Basically, anything that comes from the garden through pruning, weeding, pinching, cutting or shredding should be put back into a compost pile. Chopping up coarser woody or leafy material will speed the process. Mixing in materials of all types will end up giving you your best compost. People often layer different types to get the right mix. But layering and mixing as you go along will give you your best results. Again, remember my cardinal rule: "The greater the mix the greater the results."

CN RATIO

It is important to get the right proportion of bulky, dry, high-carbon materials to moist, green, high-nitrogen materials. Carbon is what microorganisms eat; and nitrogen is needed for reproduction. It is a frenzy of activity that builds up the heat in a compost pile. Most heat comes from the rapid reproduction of bacteria. With too much nitrogen material, your pile will go anaerobic—oxygen is lacking and your compost will go sour. When this takes place, a different set of microbes that live when oxygen is not present takes over. These are the bad bacteria, which cause an anaerobic reaction instead of an aerobic reaction. You will witness a sour smell, and if you put compost in this state on your plants, it is toxic. Turn it to add oxygen, which will bring new life into the process.

With too much carbon, microbes will run out of nitrogen and will not be able to reproduce. Reproduction and the eating frenzy are essential to breaking down organic matter. To keep it simple, go for two parts by bulk of carbon materials to one part nitrogen material. Mixing grass clippings with leaves is an excellent example of such a mix. Many add cardboard, which is made from wood, when carbon sources are lacking. Additives such as garden lime, Bio-tone accelerator and other activators, or handfuls of finished compost thrown on the pile as you go along can aid in getting the process started.

HOT COMPOSTING

There are four stages in making hot compost: 1) getting warm, 2) getting hot, 3) cooling down, and 4) maturing. Different bacteria play parts in each stage. Rich compost can be added to the soil or used as a top dressing. The benefits to your soil are incredible. Mother Nature teaches us to return all things organic back into the soil.

Microbes will thrive under ideal conditions. Bacterial populations can double every hour and this activity quickly builds up heat. Different bacteria operate at different temperatures and, as the pile warms up, the hot-temperature bacteria take over. Oxygen is what fuels the fire and this is where tumbler composters play an important role. Hot composting can take place in specially manufactured bins. Quick composting is usually finished in eight weeks and can take place in as little as two weeks. The key is in frequent turning that keeps the compost pile well aerated. The main advantage of hot composting is speed that allows you to get a finished product of 6–8 small batches in a season. Once the hot stage is over, the mid-warm to cool bacteria take over again.

Your compost needs to set and mature. At the finishing stage you can remove it from a tumbler or other composter and put it in a pile to mature. The maturation stage allows other microorganisms to take part in breaking down the more difficult cellulose products. Worms are particularly beneficial at this stage.

COOL COMPOSTING, VERMICOMPOSTING AND TRENCH COMPOSTING

A cool compost pile is where little or no turning takes place. Usually its location is in the back yard where you pile on the proper layers of organic material and let them sit for two to three years and let the cool temperature bacteria and other soil organisms slowly break them down. Cold composting does not kill weeds. It requires little or no work. If you end up turning it, you will speed up the process as oxygen fuels the reproduction process of the microorganisms.

Vermicomposting is a process where organic material is digested by worms, passes through their bodies and is excreted as granular dark castings. Worm castings are rich in nutrients that otherwise are not available to plants. You can do vermicomposting in a small bin and buy worms for this process. Worms are usually purchased on the Internet.

Adding worms to a cold composting site can be very beneficial. Red worms and branding worms are the ones most often sold by breeders.

For trench composting, dig a trench, fill it with organic material and cover it up with soil. This is a long process, taking years, but in time the organic matter will break down.

COMPOST BINS

There are lots of commercial composting bins on the market. They are all designed with good air circulation in mind. Tumblers are particularly effective if turned once or twice a week. Tumblers work well—providing you supply enough rough material to cause air openings as you turn. If you do, the pile will be fueled with oxygen. As composting has become more popular, new and better composters are being designed by engineers. Most of them are designed on the principle of supplying adequate air to the mix. Vertical composting units, some in the shape of cones, are fed from the top to allow gravity to move and mix the material.

If you would like to make your own compost bin, keep in mind that the design should allow the maximum amount of air to circulate. For this reason, many compost bins are designed with wire. A simple compost bin can be built by constructing a 3 ft. square and attaching a wire mesh to the inside.

CONSTRUCTING YOUR COMPOST BIN

* Twelve 3 ft. pieces of 2 in. by 4 in. lumber. Do not use treated wood.
* Sixteen ell fasteners or another method of mitering the wood together, 2 latches.
* A 3 ft. high roll of chicken wire fence. It is easy to work with and cuts easily with a good pair of pliers. Cut the chicken wire fence into 3 ft. lengths so that you can fasten the chicken wire to the wooden 4-sided structure once it is built.
* Build a cube out of the 12 pieces of 3 ft. cut wood. There will be 4 pieces of the pre-cut lumber forming an open square on the top which are connected with ell fasteners and 4 pieces forming an open square on the bottom. Four of the pre-cut pieces are used as uprights. An upright will be placed in each of the 4 corners holding the structure up. Hinge all the pieces of wood together to create a perfect square and have 2 latches instead of a hinge to close the last piece and create a door to the bin. This will allow you to open the bin. The bin will have no top or bottom and can be opened when you want to turn the pile or remove the finished compost. You can use your own ingenuity, material and method of construction to put something like this together. The goal is to achieve good air circulation and utilization of space.

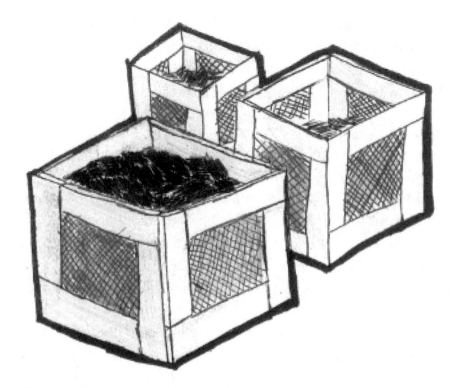

You can build 2 or 3 of these next to each other. This allows you to start a new bin while the old bin is maturing.

The chicken-wire fence principle can also be used to form a circle 3 ft. wide. Outline a 3 ft. circle and drive wooden or metal stakes 4 ft. long into the ground every 2 ft. Place a loose 5 ft. stake upright in the middle for stirring. Stirring will add oxygen to the center of the pile. Attach the 3 ft. roll of chicken wire to the stakes that were driven into the soil and hook the last piece so you can open it as a door. Bins for composting should always be placed on a well-drained area.

Old pallets, which usually can be picked up free at any nursery or lumber yard, can also be nailed together to form an open cube and lined with chicken wire creating a compost bin. Develop a method where one side can be removed or opened as a door.

Three ft. wide linear runs of any length can be constructed by running chicken wire fencing attached to stakes driven into the ground at 2 ft. intervals. Leave one end open. You can also build a bin out of wood slats, leaving spaces between the slats. 3 ft. width and height seems to be the best dimensions to work with. The larger and bulkier the bin, the less the air that gets to circulate.

These are simple, inexpensive ideas for bins that most people who are handy can easily construct. You can come up with your own method of construction or can engage a handyman or carpenter to help you. Stick to 3 ft. high and 3 ft. wide dimensions and make sure there is lots of space where air can circulate. You can build a compost pile by just throwing everything on a pile in your back yard and turning it frequently, but it will take up lots of space, sprawl over a large area and oxygen will be excluded as it gets wider than 3 ft.

SOME DO'S AND DON'TS

DO'S

❋ Use an enclosed container for kitchen waste, such as a kitchen caddy. Empty frequently into your compost bin to avoid in-home odor.

❋ Include coffee grounds and egg shells along with your other food wastes that you use for composting.

❋ Add wood chips—they are a rich source of carbon and need lots of nitrogen to break them down. They rob nitrogen and should not be mixed into the soil but are good for the compost heap.

❋ Add hair, hay and seaweed, which make excellent additives and add diversity to the mix.

❋ Turn your compost bin if it starts to have a sour odor. Turning will add oxygen to fuel new life into the process.

❋ Add mineral rock dust for a large selection of beneficial minerals.

DON'TS

❋ Don't add chemical fertilizers, pesticides, herbicides or fungicides and stay away from organic materials that have been treated with these products.

❋ Don't add kitchen wastes such as meat, poultry, fish, milk, cooked foods, grease, fats and cheese. These should only be composted in an enclosed container, as they will attract rodents. Special containers can be purchased for this purpose.

❋ Don't add cat and dog waste.

❋ Don't add diseased plants or nasty weeds except when hot composting takes place. Temperatures of 150 degrees will kill weed seeds, insects and diseases.

OTHER CONSIDERATIONS

❋ Sawdust should be added sparingly as it needs a lot of nitrogen to fuel its breakdown.

❋ Paper and cardboard are made from trees and are rich in carbon. Grass is very succulent and high in nitrogen. Dried plant stems are higher in fiber than their fleshy green leaves, which are high in nitrogen. A mixture of these is needed to create a good compost pile. The size of the material added to the pile is important in getting the right mix. Too much fine material will cause it to go anaerobic, and too much large material will cause it to heat up too fast. Large pieces are difficult to break down.

❋ Autumn leaves are high in carbon and will break down faster if ground up. Going over your lawn three times with a lawn mower after leaves have fallen and bagging on the third run will add some grass to the mixture and will make excellent leaf mold. Place it in a pile and in one to two years' time you will have beautiful rich black soil. My father used to say "leaf mold is black gold."

At the Nursery we recycle everything into our compost pile. We use 30-gallon buckets, which we usually fill two or three times every day. Into them goes anything that is compostable. Every time we pinch a plant, pull a weed, cut back a growing tip, reduce a side shoot, dump a finished plant or root prune a pot-bound plant the compost pile grows. We have a huge compost pile located out back in the nursery. Composted material coming back from a landscape job is added to the pile—old plants that are discarded, grass that has been removed to make a bed, soil that has been removed in a hardscape project. We chip all of the material that comes back from a job.

In the fall we always bring in fresh loads of leaves. We heel all our nursery stock partially into these leaves as they arrive in the spring. In the fall we fill in with leaves to cover the balls of plants and trees which provide an ideal environment and help to hold in moisture. During the winter, as composting takes place, the leaves keep the root ball warm. Adding leaves to partially composted leaves works well as the existing microbes quickly go to work on the new source of carbon. We add composted leaves to our compost pile as we build it up, which aids in decomposition. With a tractor we turn the pile once or twice a month to add oxygen to the mix.

When we mix our soil we mix one part compost with one part leaf mold and add sand for drainage. This mixture makes for a very fertile soil. When we develop our potting mix, this soil mixture is the main base for our organic soil. We steam sterilize this mix to make sure all weed seeds and other harmful pathogens are killed, as much of our composting borders on cold composting and we add to this mix coir, rice hulls, peat moss, perlite and bark. We add a mixture of beneficial microbes, mycorrhizae and other beneficials. We also add a mixture of organic fertilizers, mineral rock dust and other organic amendments to complete our mixture. People come great distances for our soil. The strength of our soil and what makes it so good comes from the mixture of products we compost. This is a far cry from the peat-lite mixes peppered with chemical fertilizers that most growers use. This large mixture of organic materials is what organic growing is all about.

Diversity is important in organic gardening. A diverse mixture of plant material grown with a diverse mixture of organic matter will attract birds, beneficial insects, butterflies and honeybees. Keep your garden organic and filled with a mixture of diverse plant material and you will attract these wonderful creatures. Composting is a great practice. Good compost added to the soil will produce great soils that will grow great plants.

COMPOST TEA

Compost tea results from brewing a finished compost product. The brewing process consists of adding good compost to chlorine-free water, adding microbial food and a microbial catalyst to grow and multiply the population, and finally bubbling in oxygen to fuel the process. Compost tea is used in addition to, not in place of, compost. The purpose of applying this tea to soil and plants is to greatly multiply the number of beneficial microbes. It contains lots of bacteria, fungi, nematodes and protozoa. The tea helps to suppress disease, provide nutrients to plants and soil, and to increase plant growth. The tea helps to develop a good food web. Everything in nature works together and together play a vital role in natural gardening.

The brewing process takes 24–36 hours. The food sources which are introduced can vary. Good food sources are non-sulfur molasses, cane syrup, maple syrup, fruit juices, kelp and fish powder or ground up fish extracts. Make sure none of the ingredients contain preservatives. Two tablespoons of any of these sugars in 5 gallons of water will help bacteria multiply. Good catalysts for fungal growth are Aloe vera extracts, rock dust, fulvic acid, yucca extracts, blueberries, apples and the pulp of oranges. Fungal mycelia can be grown in a compost prior to adding it to the tea. Cooked oatmeal mixed into compost can produce mycelia in 3 days. Through an aerobic process, you can grow large populations of beneficial microorganisms. A bacterial population can grow from one billion in a teaspoon of compost to four billion in a teaspoon of actively aerated compost tea.

There are many methods and a lot of expensive equipment that can be used to make compost tea. I will focus on a simple, inexpensive method for homeowners to use. What you will need is a 5-, 10- or 15-gallon bucket. Fill it ¾ full of water. Buy an aquarium air pump—preferably with two air outlets or use two pumps. The larger the container, the more air you will need. Attach a 2–3 ft. drip irrigation soaker to the bottom of the pail to evenly distribute oxygen into the water. If your water is chlorinated, let the air pump run for one hour to remove chlorine from the water. Rainwater is the best water source.

Twenty-five percent by volume of well-aged compost needs to be added to the water. Simply add it in and stir it frequently. A better method is to place the compost in a sock and suspend it. Tie it onto a wooden crossbar and let it hang from the rim of the barrel like a tea bag. The porous bag system eliminates the need to strain water through cheese cloth before using. Aged burlap, or other porous non-dyed fabrics can be used to form the sock. Lift and re-immerse the tea bag frequently.

Compost tea should be made at room temperature and kept out of bright sunlight. Timing is important. At the end of 24–36 hours of brewing, apply compost tea to your garden. Waiting too long can cause an anaerobic mix to take place. Bacteria multiply rapidly, deplete oxygen and end up killing each other. Before applying, smell your mixture. It should smell sweet and healthy; if it has a foul odor, it has probably gone anaerobic. Discard it and start over again since it can cause harm to your plants.

A simple method of distribution is to attach a siphon to your faucet to make the application. Drop the siphon into the bucket of compost tea, turn on the water and water your plants. The dilution rate is usually 16 or 20 to 1. The diluted mixture will distribute your microbes evenly and gently and is an easy and fast method of application. Organic liquid fertilizers can be added to your brew just prior to application. Not all compost teas are the same, nor are all compost materials the same. Compost tea is a direct reflection of the contents of the compost pile. Bacterial compost is for alkaline-loving plants and fungal-dominated compost is for acid-loving plants. Many composts are a blend of both.

A good rule of thumb is to apply 10 gallons of concentrated compost tea to 40,000 sq. ft., 3 times a year. I prefer early spring to wake things up; midsummer to replenish and increase populations; and late fall, after the leaves have fallen, to help break them down. Apply in the evening when the sun goes down so as not to expose the microbes to the sun. If your water source contains chlorine, buy yourself an inexpensive chlorine filter that attaches between the hose spigot and the hose or a water pump and apply directly from the barrel of compost tea. The Dram company sells a siphon jet which dilutes to a 20:1 ratio and a brass siphon jet that dilutes to a 16:1 ratio. You can also attach a garden hose directly to a sump pump, which is dropped into the mixture. For ease of application, dilute the concentrate. Increase application intervals for areas of poor growth. Use bacterial compost teas on lawns, ground covers, perennials, ornamental grasses, annuals and vegetables. Use fungal-dominated compost teas on trees, shrubs, evergreens, fruits or any other ornamental plant material that is acid loving. Some teas may be a combination of the above.

COMPOST EXTRACTS

Where compost tea multiplies microorganisms, compost extracts have the benefit of supplying nutrients to the soil and plants. Compost extracts when suspended in water for a period of time creates liquid fertilizer. A liquid fertilizer is made by suspending compost in a barrel of water for 7–14 days in a sock or burlap sack. The extract does not supply you with the microbial activity that compost tea does but it does provide you with a nutrient-rich fertilizer. Using compost extracts suspended in water is a technique that has been used for centuries. Many universities now recommend suspending the compost in water for only one day. The concern is that an anaerobic mix may develop when left too long; again, if your water has a foul odor, don't use it.

NOTES & OBSERVATIONS

.....OUR FAMOUS ORGANIC SOIL

The soil that we developed for growing our crops had an interesting evolution. My father was early in discovering the value of leaf mold. In the fall when leaf cleanup took place, we would accept leaves from any source that wanted to get rid of them. We had gardeners and Town of Greenburgh trucks dropping the leaves off. At first we composted them in large piles but it took a long time for them to break down. We later spread the leaves throughout our nursery stock and, with good air circulation, they broke down much faster.

We learned to heel in our nursery stock to halfway up the ball and fill the rest of the area to the top in the fall with leaves. The decomposing leaves kept the root balls warm, allowing them to absorb moisture from the ground. As a result, the leftover plants came through the winter with very little winter injury. As an added bonus, we always had lots of leaf mold for our organic potting soil. Our basic mix was 1 part leaf mold, 1 part peat moss, 1 part sand, 1 part clay loam soil and 1 part perlite. We steamed sterilized soil, leaf mold and compost and then added peat, perlite and our long list of organics. These included organic fertilizers, lime, microbes and humates.

At first we had a special steam jenny for this purpose and built a box out of 4' x 8' plywood held together by clamps. There was a pipe structure in the middle where steam was fed. When it was finished, we removed the clamps and the pipe structure and added our other ingredients. We turned it three times by hand. There was a person with a shovel on each side and we had to make sure we developed a pyramid so the soil would fall to all sides, mixing thoroughly with each shovelful we threw. I was often on one end. I always attributed my strength and athletic ability to the endurance I built up with these three-hour marathon workouts.

Through the years we kept adding more organic products to our mix. Then customers asked us if they could buy it for their outdoor containers. It became so popular that we bagged it for sale. In the spring it now takes two people bagging soil most of a day trying to keep up with the demand. On a busy weekend, we can easily go through 150 bags. Patrons come great distances for our soil.

We later put in a boiler just for the purpose of steaming. We built a pipe structure to fit our dump truck, filled the truck with the soil mixture and pumped steam into the soil. We placed the boiler on a timer overnight. When we first did this, the fire department was frequently called as people in passing cars saw smoke, which actually was steam, rising from the truck. It looked like it was a huge fire engulfing the truck that was parked next to the main Garden Center building. At one point two fire departments were called in and we were very embarrassed. The Greenville Fire Department is now aware of this problem and no longer responds to these calls. With time, we bought a tractor with a front-end loader to do the turning and a Royer Shredder to do the mixing and screening. Sprainbrook Nursery organic soil was considered to be the best on the market by all who used it.

ADD YOUR GARDEN STORY HERE

10. TRANSPLANTING (STEP 9)

It may be necessary, at various times and for various reasons in a plant's life, to move it from one location to another. When we germinate seedlings, we need to move them to a larger size pot as they grow and crowd each other out. When a houseplant becomes too big for its pot, we need to transplant it to a larger container. Plants grown outdoors can also get too big and need to be transplanted. Gardens are not static; and plants need to be moved when they have outworn their usefulness, outgrown their locations or have been planted in the wrong location.

In a garden one never gets it right the first time. Perfection is never achieved but always strived for. Many people neglect to transplant and their gardens look neglected. Plants grow and get out of scale. What fun would a garden be if we couldn't find some way to improve it? Transplanting usually takes place in an established garden when pruning no longer will do the job, when a plant is in the way of a landscape project, when a foundation planting has become overgrown or when all the plants are removed as your house gets a facelift. Transplanting is vital to the health and scale of a garden. Timing is important and techniques will vary according to the size and type of the plants and the length of time they have been planted.

LARGE TREES

Both size and costs can be a limiting factor in moving a tree. A tree that has been in the ground for more than 3–5 years should be root pruned one year before moving it. This will develop a compact root system that will allow the tree to be transplanted without going into shock. Root pruning is done by digging a deep trench around the plant that is usually the size of the root ball you want to create. Cut off all large roots and leave only those growing below the trench. Backfill the soil and move the tree one year later when it has developed a dense set of compact roots.

The safest time to transplant a plant is when it goes into its dormant state. Roots continue to grow through the winter and will help support top growth the following spring. Top growth may have to be pruned back if the root system was drastically reduced. Roots need to be in balance to support top growth.

LARGE EVERGREENS

The way to transplant large evergreens will depend on the type of the evergreen tree. Taxus with its deep root system is almost impossible to move. If large equipment is on site, digging deep huge balls can work. The trick is to transplant your evergreens before they become too large. Large evergreens are too costly to move, often do not work and are often thin and bare at the bottom. If they have grown into each other, they will have bare sides when transplanted. Smaller evergreens are easier to transplant. You can usually handle them by yourself. Young plants can be pruned back and can outgrow their deformities. Large plants will need labor; and the cost needs to be weighed while making a decision.

ERICACEOUS PLANTS

Shallow-rooted plants of this family, such as Rhododendron, Azalea, Andromeda, Mountain Laurel and Holly have a compact root system and can be moved easily and more successfully. Light pruning will help in the move.

LARGE OVERGROWN SHRUBS

Large overgrown shrubs are best handled by severely cutting them back and moving them as they reach dormancy in the fall or prior to their breaking dormancy in the spring. The cutting back allows the smaller root system to support the top growth. The plant then has a chance to rejuvenate and grow back into a strong one. Follow both our planting and pruning instructions to accomplish this task. Keep your plants well watered and well fed to encourage a lot of new growth in the first year.

PERENNIALS

We like to divide or transplant perennials in late fall or early spring. Perennials can withstand severe pruning and also can be moved successfully at other times of the year if cut back at the time of transplanting. In order to get a perennial garden right, it is

94

necessary to plant and transplant. If something does not look right, it has to be moved. If color is lacking, it needs to be added.

VEGETABLE GARDENS

Many vegetables are seeded directly into the ground. Here thinning and transplanting are needed in order to give plants adequate space to grow.

TIMING IS IMPORTANT

When planting for a show of color, timing is always an important factor. Probably the worst time to move a plant is when it has just flushed out new growth. This tender new growth needs to harden with the full cooperation of its roots to support this spurt of growth. If one is forced to transplant at this time of the year, cut back the new growth drastically. If you cut off 1/3 of the root system then you need to cut 1/3 off the top to achieve the proper balance. Root hairs greatly increase the water supply to the plant. When digging up plants from the ground, many of these root hairs are damaged. This reduction in root hairs requires a reduction in top growth.

Once we understand the dynamics associated with transplanting, we can understand why timing also plays an important part. When a plant goes dormant in the fall, top growth has stopped but roots continue to develop. This gives a plant time to increase its root system before the new growth in the spring. Disturb the root system as little as possible in the transplant process. One great advantage of buying your plants in containers is that they can be transplanted almost any time of the year without suffering transplant shock.

Organically grown plants will transplant and adapt to the soil a lot better than chemically grown plants. A lot of growers start bedding plants in peat mixes and then accelerate their growth with chemical fertilizers. The plants look great but struggle to adapt when planted. I have been told by several botanical garden directors that when they switched their growing to natural soils, using organic amendments, their plants transplanted without shock and grew rapidly. Adding microbes, particularly in the form of microbial fungi, will greatly decrease transplant shock and help develop a strong root system. A rich organic, well-drained soil is also essential to success. Keep your plants well watered after transplanting.

We as gardeners tend to be reluctant to transplant, but it is a necessary task to keep your garden in shape. We often wait too long before we make this decision. If we planted a garden based on how it would look in ten years, we'd have to live with a very sparse look in the beginning. If we plant a garden that is beautiful at the onset and then transplant as things become crowded, we will have a beautiful garden for the full ten years. Things keep changing. We need to plant for the present and the future. This can only be done if we transplant. Transplanting is an integral part of good organic gardening.

.....TRANSPLANTING

When a plant got too big for its pot in the greenhouse, my father would make us transplant it into a larger pot. By moving it up a grade, the plant would thrive rather than decline. To grow a large plant you start small and keep transplanting until it reaches the size you desire. Transplanting needs to be done on a timely and regular basis. The same advice holds true for outdoor plants. A plant that is left too long in its spot will become too large to move. If a plant is in the wrong location or has outgrown its intent, it is best to determine this early on and transplant it.

I go out every night on landscape design calls. Much of my work is ripping out overgrown plants and redoing front foundation plantings. Over the years, plants grow together and can't be salvaged, but some can be transplanted. The cost to replace large plants can be expensive. Keep an eye out and transplant evergreens from your foundation plants before they get too big. You can place them in a backyard location to give you greater screening.

My favorite tree was a juicy, sweet white peach tree that I planted when I was a kid. I couldn't wait each year to harvest the fruit. When we put the extension on our house I transplanted it before the builders could destroy it. The next year I had a great crop of delicious fruit. A happy ending to what could have been a sad story.

I had a customer who was moving to another house and wanted to transplant a large flowering tree. I said, "It looks beautiful where it is and it will be very expensive to transplant such a large tree. Why would you want to do this?" She said, "We planted this tree when my daughter was born and we celebrate her birthday each year under the tree. The tree is in full bloom on her birthday and its beauty speaks to her and makes her feel very happy and wanted." I agreed that this was a good reason to transplant a tree.

The lesson here is that transplanting is one of our great options in landscaping.

ADD YOUR GARDEN STORY HERE

11. GROOMING (STEP 10)

Plants need care to look their best. Beauty is in the eyes of the beholder and at the Nursery we tend to be control freaks when it comes to the appearance of plants. We spend a lot of time maintaining our plants. Cyclamen plants are cleaned on a weekly basis. The dead flowers on long petioles are pulled out to the right or left, removing them to the base. This prevents rot and stimulates new bud formation. Primrose flowers are picked clean as the flowers fade, allowing the inner buds more light and encouraging their bloom. Plants that get too leggy are trimmed back. Gardeners find that deadheading spent flowers cleans up plants and stimulates more flowering.

In early spring, gardeners rush to add Pansies to planter boxes. In the cool weather, they flourish and their beautiful faces smile at you, but in the extreme heat of the summer they get scraggly and heat-stall. In a focal point area they need to be removed and replaced. Grooming keeps plant displays neat, clean and full of flowers. Marguerites are a beautiful Daisy-type flower; however, when they finish flowering, they develop an ugly fruiting body. If you love to deadhead, you will love these Daisies. Once you finish deadheading, you won't believe how beautiful these plants look again.

The first person to work for the Nursery, in 1946, was Big John, a hell of a worker and a great horticulturist. He would drive my parents crazy because when the first set of flowers on our beautiful Lantana standards would come into bloom, which usually was at the time we wanted to sell them, Big John would cut the flowers back. We lost sales but three weeks later the plants were twice as compact, twice as beautiful and loaded with even more flowers. They were far superior to the ones that were not cut back. Big John was good at grooming. He knew what his plants needed to make them look beautiful.

There are many things that need to be looked after in the garden. Haircuts will rejuvenate growth and flowering. Rearranging plants will make a big difference in the beauty of your garden. If you do a little snipping here and there every time you go in the garden you can keep your plants actively growing and flowering.

Trailing plants such as Petunias will benefit from a short haircut. If a plant's energy is directed into growing a long shoot, the inner foliage will thin out. By cutting the tip you will stop terminal growth and force lateral growth, which will keep your plant full and bushy. This lateral growth will grow and produce more foliage and more flowers, keeping your plant looking vigorous and full. It is preferable to cut off some growing tips each week rather than all at one time. Grooming and maintaining are closely related. If we maintain a strong healthy plant by keeping it well fed, properly watered and nicely groomed, we will have a beautiful plant.

As plants grow, they may need staking. Peonies will need Peony hoops. Tomatoes will need cages or strong stakes. Vines will need something to climb on and give them direction. Plants rely on you to make them look their best. Spending some time in your garden working on your plants will make them more presentable. A little bit of grooming will go a long way in beautifying your garden.

.....MY BIG CHANCE TO BECOME A FAMOUS ACTOR

In the 1970s Ciba Geigy developed their first drug for hypertension. To promote it they produced a half-hour film. The story line was built on the fact that this problem could hit anyone at any time. "Without Warning" became the name of the promo film. The producers wanted a colorful environment to film in. They asked Sprainbrook Nursery for permission to film in our greenhouses. We were excited to be selected and said "yes."

We were involved in a fall flower show that year. The movie producers felt that with getting everything into bloom at the right time and getting the garden set up for the show, we would be under a great deal of stress. We provided them with the type of scenario they were looking for to promote their client's product. The script was written and the actors were brought in. Try as they might, they could not find anyone who looked natural carrying out the daily chores of a grower. In desperation, they asked me if I would take over the lead role. I was flattered and thought this was my chance to hit the big time. I was perfect for the role since by acting naturally, I was a natural.

At the film's climax I collapsed to the ground and was driven away in an ambulance, lights flashing and sirens blowing all the way to the emergency room. The film was a great success and hit many public television stations across the country and was played in the health classes of many schools. The foreman who worked on building our first large glass greenhouse called me up one day and said he was in the hospital recovering from a stroke. He saw the film while in recovery and was sorry to see I had the same problem. He wanted to know how I was doing. I wished him a speedy recovery and told him I was fine.

In payment for my time, the company did a film about the Nursery. At the time we had a white bull terrier named Josie. Children who came to the Nursery would exclaim "Look, Spuds McKenzie" or "General Patton's dog!" when Josie came up to greet them. There was always a two- or three-gallon container lying around in the Nursery and she would pick one up and carry it in her mouth. She'd also nudge the customers until they played tug the bucket with her. Our white bull terrier and the film crew got very attached to each other. In the fall when the leaves were blowing in the wind, Josie would concentrate on catching a leaf in her bucket. The highlight of the "Sprainbrook Nursery" film was capturing this feat on camera. I never did make it big in the film industry and went back to growing plants in my greenhouse. I am sure the bond to nature was a much better choice for me than the bright lights of Hollywood.

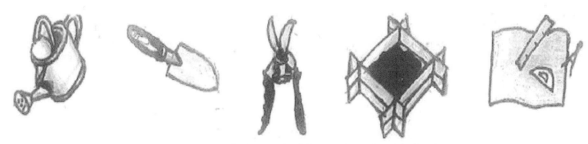

ADD YOUR GARDEN STORY HERE

12. OBSERVING (STEP 11)

Since you can't solve a problem unless you recognize a problem, one of the most important tasks an organic gardener undertakes is observing. A gardener must be in tune with his or her plants. The philosophical outlook of an organic gardener is one of prevention rather than cure. If we see a problem, we have to nip it in the bud. If we see an aphid, we bring out the ladybugs. If we see a sprinkler hitting the foliage of our flowering plants, we correct this problem because we know it will lead to fungus.

There are many signs that the observant gardener can learn to recognize and take action on. To name a few: When a plant gets out of scale with its surroundings, we need to prune it or transplant it. A plant that is suffering from being in too wet a location needs to be moved or raised in its bed. Chinch bugs like hot dry summers, and if we find our grass is running dry in the heat of summer, we need to add water to deter them. Allow Euonymus to be stressed out in the summer and you will end up with Euonymus scale. Rhododendron leaves look notched: we suspect black vine weevil. Since they chew the leaves at night, go out at night with a flashlight to see where they are and release beneficial nematodes in that area. Roses that look worn after their first set of blooms are sending a signal to cut them back. Hanging baskets that have heat-stalled need to be dead headed or cut back to rejuvenate. A perennial that has grown too tall too quickly needs to be cut back to keep it more compact. Tall plants that are falling over need to be staked. In early July, Asters need to be cut back by a third. The ground is bare and we know instinctively a mulch needs to be added. Plants look off color and we suspect lack of food. Mechanical damage such as a lawnmower hitting a tree has taken place and we need to correct the problem by creating a bed. Chemical damage is taking place from overuse of a herbicide and we know that the microorganisms in the soil will also be affected. Birds are pecking on our lawn early in the morning and skunks and raccoons are digging up our lawn each night. Check for grubs and, if present, bring out the nematodes. I have been making points at random but that is what observing is.

When we go out and observe, we don't know what we'll find. The more experience we have observing and trying out solutions, the quicker something will click in our minds the next time we encounter a similar problem. Observing is a learning process. We are learning from the signals plants are sending us. We are learning by informing ourselves on all facets of gardening.

Go into every area of your garden and look at your plants. They will tell you the problems they face and you can work on a solution. Your plants need you and you need them. We can solve more problems through observation than we can through spray programs. If we find an insect on a leaf, we can remove the insect; if we find many insects, we can come up with an organic control before an infestation reaches epidemic proportions. If we see holes in our Hosta leaves, we can suspect slugs. We can put out a saucer of beer. If we observe the saucer of beer the next day and find slugs, we know we have a slug problem. We can apply a product with iron phosphate, which controls slugs and is eco-friendly. Holes in the leaves of our trees can mean caterpillars. If weeds are taking over a portion of our lawn, we need to pull them and add more seed to compete against them. Grass is a monoculture and we need to do things to our lawn that will make grass dominate.

The organic gardener learns what makes a plant grow. A healthy plant is disease and insect resistant, develops bigger and more profuse flowers and wears a rich deep cloak. We have found that the observant organic gardener can achieve better results than those who follow the traditional chemical methods advocated by many of our agricultural institutions. The key is to be observant and make changes when problems occur, be adaptive in solutions, and follow nature's lead.

It is easier for us to see what takes place above the ground than what takes place in the ground. But if we are observant—if we touch and feel our soil and we know what takes place in our soil—we will learn what a good soil feels like. We will know what we have to do to make it better. The soil can be too wet, too dry or too heavy. The strength of any plant is in its roots, yet we can't see the roots—though we know that roots need oxygen to breathe and water and food to survive. Many people consider the roots to be the brains of the plant.

In time, you'll be able to read your plants. A customer of mine always killed his indoor cyclamen plants. His problem was overwatering. He said he finally learned the secret by reading his plant. When the leaves started to wilt, the plant told him it needed water. He said once he learned the secret of not overwatering, he kept the plant blooming all year long. There are many signals your plant can give you that its roots are in distress.

The food web is important for a healthy soil. We can't see the microbial activity in the soil but it is necessary that we know what takes place there. If our plants look strong and healthy, the soil looks dark and rich and it feels soft and spongy when we step on it, we probably have a healthy soil. On the other hand, if our plants are struggling, our soil is hard and the color is not a dark brown, we know our food web is not functioning. If high rates of chemical fertilizers are being applied we can assume microbes will be scarce.

Being observant will turn you into a plant detective and give you answers which will lead to cures. You will find that you will focus on prevention since the best cure is a strong healthy plant which will resist insect and disease invasion.

Timing is important in gardening. Gardeners have made the observation that pre-emergent crabgrass controls should be applied when Forsythia are in bloom. When a plant blooms is a more accurate indication of timing than a calendar. If we develop a phenological calendar, listing problems that have occurred in relation to plants coming into bloom, we will have an accurate alert system in place.

When we see a problem we seek a solution. In the process we develop a tremendous amount of knowledge. This knowledge will lead to action and a more beautiful garden. Many people refer to having a green thumb. A green thumb is a thumb of knowledge and experience. Observing is critical to your success in the garden. Record your observations in this book.

When you spend enough time in your garden, you will observe how happy you are there. You will feel the strength of the sun and the health benefits it affords you. You will observe a special connection that takes place between you, your plants and nature's forces. You will be inspired by your garden each day. You will observe how your garden has made a difference to you. You will understand why gardening is the number one pastime activity. Observation is your most valuable tool in making everything better in your garden.

.....MY FIRST LANDSCAPE DESIGN PROPOSAL

Upon graduation from Cornell, my friend said "Today we are graduating from college and now we will go to the school of hard knocks. Then we will really learn."

My first landscape design proposal, after I graduated from college, was in response to a customer who wanted an overall plan drawn. I worked very hard and long to produce the perfect design. It was my first chance to show everyone what I had learned. I drew everything very neatly and to scale. I took particular care to recommend the right plants for the right locations. It was a sizable proposal and when I did not get the job, I wanted to know why. I asked the customer. The customer said she chose another nursery because my design did not have enough curves in it. After that I became the curviest designer in the area.

I learned to love the Hogarth S curve and have found great satisfaction in transforming a typical square backyard into beautiful, naturally curving beds. I love areas that bay out with a mixture of flowering shrubs and perennials. Now I spend less time on draftsmanship and more time on design. When my landscape crew finishes a job, the customer is always happy. They come back years later and tell me how much they enjoy the selection of plant material and the design we developed. Most of our landscape jobs come from word of mouth. I often wondered why we do so much work in certain neighborhoods and then realized that once we got a job in an area, people saw it and liked what we had done. Then they call on us to plan their own gardens. Word of mouth is always the best advertising.

ADD YOUR GARDEN STORY HERE

13. ENJOYING (STEP 12)

Most important of all, enjoy gardening. How many times have I heard my customers say, "I love being in my garden." People who love their gardens are loving people. There are many reasons for this; but I think it is because of the bonds that gardeners develop with nature and the love they have for their plants. It can be a beautiful lawn that makes you proud. It can be walking into your garden and seeing a new variety coming into bloom that fills you with warmth. It can be the desire to escape to a quiet, beautiful place that satisfies a need. When you build a beautiful garden, each plant becomes your friend. Each plant in your perennial garden comes back year after year to greet you with a colorful display. Something new keeps popping up to capture your attention. Gardens are many things to many people. They can be quiet and beautiful with a background of birds singing to you, a refuge from the problems that face you or a place for socializing with friends, family or neighbors.

When you spend time in your garden, your perspective on life changes. Nature speaks to you. Spend your quiet time listening. In nature, the more you give the more you receive. A good gardener knows what to do to benefit his plants, and plants that receive these benefits reward him or her. A customer of mine told me that a friend came over to visit and said, "You have the most beautiful garden. It must be like living in paradise." He responded "That's true but if this is paradise, then there is a lot of hard work in paradise." Enjoying the results is what makes it all worthwhile.

Being in one's garden is healthy with fresh air, sunshine, exercise and relaxation—all in the right amounts. We all need to get one hour of sunshine each day to build that bond between you, the plant and the sun's rays. Everything in nature is connected. If you enjoy your garden, it will recharge you and invigorate you.

I am going to end this part of the book with a tribute to my mother, who many referred to as Mrs. K. She passed away at the age of 95 and enjoyed every minute of her life being with plants. She loved all the chores and became proficient in all of them. Planning, planting, watering, weeding, feeding, mulching pruning, composting, transplanting, grooming, observing and enjoying. Many attribute her longevity to keeping her body and her mind active. You would have thought that my mother had spent enough time with plants each day at work. But in her house she had a large bay window that was always filled with flowering plants. Every room in her house had foliage plants in it and she was the first one each spring to plant her terrace area with annuals.

After a hard day's work she would eat dinner and then sit down in her chair on the terrace with her dachshund in her lap, enjoying her garden. She spent her life close to nature and drew her strength from it. At the end of her life she could still outwork anyone in the Nursery and her mind was sharp as a whip. If a customer had a problem, they would first ask Grandma Krautter for the solution. There is an old German saying "Nichts sagen, Oma fragen". If you don't know the answer, ask Grandma.

We had a big winter storm when she was 94. She decided to stay in her house located on the Nursery property. She did not want to take a chance to slip or fall on ice. At her age she was afraid of breaking a bone. That night before going home I went up to visit her and I asked her how her day went. I said it must have been nice to just sit back in the house and relax without having to worry about all the work that had to be done. She said "It was the most boring day of my life. It took so long for the day to get over. All I wanted to do was be out in the greenhouse."

My mother never had cleaning help and always cooked her own meals. When my father was alive and we were kids, she always cooked a big meal for us. It was never the same and always a meal started from scratch. She shopped the outer perimeters of the supermarket and put her own meal together trying to stay away from pre packaged items. Our friends always loved to come over for dinner and she always had enough for everyone. When my father passed away, she still cooked a different meal for herself each night. When we asked her to come out to dinner at a restaurant with us, she would usually decline saying she liked her meals better. She never took vitamins and she never took medication.

I advocate in my organic program that the greater the mix in our soil, the greater the results. The greater the mix of plant material in our garden, the more beautiful and interesting it can become. Eating something different each day and eating a mixture of food may give us the same beneficial results it gives our plants. There is so much we can learn from nature and Mrs. K was in tune with nature. Everyone said she was an amazing woman. Her energy came from plants. She found that the more she gave, the more she got back. She had that bond with nature and from that bond a strength she drew upon. Enjoy your garden—it can do more for you than you can ever realize. After she died, customers would continually ask me how my mother was. I would tell them she passed away, then handed them what I wrote about the last week of her life. It was easier for me than trying to explain.

A TRIBUTE TO MRS. K

As many of you now know, my mother passed away at the age of 95 on Monday, June 2nd, 2008. With my father she started Sprainbrook Nursery in 1944. I spent every day of my life working with her and along with Heidi, my wife, we made daily decisions together. Sprainbrook Nursery isn't the same without her. We will miss her. Her last week of work was like every other week of her life.

On Tuesday she was, as usual, the first person to start work in the morning. It was important for her to be there to say "Good Morning" as the staff arrived. Her first chore before getting on with the day's work was to water greenhouse number 4. It was a day like any other day filled with hard work. When the day was finished she went home, cooked herself dinner and then went down to join the women working night crew. She enjoyed the company of the women and she loved to plant. At 9:00 p.m. the women chased her home.

On Wednesday, the last night of night crew, Mother insisted on cooking for everyone in her home. After work she made sauerkraut, spareribs and mashed potatoes, with cheesecake for dessert. That night we watched the tape of her 95th Birthday and she took everyone on a tour of her house.

Thursday was a difficult day. The silver van went up to Stephentown to pick up a load of plants from our farm. We needed to gather plants for a large planting job we did each year in North Salem. She wanted to make sure there were no mistakes and that all yellow leaves on the geraniums were picked off before the plants were packed. She had run this job for many years. The truck needed to be unloaded with the plants that came back to the Nursery and then packed and ready to go by 7:00 the next morning. We decided this was too much of an undertaking for her at her age so, instead, we decided to send Oscar and his crew. When it came time, Oscar was so overwhelmed with landscape work that he couldn't go. This job usually takes a crew of 6, but for various reasons we could not get a team together. At Heidi's insistence, I joined my mother and two other greenhouse workers to carry out the job.

At 7:00 Friday morning, Benjamin and Manuel drove the truck up and I took my mother in my car. It was nice to be away from the bustle of the Nursery and be alone with her. There was a strict procedure for unloading the truck that we had to follow; and by noon we had 269 five-inch geraniums potted into tubs and 16 window boxes of Red Dragon Begonias planted. The men turned over the bed at the gazebo and we broke for lunch. My mother and I were asked by the owners to sit in chairs at the pool but we chose instead a rock in the shade of the woods. I tried to help my mother onto the rock but she said she was all right and I needed help more than she. We had a picnic lunch together, moments I will cherish forever. Benjamin took a great picture of us, it was the last one ever taken of my mother. On our return to the Nursery, she said it was a great day and how nice it would be if she could go "home" now and join her dog—her dachshund had died in her arms just two weeks earlier on Mother's Day.

On Saturday, Mother was on a roll. I had lots of work planned for all the part-time weekend kids. One of our workers was pregnant, so Mother took over her watering in houses 2 and 3. Her watering was finished before anybody came in. She grabbed the part-time help as they arrived to accomplish major rearranging. At the end of the day she said, "Now all my houses are in order."

Early Sunday morning, my mother drove herself up to Armonk to enjoy a day off with my sister. She had a wonderful day visiting with my sister and friends. Time ran away and it started to get dark. She opted to stay overnight and drive home early the next morning. On Monday she still was the first one at work. Impatiens seedlings came in too late for night crew, so mother took it upon herself to plant them. We were busy at the Nursery and she ended up planting over 60 flats all by herself.

When the day was done, she went home a little early to have a glass of milk and some chocolate. She rested for a few minutes, then decided to go and pull some weeds, proceeding to pull down vines growing up the side of her house. At about 6:00 p.m. she called Heidi and said she wasn't feeling well and someone should come up. Heidi was ready to call 911 but mother said no. Fearing dehydration, Heidi gave her a large glass of orange juice and helped her to her bed. She complained about a pain in the back of her neck. This worried me and I looked it up in our medical book. We convinced her to have her vitals checked out and if everything was all right she would not have to go to the hospital.

We called 911 and over 10 people congregated in her bedroom. She counted them all and said, "So many people to check me out." They found she had an irregular EKG and suggested, as a precaution, that we take her to the hospital. We walked mother down the steps and the medics all went down in the parking lot to wait for her. Mother wanted to put on her sneakers. I went to get them and she said "No, not my old sneakers." As I was putting them away and as Heidi was reaching for her new ones, Mother was holding onto the kitchen counter and announced she was getting dizzy. Before we could catch her, she hit the floor like a rock. Although the paramedics rushed back up, she never had a heartbeat after that. She was rushed to White Plains Hospital where they pronounced her dead.

Mother always wanted to contribute but never wanted to be a bother to anyone. She was a teacher and a friend to her employees and to her customers. She had the talent for propagating new varieties, growing beautiful plants and creating magnificent combinations. She wanted to die the way Dad did with dignity, contributing to the end and being a burden to no one. She had a beautiful church service. Carol Demas, a talented friend who frequently visited the Nursery, sang "Bridge Over Troubled Waters." Mother had wanted me to have the hearse stop at the Nursery as her thank you and goodbye to everyone, when that time came. We had done this for Dad and she thought it would be nice if we could do it for her. The staff was gathered on her front lawn in their red Sprainbrook Nursery shirts. I spoke on her behalf to thank them and to say goodbye. Carole, unaccompanied, sang "The Garden Song" and "Bridge Over Troubled Waters." It was a moment none of us will ever forget.

I know that many of Mother's friends who have been coming to the Nursery for years are just learning about her death. You have enjoyed her friendship and I am sorry that I couldn't let you know earlier. I am writing this now so you can feel part of the celebration of her life. Thank you for being a friend.

NOTES & OBSERVATIONS

.....A MARATHON RUNNER

I was a marathon runner and continue to run 5–6 days a week. I am not sure you can call it "running" anymore but I try. In my best New York City Marathon I ran a 3:08.56. This was in the early 1980s. I trained four 100-mile weeks prior to running it. I was in the best shape of my life. As a runner, you share lots of stories with your friends. We found all the paths and trails that would keep us off the busy roads. I was an early morning runner, on the road from 5:45 a.m. to 7:45 a.m. to be at work at 8:00 a.m. The morning runs were part of my routine and I ran 3½ years without missing a day. Only a broken ankle would end my streak.

I loved the morning runs. They put me in close proximity to nature. They changed with the days and seasons. I would see the sun rise in the morning, I would feel the wind against my body, the rain on my skin and the coldness of snow penetrating my body. In the spring I would see the first flowers burst into bloom and in the fall I would marvel at the color. We met as a group and had seven different routes, one for each day of the week. I loved going through winding paths in the woods and meeting up with deer and other animals. I felt a closeness to nature which made me feel indestructible. I ran hard up her steep hills and glided down them on the other side. There is no question that I was hooked, but I was happy and felt accomplished.

A runner friend of mine said this was the toughest part of the day and once you got through that early morning run, the rest of the day was easy. I was lucky because I spent most of my day with nature. My work took me back to the greenhouse where watering, production, growing and organizing took place. Customers kept me on my toes with their questions and the field of horticulture offered daily challenges. Once you form a bond with nature you have taken the first great step that leads to happiness. This bond with nature is what I am hoping that you will be able to find too.

ADD YOUR GARDEN STORY HERE

14. PART TWO: PUTTING YOUR GARDEN TOGETHER

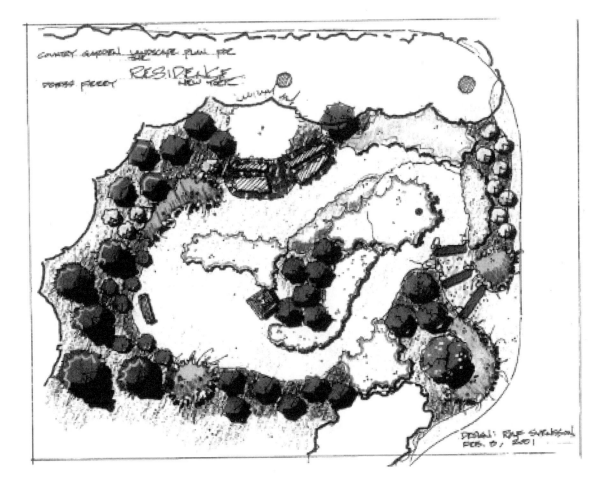

A STEP-BY-STEP GUIDE

The second part of this book will help you implement and enhance parts of the Natural Garden. I have written about topics in response to the needs of home gardeners. The information in this book will help you develop natural gardening on your own property. The natural garden preserves a place so that you can coexist with nature and enjoy outdoor living.

There are many parts to a landscape. Developing your grounds is an endless challenge. True gardeners find ways to improve their gardens each year. They read about a new plant and want to incorporate it. They observe and supply what is lacking. Life styles change as children grow and we need to accommodate these changes. Whether you plan a big project or a small one, change is what makes gardening such an exciting and evolving pastime.

There is so much to learn and the nice part is we never know it all. Each time we work in the garden we learn something new. Our organic programs will guide you with monthly "to do" lists. If we work with nature, nature will work for us. If we work against her by using toxic sprays, chemical fertilizers and harmful herbicides, we destroy the complex system that supports the food web. When we work against nature, we ultimately work against ourselves.

The parts of a natural garden include:

* Front Yard
* Back Yard
* Lawn
* Vegetable Garden
* Annuals
* Perennial Garden
* Herb Garden
* Ground Covers
* Plants that Attract Butterflies
* Plants that Attract Birds
* Plants that Attract Hummingbirds
* Indoor Gardening

MY GARDEN STORY

.....A NEW NEIGHBOR MOVES IN ACROSS THE STREET

Across the street where F. A. Young once ran Happy Valley, two sisters occupied the small, now remodeled house. After about five years, one sister got very sick and died of cancer. The other sister, Miss Lasher, who was a bookkeeper with a plumbing company, retired. She always had a dog—a boxer named Bambi. Boxers need to run and she built a large lawn where Mr. Young once grew his crops. She religiously mowed it several hours each week. Miss Lasher would go out every day and run her dog there.

I don't know when it happened, but in her retirement she got bored and ended up working for us as a bookkeeper, buyer and stock clerk. Salespeople had to go through her for orders. They said she was a character but they loved meeting with her each week. Years later a customer told me he would rattle the clay pots while she was working in the office to aggravate her and get her attention. She would come running out of the office yelling "Can I help you?"

We loved her and if we pried hard enough she would tell us great stories of her past. She was very secretive about that part of her life which made us curious. We would invite her to the house for a meal but she would never come. So we stopped inviting her and she became upset. She said "You know I won't come, but I want to be invited." She was a tough old lady and when the two sisters lived together she was like the man of the house. She did the heavy gardening and lugging. In the Garden Center when stock arrived she carried it to its proper place and unpacked the stock immediately.

One day she was chopping down some brush with an ax and cut a huge gash in her leg. She called us and we rushed over and tried to stop the bleeding. We needed to get her to the emergency room in a hurry. I ran to get the car but she refused. We were beside ourselves and told her she had to get stitches for the wound. She refused and wasn't going to a hospital. We realized it was useless so we made her apply Aloe vera to this wound three times a day. This she agreed to and we brought her three big Aloe vera plants so she could apply the juice directly from the leaf. It is amazing how the wound healed without infection or leaving a scar. When I talk to customers about the virtues of Aloe vera, I always remember these amazing healing results.

Miss Lasher worked for us for many years and she was very close to all of us. She was getting on in years when she sensed her heart was getting weak. She had Heidi, my wife, promise her that if anything ever happened, Heidi would take care of her dog. This was her only family and she needed assurances that her dog would live a happy life and never suffer. One morning Miss Lasher never came to work. We called her but there was no answer. We went over and knocked on the door. There was no answer but the dog was barking. We tried the door but it was locked. We called the police and they broke in. Miss Lasher was lying on the couch and her body was already cold.

Heidi immediately took the dog and brought her over to our house. She pampered the dog and kept her promise. She took the dog down into the office each day. The dog was sad and lonely and wouldn't leave Heidi's side. When anyone entered the house, Bambi would fiercely defend my wife. The only one who could calm her down was Heidi. We had just acquired a new bull terrier pup who would annoy Bambi by nipping at her feet. They never really became great friends but they tolerated each other. About a year later, Bambi developed a tumor on the brain which the vet said was terminal and we had to put her to sleep. Heidi would not allow her to suffer.

We buried Bambi on Miss Lasher's property which we had purchased from the estate after she died. Miss Lasher would have been pleased that Bambi was laid to rest where she spent her happiest years—in the field that Mr. Young grew his crops for Happy Valley and which Miss Lasher turned into a field of grass just for her Bambi.

ADD YOUR GARDEN STORY HERE

15. FRONT YARD

Unlike the back yard, the front yard puts you on display. It is not your own little hideaway. There is neighborhood pressure to conform and fit in. You are judged by the front of your house. Men become obsessed with a beautiful lawn and women strive for curb appeal. The front yard shows off your house and people form an opinion about you.

Front yards vary from neighborhood to neighborhood. Some people will hedge their whole property and will screen their house from sight. This is more often done on larger plots with longer driveways, preserving the valuable open space for one's private use. Some people just can't stand a noisy main road or an ugly sight. Some can't deal with the lack of privacy. Some houses don't face the front of the road, so they don't actually have a "front" yard. This group of people hedge themselves in. However, most front yards in a neighborhood conform to what I call the traditional front yard planting. It is this planting that we will be exploring in this chapter. The front door is the focal point and the house and the landscape plants radiate from it. The house is seen from the road and it is part of the local landscape.

Individual styles and tastes vary, creating an interesting mix as you walk or travel down the street. Window boxes in the front of a house, baskets hanging from a porch area or planters as you approach the front steps of your house add to the charm. Each person puts these together with a great deal of thought. Front yard plantings rely on the topography of the land and plantings need to be based on terrain. Side yards often become part of the front or back yard and you may find it necessary to screen this portion off to preserve privacy. These partial screens often leave openings large enough to frame the house.

Practical solutions are as important as aesthetic ones. Driveways need to be designed to accommodate the number of car spaces needed. Walkways to the front door need to be fitted as well as walls and steps to accommodate your needs. Easy access is necessary. Hardscapes need to be thought out and sometimes redone to provide the most practical solution for your piece of property. Put them on graph paper to scale and then work out a design. They can be removed more easily with an eraser than with a sledge hammer. Integrate design with convenience and make compromises. There are a lot of choices to be made in hardscapes. It is environmentally important to reduce impervious surfaces with surfaces that allow water to penetrate. Runoff causes erosion and leads to water pollution.

The goal of a foundation planting is to integrate the man-made structure of a house with nature. This is achieved by planting evergreens, shrubs, perennials and annuals around the foundation of a house following a landscape design. Give particular attention to choosing plants that will not overgrow the area. You want to choose plants that will complement and soften your house, not hide it. The front door is the focal point, your eye should lead to it. Balance needs to be achieved. This does not mean that you need symmetry—an asymmetrical planting is usually much more interesting. Balance can be achieved in many ways. A simple thing like a small evergreen, such as a pyramidal boxwood, planted on either side of the front entrance will lead the eye to the front door.

Most foundation plants are a mixture of spreading plants and upright plants. Try to get a mixture of textures, colors, shapes and heights. The upright plants serve to soften harsh corners, create interest on blank walls and lead the eye to the front door. The spreading plants should complement the beauty of your house and help create and further the transition to nature. Unattractive sights need to be blocked from view. Landscaping can hide many architectural weaknesses. A good landscape plan will fit your house into your property and will give your house a more natural setting.

When designing your front yard, move your thinking away from a straight line of shrubs planted in front of your house. Design your total space. Start with your plants radiating out. Corners can be softened with curving beds. Far enough from the corner of the house, a small flowering tree can be planted to soften the corner of your house. Bold, curving lines will make your plants look more natural. In the bays, color can be added for greater appeal. The cars in your driveway can be blocked from view by using beds of perennials, flowering shrubs or ornamental grasses. Banks need ground cover or a rock garden and always keep in mind that color is very important by your front entrance. It leads the eye, creates a cheerful atmosphere and adds interest.

Hedges are often desirable on the sides of a property to block the view of your neighbors' driveway, to define your property line and create a background for your plants. These side yard screens can also be made up of a mixture of tall growing plants. Make sure you pick the right plants for the right location and maintain them so they remain full and healthy. Watering, feeding, pruning and mulching are essential to their success.

Once you have scoped out your needs, your creativity can kick in. You can make your front yard whatever you want it to be. Flowering trees may be added, as may specimen evergreens, colorful islands of annuals, landscape roses, ornamental grasses or perennial beds. The lists of plants and the solutions are endless and can be constantly modified. Each front yard takes on its own personality. Make sure you strategically place flowering trees, specimen trees and island plants so they do not clutter up your front yard or block the view of your house. The neighborhood remembers your house by the spring color, the fall color, the beautiful specimens and the unique design and arrangement of plants that you have created. Some home owners will opt for a very simple arrangement with low maintenance. Some will want a picket fence, a low stone wall or a low front hedge as a border. Each property will be different and reflect the person who owns it.

Most landscape renovations take place when foundation plants have become overgrown—maintenance and pruning were not done in a timely fashion and the plants no longer complement the house. Perhaps the house has become hidden by the overgrowth, or the walkways are encroached and breaking down. A new owner may want to correct the mistakes made in the original planting and design. It is time to start anew. Many overgrown plants can be utilized in back yard or side yard plantings while others will not be salvageable. Ripping out and starting over will make all the difference in the appearance of your house. Save what makes sense, aim for a new start. Curb appeal is what sells your house and your house is a big investment.

Since you share your front yard with your neighbors, you will receive compliments, criticisms and suggestions. Your care and maintenance practices will also be critiqued. Variety is what makes the neighborhood interesting and most people will appreciate what you have done. Some will even copy you, and you'll take pride in a job well done. What is most important is that you are happy with your front yard—it is you and your family's happiness that counts. If your plantings can inspire you each morning and each evening when you come back from work, then they have done their job. They are making you proud of your home and there is no place like home. It is amazing what a beautiful front yard can do for both you and your neighborhood.

.....I NEEDED SOMEONE TO TAKE OVER THE LANDSCAPE DEPARTMENT

The business was growing and my chores were also growing. I needed someone to take over the Landscape Department. We had on staff Jan Berends, who once worked with the Dutch Consulate and joined Sprainbrook Nursery because he wanted to get into horticulture. He was well educated and had taken many courses at the New York Botanical Garden. He was a very talented individual and he loved flowers. I asked him if he would be willing to run a Landscape Department for me. He agreed and built himself an office in the upstairs of the Garden Center, hired himself a crew of hard-working Salvadorans and went to work to build up the department. Customers loved him and the two foremen he hired—Oscar and Tavo—are still with us.

Jan worked on the catalogue during the winter months and for many years worked on refining the cultural requirements of each plant we listed. He won several awards in the New York City flower shows. Sprainbrook Nursery became known for beautiful designs and its great installation crew and I got to spend more time with my family. In my spare time, I wrote handouts on every aspect of horticulture. This was the start of my book.

ADD YOUR GARDEN STORY HERE

16. BACK YARD

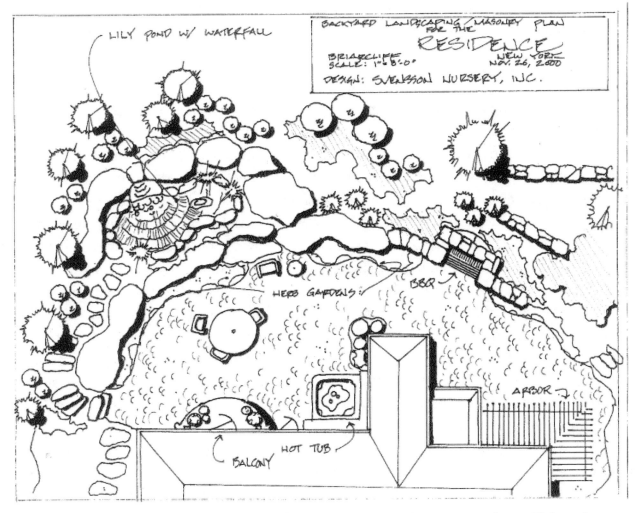

The back yard is for you. It is your own private playground, your own beautiful garden to sit, enjoy and entertain in. It's a place to lose yourself in, a place to bond with nature. Your back yard is anything you want to make it for you and your family to enjoy.

The first step is to screen your property from your neighbors' houses and from their view. Whether you love your neighbors or not, you need your privacy. It is important to be able to enjoy your back yard—to be surrounded with nature, not houses or other undesirable sights. If you have a beautiful view, preserve it; but if not, screen it from your sight and replace it with tall-growing evergreen trees. Screening in your back yard is one of the most important decisions you will make toward enjoying your back yard. You can start with hedges that are relatively small 5–6 ft. or 6–7 ft. tall. Let them grow. Your property value will increase as they grow. You may want to start with larger specimen plants. When selecting a hedge, there are many variables you will need to consider, such as

❋   Location: Sun, shade and soil conditions need to be matched to the proper plant.

129

* Width: Some hedges grow narrow, taking up less space; others grow wider, needing more space.
* Rate of growth: Choose fast-growing types to screen tall buildings; keep to slow-growing types for shorter hedges.
* Aesthetics: Choose single species or a mixture, broad-leaved or narrow, color and texture.
* Deer: If you live in deer country, you need to choose deer-resistant varieties.

There is nothing more beautiful to a home owner or prospective buyer than to walk into the back yard and find it surrounded by nature—with not another home in sight.

Hedges are an investment and require proper maintenance to keep them full, healthy and growing. Proper installation is very important and needs to be done the organic way. Add organic matter to your soil and use an organic fertilizer such as Bio-tone Plus, which contains mycorrhizae for better root development. Mulching, organic feeding throughout the year and adequate watering are necessary maintenance procedures to develop great hedges. Pruning is essential in keeping hedges full and dense. Lower branches fail due to stress and lack of proper pruning. It is sad to see beautiful hedges become bare on the bottom exposing all that you were trying to screen. Once you have reached the stage where your lower branches have thinned out, you have two choices: 1) rip the plants out and replace them with a new hedge, which becomes expensive, or 2) if you have enough property, you can do foreground planting with different shrubs to fill in the empty spaces by forming a lower screen. It pays to spend some time keeping your hedges healthy. Great hedges make great gardens.

Once you have solved your screening problem, you can start designing the back yard. Your back yard needs to fit your and your family's needs. If you have young children, you will want to carve out enough lawn for them to play on and enough property to put up their swing and play sets. Your back yard will change as the ages of your children change. The back yard is for everyone to enjoy at all times. Curving lines and foreground plantings can greatly improve the beauty, taking away from the rigid look that hedges create. Design areas with Hogarth S curves and graceful baying out protrusions that can create wonderful planting beds. If you are a gardener, you will love to incorporate perennial beds and flowering shrubs in these locations.

Terraces and patios will provide you with sitting areas and a place to barbecue. These areas become an extension of your living area, where entertainment takes place for the entire family. Small kids find it a place to ride bikes and play. Grown-ups find it a place where they can enjoy dinner or invite friends over for a drink. Or it can be a quiet place to sit and read a book. A designer will often plan a garden from a terrace or deck and create focal points with color, something beautiful to see and enjoy. The design may include a water display in a corner, a vegetable garden around the side of the house or a woodland path with a woodland garden leading to the back of the property. The possibilities are endless. Your dreams need to emerge for it to be a good design.

The back yard is yours to enjoy and yours to develop. This is where gardening takes place. This is where your creative side comes into play. If you love gardening, here is where you can spend hours immersed in sunshine, close to nature amongst beautiful plants, exercising your body with planting and maintenance chores and exercising your mind with thoughts of how to make it better. This is where you find the calm and beauty that Mother Nature offers to us all. If you build a beautiful garden, you and everyone that comes to visit will be filled with the happiness that your dream space will provide. It sets the tone of the visit.

The back yard often flows or extends into the side garden. Some of these side areas can be out of sight and lend themselves to special gardens or special treatments; they can become great places for vegetable, herb and woodland gardens or an extension of your lawn area or a play area. Make your private area as large as possible. Make out your wish list and then make it a beautiful reality. The back yard is for the family.

As a country, we spend a lot of our time on the computer or watching television. We need to spend some of our time enjoying the outdoors. Nature teaches us many lessons that we can only learn from her. Appreciating nature is a part of bringing up our children and it is part of enjoying a side of life that we often forget. It is a part of replenishing our souls by spending some time alone in thought or receiving that one hour of sunshine that is needed for healthy living.

You may need help in design. But whomever you choose, the designer needs your input and ideas. The back yard needs to be tailored to your desires and the special needs of your family. This is your hideaway that gives you a chance to spend time close to nature, your place to refresh from stress and to dream your dreams.

NOTES & OBSERVATIONS

.....A SPECIAL BACK YARD

One of the most beautiful gardens I ever designed was in the back yard of a ¾-acre lot. The home owner's back yard property faced four big houses that loomed over him every time he went out to suntan. Our first priority was to get large evergreens to screen all the houses from his view. He spent a lot of time and money with us, picking out each individual evergreen tree to form his back border. He chose conifers, mixing in some very unusual specimen plants. When he was finished, he had a barrier of different textures, tones and colors creating a very natural look. It looked like he lived in another world, devoid of any man-made structures.

Once the background was completed, he focused on the foreground. In the left-hand corner he wanted us to create a water feature. He chose a small circular pool where you could swim against the current. Cascading into the pool was a waterfall. The waterfall and the rock formations that surrounded it were built, then the pockets between the rocks were filled with dwarf evergreens, a dwarf cutleaf maple, flowering shrubs, colorful perennials and eye-catching annuals that created a spectacular display. On the other side of the pool, I built a berm filled with lots of colorful plants and to the right a large perennial garden following a Hogarth S curve. The perennial garden was filled with a diverse selection of flowering plants that created dramatic splashes of color throughout the year.

The entrance to the back yard was an arbor covered with roses and the house was lined with blue hydrangeas. The terrace on the lower level was enclosed with natural stone and on the bluestone patio were potted containers filled with beautiful combinations of flowers. The porch on the upper level was lined with window boxes filled with annuals that trailed with a profusion of color down to the second level.

The garden we installed followed our organic approach and was maintained by following Sprainbrook's organic programs. The birds, the bees and the butterflies all swarmed to this natural oasis. When the garden was finished, the owners had a party celebrating a special birthday. As the guests walked into the back yard, their faces lit up and the beauty of the plants put smiles on all of them. Beautiful flowers have a positive effect and there is a close relationship between humans and plants. Everyone was caught up, feeling a bond to nature. All had a great time. People still talk about this great party.

ADD YOUR GARDEN STORY HERE

17. THE ORGANIC LAWN

Lawns can be many things to many people and for some it is the most important part of outdoor living. For dogs it's a place to run, for children it's a place to play, for grown-ups it's a place to spend recreational time with the family. It's a way to move from one place to another. It frames our gardens. And for many, a beautiful front lawn is a status symbol. We pour more money into our lawns than any other part of our property. In the process we have abused our soils and polluted our environment through the excessive use of chemical fertilizers and poisonous pesticides, herbicides and fungicides. A lawn that is environmentally friendly, healthy for your children, pets and family and free from chemical fertilizers, toxic pesticides or harmful herbicides is an organic lawn.

Even though I always felt my company did the best job, I hated to put in a new lawn because lawns are always trouble. Cool-weather grasses take a beating in the heat of summer. And, since grass is a monoculture, weeds look different and are a source of great frustration. The common thinking is to kill the weeds, kill the pests and get rid of the fungus—a negative approach to obtain a positive result. An organic approach is a positive approach, one that concentrates on building up the strength and resistance of our grasses, making them so aggressive and strong that they will crowd out weeds and ward off insects and diseases. The organic approach asks what is natural for our soils and what will make roots grow deeper.

Our best ground covers are lawns, as they prevent erosion and erosion is what causes many of our environmental problems. Lawn care has suffered through an era of chemical applications and chemical programs. Phosphates in chemical fertilizers are water soluble and will wash into our water streams. Organic fertilizers have phosphates that are broken down by microbes, then released into the plant roots or into the soil. These phosphates do not dissolve in water and do not wash into our water streams. Nitrates in chemical fertilizers are also water soluble and leach into our water streams. This again is not the case with organic fertilizers that use microbes to break the organic matter down. In this break down process nutrients are released to plants. Chemical fertilizers with their high salt content kill microbes and provide an unfriendly environment for them to function in. They also release nutrients quickly to the roots of the grass and cause a spike in growth. Many organic experts say it is like feeding drugs to your plants. We create superficial growth responses without building a deep root system or healthy immune system. We end up with a myriad of insect and disease problems that require toxic pesticides and fungicides to cure them.

As we pour these products into our lawn, we further weaken our food web and we poison our soils. These poisons affect our ground water and the health of anybody spending time on a lawn. More and more severe health problems have been developing for our pets, our children and ourselves. These have been reaching alarming proportions. As more research is done and more facts come out, the harm that we are doing to ourselves is mind-boggling. Who would want to follow a chemical lawn program knowing all the problems that result?

The reason we got ourselves into this situation is interesting. After World War II, the agricultural community bought into the fact that we had lots of cheap chemical fertilizer left over from explosives used in the war. The idea was that we could utilize this technology to revolutionize the way crops were grown and we could develop programs of accelerated growth that would solve the world hunger problem. Large chemical companies became very powerful and rich. They gave grants to agricultural universities that enabled professors who published papers to earn status in their respective fields. The results of their findings were the basis of our classroom discussions.

The chemical world was a new world that led us down untested paths. Although crops could now be grown tailored to specific needs, problems arose and weaker plants resulted;

cures were developed and we poured more pesticides and fungicides into our earth. We could alter our plants by genetically engineering our seeds. We could even solve the labor-intensive weed problem by spraying more toxic herbicides into our soil. In our attempt to take control of nature we contaminated our soils, weakened our ecosystem and ruined our food supply. Now our country is facing a crisis which I fear will potentially lead to food shortages. My intent is not to talk about our agricultural dilemma but to talk about horticulture. I talk about it because agriculture influenced horticulture and the way we were taught at our respective universities.

When we studied turf management, we studied the relationship in chemical fertilizers of nitrogen to phosphate to potash. We wanted to come up with the best formula to grow turf. We found a 10-6-4 fertilizer was better formulated for growing turf than a 5-10-5. As the years passed, the nitrogen levels were increased to push more green growth and programs dealing with the ailments of grass were addressed. We followed the same destructive path that our agricultural counterparts followed and we are witnessing the same path of destruction.

The chemical approach has become ingrained in our universities. Students, in turn, wholeheartedly accept the chemical model and follow in the same footsteps. In most universities, the change to an organic approach is moving very slowly, if at all.

For years consumers have been bombarded with television and newspaper ads about the four steps that will give you a beautiful lawn. The picture of the lush green lawn is irresistible. The simplicity of such a lawn by following four easy applications per year is comforting. These are ads put out by chemical companies. The public is blinded by lack of knowledge and beautiful pictures.

Typically, the first step is a pre-emergent crabgrass and weed control and chemical fertilizer applied together. The second step is a post-emergent weed control and chemical fertilizer. The third step is an insect control and chemical fertilizer and the last step is usually just a fertilizer with the advice to apply seed at this time of the year. These programs usually require additional fungus controls, weed controls, insect controls and a winterizing chemical fertilizer to be applied in late fall. The chemicals are blanketed across the whole lawn and applied on a regular basis, whether they are needed or not. The large amount of chemical fertilizers with their high salt content kill most of the microbes in our soils. The herbicides, fungicides and insecticides that are used contaminate our soils and we grow a lush grass that is constantly weak and vulnerable. The frequently applied weed controls provide more toxins to our soil. Short-term solutions lead to long-term problems. The grass constantly needs to be treated. There is no end to the cures that need to be applied.

There is a better way. Learn to work with nature and not against her. Learn about the soil and the food web. Follow the path into natural gardening.

The organic lawn can become a great lawn filled with a deep root system and strong, resistant grasses. A chemical lawn will always be a weak lawn filled with constant problems. To me the choice is clear and my emphasis is to change the way we look at and treat our soils. The organic movement is in full swing and we need to get everybody on board; we need to support the health of all living things.

Timing is important on lawns and I have written an organic lawn program with steps to take on a monthly basis. Once we develop a great food web in our soils, we can limit our number of applications. Many things will become self-sustaining.

To grow a good lawn we need a good soil, adequate light and adequate water. With any new lawn, emphasis should first be on developing your soil. If you have a good soil, you have a fighting chance to have a great lawn. There are many things you can do to improve your soils but if your soil is either heavy clay or mostly sand, it will be greatly improved by adding organic matter. I will provide you with my step-by-step formula for how to build a new lawn.

Mixing enough organic matter into your soil initially will allow the food web to grow and develop. Carbon is microbe food. Microbes are essential and needed in great numbers, along with earthworms for aeration and lots of little arthropods to add to the porosity of our soils. A rich soil is filled with a diverse mixture of microbes, which leads to greater soil life in the form of mites, protozoa, nematodes, arthropods and even higher forms of life where worms are prevalent. Along with feeding plants, they coexist with each other to create a healthy environment that will make a great soil to grow turf on.

A healthy food web will encourage a deep root system. Mycorrhizae will form a symbiotic relationship with roots and the roots will flourish. The strength and overall health of your lawn will depend on the root system you can develop. It all starts in the soil. We can all see top growth but root growth is hidden below the surface and hidden from our sight and minds. It is amazing what takes place in our soils. The strength of any plant is in its roots, so it is necessary that we understand what grows good roots. Feed the soil and the soil will feed the plants. Follow my program. Each application contributes to the development of a healthy food web.

The greater the mix of organics added to the soil, the greater the results. Diversity is important. My program does not stick to any one brand of fertilizer; rather, my recommendations require a mixture of organic supplements to be applied to the soil. Organic fertilizer is food for the microbes and as it is broken down, it becomes food to be absorbed by the roots of our grass. There is more to food than NPK. Our universities taught us that Nitrogen, Phosphate and Potash is the key to growing good plants. They are now finding that other nutrients are needed. The key to growing strong healthy grass is to supply it with important micronutrients as well. If we apply the right mixture of organics to the soil, we will supply the rhizosphere with all the nutrients it needs to grow a strong healthy turf. Having to add supplements is a direct result of deficiency in our soil.

Remineralizing your soil is another sound organic practice that is beneficial to living soil. This process replaces minerals once spread by glaciers, floods and winds. Mineral rock dust may be hard to find and usually comes in 40–50 lb. bags. It provides ingredients to the soil that are not usually available from other sources. When added to the soil, the results in an improved turf can be astounding. Again, the greater the mix of beneficial ingredients to our soil, the greater the results.

Oxygen is critical to any good soil. Both the roots of the grass and the microbial activity within it require oxygen to sustain life. We talk about the importance of well-drained soil. Areas that are saturated with water lack oxygen and plants die. Water is critical to growing good turf but drainage is also critical. Areas that are saturated with water need to be remedied by building up the soil or draining off the water.

Compaction can be a huge problem on lawns. Porous soils support oxygen, but, when compacted, the pores are closed off. Lack of oxygen will cause grass to die. Aeration and applications of gypsum can help this problem. Steps to reinstall the food web need to be taken to bring the soil back to its healthy state. Once we have a healthy food web and soil plentiful with worms, aeration will take place naturally and oxygen will be available to the roots of our grass.

Water is an essential part of any living plant and is one of the most important factors in keeping a lawn lush and green through the growing season. In an organic lawn we are striving to develop a deep root system. The key is to water deeply but less frequently, to send the roots deeper in search of water. Watering your turf daily causes a superficial root system. Excessive watering can do more damage to a lawn than drought. Your turf should receive one inch of water each week. If Mother Nature does not provide it, apply ½ inch of water two times a week. An empty cup on your lawn will tell you how much water Mother Nature provides, and it will allow you to determine the amount of time needed on your sprinkler system setting to apply a ½ inch of water. During extreme heat conditions and long days, you may need to apply more water.

Roots are dependent not only on the soil with its supply of oxygen, microbes and organic matter but also on the food supplied from the plant above. When we cut the grass too short, we are cutting off food supply. We need to always strive to develop the best root system we can.

MYKE is a new line of products in our arsenal to produce a strong healthy turf. Establishing a large selection of beneficial microbes in our soil is the key to a successful organic soil. MYKE TURF has worked hard to produce the best selection of microbes to incorporate into a turf soil. It is best applied by mixing directly into the soil. A topical application is available. It is placed on a clay soil carrier which carries it down to the soil level. Other similar products are available and more will be developed in the future.

When trying to grow a great lawn, you need to consider that which takes place in the soil and that which takes place above the soil. Green leaves derive their energy from the sun. The sun's light and energy are critical to growing good turf. If your location is too dark, trim off the lower limbs of your trees. Let some sunlight in and use a good shade mixture of high-quality seed. The best lawns are grown in full sun or light shade. Photosynthesis is a process that takes place when the energy from the sun in the presence of chlorophyll facilitates the synthesis of sugar from CO_2, a gas absorbed through the stomata of the leaf blade and water absorbed and translocated from the roots. This process supplies the plant with essential carbon and oxygen. Sugars produced by photosynthesis provide food for the plant. Oxygen is released back into the atmosphere. Plants need green leaves filled with chlorophyll to carry on the photosynthetic process. A green turf is a healthy turf. The sun, the roots and the green blades of grass work together to produce a great turf. A great turf gives back oxygen to the atmosphere. It is nature's way of maintaining balance and keeping our air healthy.

In the selection of seed, all environmental factors need to be taken into consideration. Determine exposure for good success. Select your seed for a sunny location, for a sun and shade location or a shady location. A location on a hill may need to stand up to drought, and an area on the bottom of a hill may be moist. Different varieties of grass seeds do well under different conditions. Pick a mixture that best meets your requirements.

Most grass types blend beautifully together. It's the dark green color that most people are interested in. Fescue, perennial rye grass and blue grass make up most mixtures. If one type doesn't succeed another type will. Always buy high-quality seed. High-quality seed is in short supply because it is difficult and costly to produce. It can best be found at your local garden center. There is not enough high-quality seed to supply the big boxes and the chains. The strength of any organic lawn is in the high number of grass seedlings that grow so strong that it will crowd out all of your weeds.

Whenever you find a bare spot, add grass seed to it. In areas of high-weed population, pull weeds then add seed. If you don't have the time to pull weeds, add seed anyway and crowd them out. Seed needs to be in contact with soil. Brush, rake or shake so that the seed touches the soil. Use a high-quality weed-free organic topsoil, usually supplied in a bag and cover the seed with a 1/8 inch of soil. This will keep your seed from drying out and the birds from eating it. Water three times a day for 14 days for ten minutes each time. Make sure your new seedlings do not dry out before they reach maturity. Patch seeding should take place throughout the growing season but early fall is the best time of the year to do major seeding.

Dormant seeding is an easy way to add more seed to your lawn. It occurs when temperatures are too cold for germination to take place and your seed lays dormant until spring. Prior to the first snowfall, broadcast the proper seed mixture onto your lawn. With a good snow cover the seed will be conditioned and will germinate with warm weather. Success depends on adequate snow cover.

A school groundskeeper complained to me that he could never find a time to seed. His fields were always in use. I suggested that he try dormant seeding. The next year he came back and said it worked so well he didn't want any of that regular seed anymore. He wanted that dormant seed. At the nursery we couldn't stop laughing.

A trick for home owners who need to patch small areas is to pre-germinate seed by mixing it into compost, placing it in a wheelbarrow and keeping the soil moist. As the seed begins to germinate apply the mixture to a bare area. Another trick is to soak seed overnight in a cheesecloth bag which can save you a week's time. There are also patch seed formulas where the seed is impregnated into a mulch and you apply that to bare areas. Many grass seed mixtures contain grass plants carrying beneficial fungi called endophytes. While living synergistically off the grass plant, endophytes produce defense compounds called alkaloids. These are detrimental to above-ground feeding insects. They are natural and remain over time in the living grass plant.

Compost teas can be very beneficial to your lawns. In the era of 0 phosphate laws they can supplement your soils with phosphate which otherwise could be lacking. Compost tea is made directly from the compost that you create. You can add fish emulsion, seaweed extracts and seed-based liquids (such as Daniels) to your brewed tea just prior to application.

This will provide your soil not only with a mixture of microbes but also with a mixture of microbial food. Three to four applications of compost tea can produce an incredibly beautiful lawn at very little cost, especially if you brew and apply the product yourself. Soil equalizer and other microbial products can be bought to make instant teas. (See the section on Compost Tea in chapter 9 COMPOSTING.)

Grass needs to be cut and mowing practices are critical to growing a good organic lawn. Make sure your blades are sharp so you cut your grass, not rip it. Mowing high can eliminate many of your weeds by crowding them out, which will further increase your root mass. The more leaf surface, the greater the photosynthesis. Rhizome activity tremendously increases when you mow high. Mowing at 3½ in. high suppresses crabgrass; many consider this more effective than using herbicides. I like to keep my grass at 3-3½ in. high all year round and only at the last cut of the year do I lower my blade. This is because long grass can be matted down and snow mold will develop. Grass should be shortened before the snows appear.

Never cut more than 1/3 of your grass off at one time. During periods of rapid growth, cut your lawn more frequently. Leave grass clippings on your lawn. You will be recycling much-needed food back into your soils. During periods of high temperatures and long days, grass clippings act as a mulch, conserving much-needed water. Clippings suppress crabgrass growth, increase earthworm populations, suppress disease, reduce thatch and help reduce water runoff.

In the fall, leaves need to be removed from the grass with frequency. Fallen leaves can cause rotting and suffocation. But Mother Nature rewards us with products to put back into the earth. If you have enough space, compost your leaves. They can be reapplied to the lawn in the form of compost tea. If the leaf drop is not too heavy, you can recycle them back into the turf by crosscutting your lawn with several passes until the pieces are small enough to decompose. By chopping these leaves into small pieces, you will be amazed at how quickly they disappear into your lawn. Leaves will provide necessary carbon to the soil.

Introducing beneficial insects is an organic method to control grubs in your lawn. Nematode, a very small worm barely seen by the human eye, enters the body of the grubs and releases a bacterium that infects and kills the grub. The nematode uses the remains to carry on its breeding process. Nematodes like a porous soil with adequate moisture. Milky spore is a biological control for Japanese larvae. The bacterium is ingested by the grub and kills it. The bacterium reproduces within the grub, inoculating the area. After three to four years of application, the area can become self-sustaining in its control of Japanese beetle grubs.

Knowing the pH level of your soil is critical. A pH soil test may show a level you need to correct. Grass grows best at a high pH and most weeds grow better at a low pH. I like my soil to be at a 7 pH. Many soils tend to be acidic and a high calcium lime applied once or twice a year may be required.

Many people consider weeds to be the biggest problem in an organic lawn because toxic weed killers and herbicides are not applied. Cultural practices and hand weeding are the preferred method. I am a runner and after finishing my morning run I stretch my hamstrings by pulling weeds from my lawn. Do a little bit each day and the job won't become so daunting. Corn gluten is an organic preemergent weed control that is applied when Forsythia are in bloom. It prevents weed seeds from germinating. Selective organic postemergent weed controls are in use and more are being developed. They work on a limited number of weeds. Another product that's now available is derived from iron, which occurs in nature. It causes the foliage of the weed to burn and the weed collapses. We will hear more about new methods for organic weed control as organic lawns become more popular and research takes place. Both of these applications for weed control are recommended for use on organic lawns.

I'll end my discussion on lawns with the story of my mother's front lawn. My mother's house, the one I grew up in, is a red brick house located in the front of the Nursery. My mother was always concerned that the first thing people saw when they entered the Nursery was her lawn. She wanted to have one that was beautiful and green all during the year. We at the Nursery took care of her lawn and followed the chemical program I was taught in college. She always complained that her lawn looked terrible. She felt like the shoemaker's daughter who never had soles for her shoes. She said running a

Garden Center and advising people on lawn care with a terrible looking lawn was not good advertising.

The problems started each year by the end of June. Her lawn suffered from a fungus called "melting out." Just when we were getting the problem under control, chinch bugs popped up. We got out the insecticides and trounced the lawn area and tried to reseed the brown spots. At about the time we solved this problem, animals started digging in search of grubs. We would run to our arsenal of chemicals and apply Dylox for a quick grub kill. The lawn was filled with crabgrass even though we applied preemergent crabgrass killers every year. The weeds had an easy time competing and in the spring the lawn was a sea of yellow when the dandelions came into bloom.

We put in an irrigation system which would water the lawn every morning at 6.00 a.m. We prepared the soil adding in lots of organic matter. Even so, our roots were always too shallow. I will admit we were delinquent with some of the timing of our applications but the lawn looked terrible for a large part of the year. It looked green in early spring and again in the fall but it took a beating for the rest of the year. I was in the business and I was letting my mother down.

A year and a half before she died, I switched our Garden Center over to the organic approach. I researched and wrote an organic program for every phase of gardening. I followed to a "T" my own recommendations that I wrote on the organic lawn. Following the monthly application I was astounded with the success in my first year. That year or any year thereafter I did not have fungus in the spring, chinch bugs in the summer or grubs in the fall.

Each year the lawn gets better and now there are very few dandelions blooming in the spring. Most of the weeds and crabgrass are being choked out. Nematode and milky spore disease take care of the insect problems. Compost top dressing takes care of the disease problems. Grass is dominating and the color is a rich green. The roots are penetrating deeply into the soil, and in drought conditions when many of the other lawns are suffering, this lawn holds up and looks beautiful. I know the grass is healthy and the microbes have eliminated all the toxins in the soil. It takes 3–5 years to build up a good organic lawn and for the food web to become self-sustaining. At that point, reduction of applications can take place. My mother's lawn convinced me that I have come up with a great program.

DIAGNOSTIC SHEET FOR INSECTS AND DISEASES ON LAWNS

INSECTS

The following insects are most commonly active and are likely to damage turf. Once you diagnose the problem, you can come up with a solution.

INSECT	DESCRIPTION	TIMING
GRUB	Soft-curved 1-1 ½ in. larvae of various beetles including the Japanese beetle. Roots are chewed off and the turf can be rolled back like a carpet. The larvae are quite visible and about the size of a large fingernail. Raccoons, skunks and moles tear up the lawn to search for grubs. Birds are present in the early morning. Organic control: Beneficial nematodes and Milky Spore disease applications.	Late spring to early fall
SOD WEBWORM	They are 3/4 in. greenish-brown segmented caterpillars with stiff hairs on dark spots Small, irregular, dead spots form on the lawn. Sod webworms eat blades, promoted by thatch and hot, dry conditions.. Lawn moths can be seen flying in a zig-zag pattern over the lawn dropping eggs. Organic control: Soak the area with a horticultural soap and rake to remove pests. Add beneficial nematodes to the soil. Spray with pyrethrin in heavily infested areas.	Several generations during the growing season

CHINCH BUG	Adults are tiny 1/4 in. insects with black bodies and folded white wings. Yellow, round patches on the lawn that keep growing. Chinch bugs suck the juices out of the grass, causing it to turn brown; they continue to feed on the good grass, expanding their damage. Take a coffee can and remove both ends and place the open cylinder on the ground, covering 2/3 green area and 1/3 brown area. Press container two inches into the ground and fill with water. If present, the Chinch bug will float to the top within ten minutes. Chinch bugs are usually active when temperatures are above 70 degrees. Damage usually starts along hot walks and driveways. Organic control: Seed endophyte-containing resistant strains of grass. Keep area well watered.	As soon as temperatures reach 70 degrees or above.

DISEASES

Fungal diseases can become active and destroy large areas of turf in a short time. Diagnosis is more difficult than with insects, but careful study of the grass leaf blade, coupled with occurrence time, will help you identify the problem. Once you diagnose the problem, you can come up with a solution.

DISEASE	DESCRIPTION	TIMING
BROWN PATCH	This fungus causes circular areas up to two feet to turn brown. "Smoke rings" around the edge of the affected area. Most severe on grass cut too short. Most likely to occur during high temperatures and high humidity. Close cutting, poor drainage, over-watering, excessive nitrogen, and low pH all contribute to the disease. Organic control: Reduce nitrogen, mow less frequently, aerate and dethatch. Water less frequently and only during the day so grass dries off quickly. Rake out dead grass, top dress with Lobster Compost, 1 bag per 1,000 sq. ft. And seed with disease-resistant strains.	May through September.

DOLLAR SPOT	This fungus causes tan or straw-colored blotches about the size of silver dollars to appear on lawns. Hourglass shaped lesions on grass blades. Most damage is done when the lawn is dry and not properly fertilized and also on poorly drained lawns. Organic control: Aerate the soil, top dress with Lobster Compost, 1 bag/1,000 sq. ft. Fertilize and apply seaweed extracts. Overseed in fall with disease-resistant cultivars.	May through mid October.
FAIRY RING	Circles or arcs of dark-green grass occur in the lawn. The circles may be small or large. Mushrooms may grow in the dark-green area. A ring of grass around the green spots turns brown; the green areas will eventually brown out too. Organic control: Rake and discard the mushrooms as they appear. Spike the area with a spading fork each day. Water well. Encourage beneficial soil microbes by top dressing with compost. Remove the ring of soil carefully so as not to contaminate remaining soil, replace with finished compost and reseed.	Year round.
FUSARIUM BLIGHT	'Frog-eye' pattern. 'Cobwebby' material in crown of plant. Grass has a soapy feeling. Reddish brown, tan or yellow patches develop on lawn. Roots rot and are covered with a pink mold when temperatures reach 70 degrees or over. Recurs in the same patch each year. Organic control: Dethatch and aerate the lawn. Apply 1 in.-2 in. of water each week. Don't fertilize in late spring or early summer. Rake out dead grass and replant with fusarium-resistant cultivars.	June through September.

146

LEAF SPOT	Conspicuous leafspots on the grass blades which continue into the crown and root system. Grass blades develop reddish brown to black spots on the leaf blade. Grass shrivels and roots rot. Hot, humid conditions favor fungal growth. Organic control: Apply one bag of Lobster Compost per 1,000 sq. ft. each June. Restore diseased area by raking out diseased grass and top dressing with a finished compost. Reseed or overseed with resistant cultivars.	May and June.
POWDERY MILDEW	Most often in shaded, moist areas with poor air circulation. First appears on grass blades and soon the entire plant looks as if dusted with a white, powdery substance. Occurs with the onset of cool nights. Organic control: Water in early morning to allow grass to dry. Provide good air circulation; you may need to cut some lower tree branches.	March through October.
RUST	Grass blades develop yellow to rusty red, powdery spore blisters. Rusty appearance on turf. Orange-red dust comes off on shoes and clothing. Seriously infected lawns turn yellow and wither. Most common during July and August on dry lawns lacking nitrogen. Organic control: Water the lawn in the early morning so the grass dries off quickly. Fertilize using a seaweed extract. Rake out dead areas and overseed with resistant cultivars.	May through October.

147

SLIME MOLD	Slimy masses growing over the grass in irregular patches after heavy rains or after excess watering during warm weather. Pythium fungi cause patches of grass to turn black and look water soaked. In humid conditions, a cottony mold may appear. The disease usually occurs in wet, poorly drained areas that have been overfertilized. Spreads rapidly. Organic control: Aerate and dethatch lawn. Add calcium and reduce nitrogen. Enrich soil with organic matter. Improve drainage and reseed.	Early spring, summer and early fall.
SNOW MOLD	There are two types of snow mold. Grey snow mold has tan to greyish-white halos. Pink snow mold has pink web-like mycelium growing on the grass surface. In both grass is flattened against the ground. Occurs when excessive snow or snow melt water is present. Organic control: Cut grass shorter on your last mowing of the year. Lightly rake matted areas.	Late fall through early spring.
STRIPED SMUT	Turf takes on yellow-green to black appearance. Rubbing a white cloth or your hand across infected area leaves streaks. Most prevalent on Kentucky bluegrass. The spores infect the plant's crown and adjoining underground stems. Diseased plants die during the next period of hot weather. Organic control: Top dress with Lobster Compost every 6 weeks. (2 bags per 1,000 sq. ft.). Spray compost tea 3 times a year. Reseed with disease-resistant cultivars.	March through October.

MY FORMULA FOR BUILDING A NEW LAWN

The following is my formula for building a new lawn. Many who have followed it have reported back to me how beautiful their lawns look.

THIS PROCESS SHOULD TAKE PLACE FROM MID-AUGUST ON

I have developed and tweaked this formula over the course of many years. It turns a poor soil into a great soil. It allows grass roots to develop and penetrate into the soil.

1. On top of your existing lawn, per 1,000 sq. ft., evenly spread 3 bales of peat moss, 2 blocks of coir, 6 bags of Lobster Compost, 10 lbs. of Bio-tone Starter Plus and 2 bags of Penobscot Blend.
2. Apply and evenly spread 50 lbs. of lime per 1,000 sq. ft.
3. Rent a rototiller. Make sure it is large enough to till to a depth of 6+ in. Till the area twice, making sure the ingredients are well mixed into the soil. On small areas, hand digging can be done.
4. Rough rake the lawn area to remove large rocks and clumps of weeds and to establish your desired grade.
5. Apply over the surface of the soil Dry Formula Roots or Jonathan Green Humates, MYKE TURF and Azomite (mineral rock dust).
6. Finely rake the area, establishing the final seeding bed. Do not allow the prongs of your iron rake to penetrate too deeply into the soil and use the opposite side of the rake to develop a smooth bed.
7. Seed your lawn using the seed mixture that is right for the lawn's location. Use a hand-held spreader and seed by walking backwards.
8. Lightly rake in the grass seed, covering it with only 1/8 in. of soil. Cover the seed with salt hay.
9. Water the seed 3 times daily: 10:00 a.m., Noon and 4:00 p.m. Do this for three weeks until all the grass has germinated. You can make it easier on yourself by setting up sprinklers and automatic timers.
10. Cut the grass as soon as it is 3½ in. high.
11. Follow my Monthly Organic Lawn Calendar at the end of this chapter.

MY FORMULA FOR RENOVATING AN EXISTING LAWN

To renovate an old lawn, I have developed a formula for you to follow. Cut your lawn slightly shorter just prior to this procedure to allow better contact to soil, but set your blades back to 3–3½ in. for the next cut.

1. Rent an aerator. This will plug holes into your grass and bring oxygen down into the soil. It will open up areas for mycorrhizae and seed to enter.
2. Apply gypsum at the rate of one bag per 1,000 sq. ft. Gypsum will break up heavy soils.

3. Add Myke Turf to the soil. Myke Turf contains mycorrhizae fungi, which improve root development and plant vigor.

4. Add Jonathan Green "Natural Beauty" Organic Lawn Food to supply the necessary nutrients.

5. Add seed. For all difficult areas that have sun to part shade, I am recommending Black Beauty or Black Beauty Ultra at double the recommended rate. Black Beauty Ultra has blue grass added to its mixture. I am recommending the Black Beauty mixtures in my renovation program because they add genetically superior lawn grasses from three different families of grass bred to be drought and disease resistant. These grasses root deeply to reach available water underground. There are a lot of other great mixtures that have been developed. Pick the right grass seed mixture for the area. For shady areas, choose a grass seed such as Shady Nook. Remove lower branches on trees to allow more light in. There are many formulations of seed on the market. Study the ingredients and apply the right seed to the right location.

6. Spread the grass seed and rake or broom it in so that the seed comes in contact with the soil.

7. Top dress the area with 8 bags of topsoil per 1,000 sq. ft. Here again, rake or broom it in.

8. Water your seed 3 times a day for five minutes. 10:00 a.m., Noon and 4:00 p.m. Continue to water on schedule for at least 10 days. This is the most important step.

MONTHLY ORGANIC LAWN CALENDAR

I do not endorse any one brand and strongly believe the greater the mix of products, the greater the results. Similar brands can be substituted. For example, in place of Lobster Compost, you can use any akaline-based compost. Timing and purpose are the key ingredients to a successful program.

MARCH

* MILORGANITE (6-2-0). Organic ingredients rich in iron and calcium with nutrients derived from bio-solids. Purpose: A high-organic, nitrogen fertilizer rich in iron to get the season started. Also acts as a deer repellent. Application: 40 lb./2,500 sq. ft. Preferred application is as soon as the ground thaws.

* COMPOST TEA. Purpose: To add microbes to the soil and give your lawn an early and healthy start. Application: For those making their own brew, we recommend applying compost tea three times in the year, starting in March. See Chapter 9 COMPOSTING, Compost Tea, for detailed application instructions.

* MINERAL ROCK DUST (Azomite). Purpose: Applying mineral rock dust mimics the actions of Mother Nature by replacing minerals once spread via glaciers, flooding

and wind. Using mineral rock dust on your land is a sound organic practice beneficial to living soil. Application: 50 lb./10,000 sq. ft.; 5 lbs./1,000 sq. ft.

✳ GYPSUM. A naturally mined product containing 23% calcium and 17% sulfur. Purpose: To alleviate compaction in clay soils by causing a chemical reaction. Application: 36 lb./5,000 sq. ft.

APRIL

✳ CORN GLUTEN (Jonathan Green Organic Weed Control Plus Fertilizer). This is a non-chemical method to prevent the germination of crabgrass seeds and an excellent slow-release form of nitrogen. Purpose: Crabgrass and weed control and to add nitrogen to the soil. Application: 25 lbs./2,500 sq. ft. Apply when Forsythias are in bloom.

✳ SEED YOUR LAWN. If you need to seed, DO NOT apply corn gluten. This is a choice you are going to have to make. Corn gluten prevents new seeds from germinating. If you have small spots to patch, you can seed above the barrier by applying soil, then seed and top dress with soil again. Water three times a day.

MAY

✳ KELP BOOSTER PLUS. A natural bio-stimulate comprised of calcium and kelp. Kelp is rich in plant-growth compounds, micronutrients, amino acids and vitamins. Calcium is essential for plant growth and development. Purpose: Promotes root growth, increases resistance to insects and disease, increases healthy plant growth and development and improves seed germination. Application: 35 lbs./5,000 sq. ft.

JUNE

✳ LOBSTER COMPOST. Purpose: To enrich the microbial activity in the soil and add organic matter, making your plants stronger in resisting insects and disease. Fungus is rarely a problem on an organic lawn when this step is applied. Application: Apply at rate 50 lbs./1,000 sq. ft.

✳ MILKY SPORE (St. Gabriel Labs Milky Spore Grub Control). Bacillus popilliae. Purpose: To control the larvae of the Japanese beetle grub. Application: 20 oz. bag/ 7,000 sq. ft.

✳ BENEFICIAL NEMATODES. Comes in small refrigerated containers containing 50,000 or more nematodes. Purpose: Used to control grubs in the lawn. Application: Apply by diluting in water or mixing in compost. You can release the full quantity into the soil. Spread evenly and it will be effective on a large or small area.

JULY

* NORTH COUNTRY ORGANICS "Natural No Phos" fertilizer (6-0-6). Feather meal, peanut meal, natural nitrate of soda, natural soda of potash and pasteurized poultry litter. Purpose: To feed the grass in summer and provide a different set of organic ingredients. Fill the soil with as many organics as you can find. This is a total well-balanced organic which will not burn. Application: 50 lb./5,000 sq. ft. Apply with a spreader.

AUGUST

* INSTANT COMPOST TEA SOIL ECOLIZER EM3 (Mother Earth Organics). It contains fulvic, humic and ulmic acids, kelp and microbes, including endo and ecto mycorrhizae. Purpose: To add high levels of microbes to the soil. Application: Apply at the rate of one teaspoon in a gallon of water.
* COMPOST TEA. Purpose: Second application of the year to add microbes to the soil. Application: For those making their own brew, we recommend applying compost tea three times in the year, starting in March. See Chapter 9 COMPOSTING, Compost Tea, for detailed application instructions.
* MILKY SPORE (St. Gabriel Labs Milky Spore Grub Control). Purpose: Second application of the year to control the larvae of the Japanese beetle grub.
* BUILD A NEW LAWN. Follow our installation program found in this chapter.

SEPTEMBER

* LAWN FERTILIZER (Jonathan Green Natural Beauty 10-0-1). Organic ingredients are feather meal, blood meal, kelp meal, wheat shorts, amino acids and humic acid. Purpose: To provide a high-grade organic lawn fertilizer at the most important time of the year for grass growth and rejuvenation. Application: 20 lbs./5,000 sq.ft.
* SEED AND PATCH YOUR LAWN. Follow our Renovation program in this chapter.
* MYKE TURF: Mycorrhizal inoculant (Glomus intraradices). A natural beneficial microoganism that colonizes grasses and enhances macronutrient uptake, which contributes to plant survival and growth. Purpose: To quickly develop a deeper root system that requires less watering and with the ability to withstand drought and heat stress. Use when seeding and for maintaining established lawns. Application: One 7.1 lb. bucket covers 3,750 sq. ft.

OCTOBER

* TOP DRESS LAWN (Fafard Premium Compost (Shrimp and Seaweed). Purpose: To inoculate beneficial microbes and organic matter into your soil. Application: One 40 lb. bag (30 qts.)/1,000 sq. ft.
* COMPOST TEA. Purpose: Add microbial food to your soil to build up the strength of your roots and to increase plant health. Application: For those brewing and applying their own tea, this is the third and last recommended application. See Chapter 9 COMPOSTING, Compost Tea, for detailed application instructions

NOVEMBER

* JONATHAN GREEN HUMATES: An all-organic, highly concentrated carbon source known as Leonardite or Humates from Utah. Purpose: Stimulates soil microbes and promotes rooting with increased biomass. Conditions the soil, making it healthy, disease and pest resistant. Application: 50 lbs./5,000 sq. ft.

DECEMBER

* MAG-I-CAL: (35% Calcium Lime). Purpose: Bring soil pH to 7 and add calcium. We like soils to be at a pH of 7, where lawns grow best and have a competitive advantage over weeds. High calcium aids in the fight against weeds. Application: 45 lbs./10,000 sq. ft.

NOTES & OBSERVATIONS

.....GOING GREEN

We were in a tough economy when a customer told me he wanted to go green. He believed in the organic solutions that we kept advocating in our weekly e-mail. He had small children and wanted them to play safely on his lawn. He refused to have anyone put anything toxic on his grass and he needed to cut back on personal expenses. He could not afford to give up exercising for health reasons and he needed to utilize his time in a productive manner. He came up with a set of solutions.

To cut back on expenses he gave up his gym membership and decided to take over the gardening chores that he was paying someone to do. He rode his bicycle to and from the railroad station each day, saving on both parking and gas while getting a good workout. He bought an extra-light hand-push lawn mower and in return got a great workout each weekend by cutting his lawn using his own power instead of the gas engine that polluted the air. The hand-push lawn mower also enabled him to assure a high cut on his grass and kept heavy equipment from compacting his lawn. In the fall he bought a rake to take care of the leaves. He did not pollute the air with powered blowers. He felt he was in great shape and enjoyed getting things done the right way.

He followed our organic solutions and said he had the best lawn ever. The gardening chores brought him a sense of satisfaction and he formed a bond with nature by redirecting his efforts toward her. He enjoyed the results he got in return and by double-tasking managed his time more efficiently.

He told me operating a typical gasoline-powered mower for one hour produces the same amount of smog-forming hydrocarbons as driving an average car almost 200 miles under typical driving conditions, and that exhaust pollution per leaf blower per hour is the equivalent to the amount of smog from 17 cars driven one hour. This was a man who did his homework and was concerned with saving our environment.

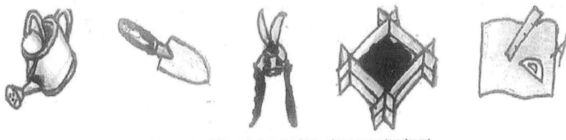

ADD YOUR GARDEN STORY HERE

18. VEGETABLE GARDEN

Any of us who own land can start a vegetable garden. All you need are the three basic ingredients: soil, sun and water. You can amend the existing soil to develop a rich organic medium, you can find a sunny location or create more sunlight through pruning or removal of vegetation that shades the area and you can add water when needed. We all have the ability to grow vegetables. If you are growing vegetables, you want to grow them organically.

Organically grown vegetables have greater nutritional value and are free of toxic chemicals. By converting your whole property to an organic garden you can plant vegetables in any part of your property. One of the newest trends in gardening is to incorporate vegetables and herbs into a landscape design. This is called edible landscaping —the intermixing of vegetables into flower gardens and perennial beds, giving them a whole new look.

Your parsley patch can border a rose bush, your rosemary can be part of a perennial bed. An ever-bearing strawberry patch can be part of the annual bed surrounding your terrace and a cherry tomato plant can end the bed as it approaches the upright walls of your house. The whole family will love to pop a small tomato into their mouths each time they walk out onto the terrace, and children will love the strawberry patch. A grouping of red pepper plants can create a focal point in a flower border and Swiss chard can add color to your perennial display. Edible gardening requires some creativity and imagination. Try adding some vegetables to your garden this year. Each year you will get better with this approach and will find places to tuck in a few veggies and herbs.

The traditional approach to developing a vegetable garden is to find a separate sunny location on your property. People who enjoy a beautiful back yard and don't want to disturb that look will often use a side yard or a location against a freestanding garage. To increase the beauty of a vegetable garden, border it with flowers. Winter is the time to put some thought into finding a great location for your vegetable garden. It may require some removals and some new paths. While you have the time, play with different ideas and put them on paper. Consider access and available water. Once you start working out layouts on graph paper, you will be surprised at the interesting ideas that can develop. Picking the right location is the most important step in having success with growing great vegetables.

My suggestion is to start small and plant things you love to eat. The most popular homegrown crop is the tomato. You can't beat the taste of a homegrown organic tomato. Raised beds can be expensive but are very convenient to work in and tend to have a superior growing environment; the soil is well-drained and thus properly aerated. Raised beds may be necessary in areas where rock formations are close to the surface. Irrigation is important and fencing may be necessary if animals are a problem. Once you commit to a vegetable garden, you will find ways to make it work..

Historically, before World War II, all crops were grown organically. After the war, America found a way to increase production through the use of cheaper chemical fertilizers. The chemical companies provided large grants to our agricultural colleges and influenced the teaching and learning process. In our quest for increased production, America as a society lost sight of nutritional and health values in the vegetables and the grain crops we grew. Agriculture is the strength of any nation and the American businessman put together a marketing plan that would sell our agricultural products. The American consumer bought into this plan. Now we are trying to sort out the facts and return to healthy eating.

We are overwhelmed with choices and tempted by fancy packaging. We are not well equipped with the knowledge of what's best to buy. Our country is suffering major health problems and we need to make changes. We have altered our food crops by genetically modifying seed, so that herbicides could be sprayed by farmers without injuring the plants being grown. We are guinea pigs eating food we never ate before on the assumption we have been eating it for centuries. We have processed our foods, making sure they look good and taste good but it's at the expense of good nutrition.

A mismanaged agricultural philosophy is causing the health of our younger generation to be in jeopardy. Parents who have become enlightened to these issues are in distress and search out organically grown produce. The healthiest vegetables are organically grown. They are started from an organic seed and grown in an enriched organic soil. When grown in your own back yard, they can be picked at their prime. When harvested directly from the organic garden, vegetables have the most nutritive value. Starting your own vegetable garden is making a start toward healthier living.

We need to explore the question of why growing organic is so important to nutritional value. It all goes back to the soil. In organic growing we feed the soil and the soil feeds the plant. Microbe populations thrive in a rich organic soil. The microbe is the key to growing nutritional vegetables. Chemical fertilizers such as the old chemical 5-10-5, which were so popular at one time, are not conducive to microbial activity. The high salt content in these fertilizers is detrimental to microbe populations. With organics, microbes are a gardener's best friend and work silently for you day and night by digesting the organics in the soil and then releasing nutrients to the plant. They release more than just NPK; they release a full spectrum of nutrients which make for nutritional food. Chemical fertilizers directly feed the plant, not unlike injecting them with drugs to stimulate growth and production. A rich organic soil is the key to growing healthy nutritious vegetables. Your vegetables will be filled with not only the three basic fertilizer groups but also with all of the micronutrients that make for healthy eating.

For those who would like to start their own organic vegetable garden, make sure you choose organic seed. Make your choices early to ensure a good selection.

A few things to consider: Healthy plants resist insect and disease infestations. Overhead watering in your garden promotes fungus problems; drip irrigation is a great solution. Keep a vigilant eye out for insects and use organic controls before populations reach epidemic proportions.

Initial soil preparation is extremely important when you develop a new planting bed for vegetables. Prepare your soil properly by incorporating my list of organic products into the soil. This will develop and establish a good food web. The following year, do not turn the soil so as not to disturb your food web, and add your amendments to the top 3 in. instead.

NEW BEDS NEED TO BE PROPERLY CONDITIONED.

I have developed a formula that I have recommended and used for many years. My customers thank me for the advice and the great yields of vegetables they're able to produce using my formula.

MY FORMULA FOR THE PREPARATION OF A NEW PLANTING BED FOR A VEGETABLE GARDEN

Per 100 sq. ft. of area, dig and mix into the top 1-foot.

- ❋ 1 bale Peat Moss (3.8 cu. ft.)
- ❋ 1 Coir block
- ❋ 3 bags Lobster Compost (1 cu. ft.)*
- ❋ 1 bag Penobscot Blend (1 cu. ft.)*
- ❋ 2 bags Dehydrated Cow Manure (1cu. ft.)*
- ❋ 2 bags Fafard Top Soil (1 cu. ft.)
- ❋ 4.5 lbs. Bone Meal*
- ❋ 1 lb. Mineral rock dust*
- ❋ 5 lbs. Lime*
- ❋ 1.4 qt. Myke Vegetable Garden*
- ❋ 8 lbs. Plant-tone (Espoma)*
- ❋ Add Soil Perfector to heavy clay or sandy soils

* Items followed with a star should be added after the first year and every year thereafter to the top 3 in. of the soil. Mixing deeply into the soil will injure the food web that developed during the previous year.

Your vegetable garden needs to be planned because there are many variables to consider. Choices depend on the size of your plot and the amount of space you are willing to give to this garden. Large vegetable gardens lend themselves to row planting and fencing in to prevent animal damage. Raised beds provide greater air circulation in the soil and usually greater crop yields. Container planting provides another choice where little or no adequate land is available.

Whatever your choice for containing the plants, decide what crops you want to grow and make a plan for where you want them to grow. Vegetable gardens are not particularly pretty to look at, but by planting perennials and annuals in the foreground or around the circumference of the vegetable garden, you can achieve a more attractive appearance. You don't have to keep to the more efficient rectangular design, you can play with various shapes and designs to see what fits into your overall scheme. Think about all of these variables and come up with a plan that best suits you and your family.

COOL-WEATHER CROPS

These cool-weather crops should be planted about two weeks before the last killing frost in the spring:

- ❋ Beets
- ❋ Broccoli
- ❋ Brussels Sprouts
- ❋ Cabbage
- ❋ Cauliflower
- ❋ Celery
- ❋ Garden Peas

* Kale
* Lettuce
* Onions
* Radishes
* Spinach
* Turnips

Listen to long-range weather forecasts for your area.

WARM-WEATHER CROPS

These warm-weather crops should be planted just after the last expected frost in the spring:

* Cantaloupes
* Carrots
* Corn
* Cucumbers
* Peppers
* Pumpkins
* Snap Beans
* Squash
* Swiss Chard
* Tomatoes

Listen to long-range weather forecasts for your area.

HOT-WEATHER CROPS

The following hot-weather crops should be planted about 3 weeks after the last frost in the spring:

* Eggplants
* Field Peas
* Lima Beans
* Okra
* Shell Beans
* Sweet Potatoes
* Watermelons

Listen to long-range weather forecasts for your area.

OTHER CONSIDERATIONS WHEN PLANNING A VEGETABLE GARDEN

HARVESTING. The art of harvesting your vegetables at the right time is important. The basic rule is to harvest vegetables early and often. If you eat your vegetables on the same day that they are harvested and if they are harvested at the right time, you will be eating them at their nutritional peak. This will require tending to your garden frequently.

WATERING. Watering is the most critical aspect of growing a good plant. Overhead watering often has disastrous results. Drip irrigation is my watering method of choice. A simple, inexpensive system can be attached to your outdoor faucet with an automatic timer. If you choose to water by hand, water the roots, not the foliage. Water deeply and less frequently. A good grower will spot-water plants that are dry rather than watering everything. Too much or too little water can be detrimental to your plants. But in general most vegetables need a half-inch to an inch of water each week.

STAKING. Plants that are staked require special attention. Tomatoes need to be attached to their growing structure as they grow. Many vegetables require trellises to keep them off the ground to avoid rot. Check your local garden center for the many methods of staking that are available.

WEEDING. Keep up with weeding from the start. Mulching is beneficial for your plants as well as aiding in weed control. In difficult-to-control weed areas, apply double layers of newspaper or brown paper covered with a 3 in. layer of mulch. Weed in the evening or early morning hours as weed seeds exposed to sunlight germinate rapidly.

FENCING. Where rabbits, woodchucks, deer and other animals are a problem, fencing may be your best answer. Deer require a 7 ft. or higher fence, but for other animals use inexpensive 5 ft. chicken wire. 18 in. to 2 ft. should be folded facing it to the outside of the garden and covered with 3 in. of soil. 3 ft. should be left to attach to stakes 3 ft. tall and leave the top 1 ft. unattached. A friend saw a woodchuck go to the fence and start to dig under it. It hit the underground fence, backed up and dug again with the same result. It backed up one more time and after hitting the underground chicken wire again, gave up and decided to climb the fence. When it got to the top, the weight of the woodchuck propelled the loose part of the fence backward throwing the woodchuck to the outside of the garden. The woodchuck had enough and gave up.

MONTHLY VEGETABLE CALENDAR

I do not endorse any one brand and strongly believe the greater the mix of products, the greater the results. Similar brands can be substituted. For example, in place of Lobster Compost, you can use any akaline-based compost. Timing and purpose are the key ingredients to a successful program.

MARCH

* MINERAL ROCK DUST (Azomite). Purpose: Applying mineral rock dust mimics the actions of Mother Nature by replacing minerals once spread via glaciers, flooding and wind. Using mineral rock dust on your land is a sound organic practice beneficial to living soil. Application: 50 lb. bag/10,000sq. ft.; 5 lb. bag/1,000 sq. ft.
* Plant-tone 5-3-3 (fertilizer) Purpose: To feed the soil with a total well-balanced organic fertilizer which will not injure the roots of the plant. Application: 50 lbs./ 2,500 sq. ft.

APRIL

Incorporate these organic materials into the top 3 in. of your soil. Once this is accomplished, cool-temperature crops can be planted. Add Myke Vegetable Garden at planting time.

Per 100 sq. ft.:

* 2 bags Dehydrated Cow Manure (1 cu. ft.)
* 3 bags Lobster Compost (1 cu. ft.)
* 1 Penobscot Blend (1 cu. ft.)
* 1 4.5 lb. Bone Meal
* 1 lb. Mineral Rock Dust (Azomite)
* 5 lbs. Lime
* 1.4 qt. Myke Vegetable Garden (use at time of planting)
* 8 lbs. Plant-tone (Espoma)
* Add Soil Perfector to heavy clay or sandy soils

MAY

* BRADFIELD ORGANICS LUSCIOUS LAWNS AND GARDENS. Purpose: To feed the soil with a diverse mixture derived from alfalfa, molasses, sulfate of potash and poultry byproduct meal. An excellent organic fertilizer for vegetables. Application: 20 lbs./1,000 sq. ft.
* MYKE VEGETABLE GARDEN should be added at planting time to ensure microbial activity in the soil, reduce transplant shock and ensure strong plant growth.
* PLANT. May is the month to plant your warm weather vegetable garden. Buy plants grown from organic seeds and that are grown organically.
* MULCH. Once your garden is planted, make sure you apply a 2 in. layer of mulch.

JUNE

* KELP BOOSTER PLUS. A natural bio-stimulate comprised of calcium and kelp. Kelp is rich in plant-growth compounds, micronutrients, amino acids and vitamins.

Calcium is essential for plant growth and development. Purpose: Promote root growth, increase resistance to insects and disease, increase healthy plant growth and development, improve seed germination. Application: 35 lbs./5,000 sq. ft.

❀ OBSERVE. Keep a vigilant eye out for insects and diseases and treat early with an organic solution before it reaches epidemic proportions. Inspect your garden on a weekly basis. It is essential to eliminate weeds. Make sure plants get adequate water. Water the soil. Overhead watering leads to disease and poor fruiting. Release beneficial insects to reduce potential problems. Keep slugs under control by applying Sluggo.

JULY

❀ DANIELS 10-4-3, a liquid fertilizer. Purpose: It is organic in nature, environmentally friendly and promotes microbial growth. Increases plant vigor and flowering. Promotes disease and insect resistance. Application: 1 tbs./gal. water as a thorough drench to the soil.

❀ WATERING. Keep your vegetables evenly watered to avoid cracking and splitting. Avoid overhead watering. Drip irrigation is your best option. Keep your beds weed free. Check plants for insect damage and, if present, use an organic control early on. Many crops may need staking or hilling. Check for slug damage.

❀ OBSERVE. Keep a vigilant eye out for insects or diseases and treat early with an organic solution before it reaches epidemic proportions. Inspect your garden on a weekly basis. It is essential to eliminate weeds. Make sure plants get adequate water. Water the soil. Overhead watering leads to disease and poor fruiting. Release beneficial insects to reduce potential problems. Keep slugs under control by applying Sluggo.

AUGUST

❀ FEEDBACK LIQUID COMPOST. A gourmet meal for soil microbes, it's 100% organic soil food and a catalyst for soil activity. Purpose: Feed microbes, increase root bio-mass, balance soil and reduce stress on plants. Application: 1 oz./gal. water, 3 oz./1,000 sq. ft.

❀ COMPOST TEA. If you brew your own you can add it instead of the above. See Chapter 9 COMPOSTING, Compost Tea, for detailed application instructions.

❀ OBSERVE. Keep a vigilant eye out for insects or diseases and treat early with an organic solution before it reaches epidemic proportions. Inspect your garden on a weekly basis. It is essential to eliminate weeds. Make sure plants get adequate water. Water the soil. Overhead watering leads to disease and poor fruiting. Release beneficial insects to reduce potential problems. Keep slugs under control by applying Sluggo.

SEPTEMBER

❀ NEPTUNE HARVEST FISH & SEAWEED FERTILIZER. This liquid, all-natural organic fertilizer combines several species of fish, has no offensive odor, is cold processed, has no oils or proteins removed, contains no chlorine and won't clog your sprayer. Combining this with kelp makes it an incredible product. Kelp is derived from seaweed harvested from Nova Scotia and has 60 naturally occurring major and minor nutrients, carbohydrates, amino acids and other naturally occurring substances that specifically promote plant growth. Purpose: Enhance crop yields, quality and vigor. Application: 1 oz./gal. water applied as a thorough drench.

❀ PLANT COOL WEATHER CROPS. Extend your harvest into late fall.

OCTOBER

❀ TOP-DRESS COMPOST. As crops have been harvested, remove remaining plants to avoid insect or disease complications and compost them. Add leaves and other materials to develop a rich compost. If this process was done the year before, mix the finished compost into the bare areas. If not, incorporate Lobster Compost and Penobscot Blend into bare areas. Keep the bare areas cultivated, allowing birds to feed on grubs and other hidden larvae. Frequent cultivation prevents weed seeds from developing. Allowing existing seeds to germinate and removing them before they go to seed is another weed seed reduction technique used effectively by many home gardeners for controlling weeds on next year's crop.

NOVEMBER

❀ PLANT A COVER CROP. Winter rye can add a lot of bio-mass, effectively covering the soil once it germinates. Cover crops are known as organic manure. The bio-mass of a crop of winter rye, for example, keeps weeds crowded out of the garden and prevents erosion. Turned into the soil the following spring, they add great nutritional value as they break down in the soil.

DECEMBER

❀ LIME SOIL. Add a high-calcium lime to your soil if the pH is below 7.

.....THE VEGETABLE GARDEN

One spring, I went on one of my nightly landscape appointments to find that my client wanted us to lay out and build two 6'x12' raised beds for a vegetable garden to be installed in front of his house. We discussed the project and I advised him that, for aesthetic reasons, we should come up with a compromise since when plants dieback, the ground will be bare and the house would look naked.

The house faced a road. Parallel to the road was a hedge of Arborvitae, which gave him screening from the noise of traffic. His driveway created a border on the right side. To the left side of the front door was an open grass yard that he was very protective of, as it was the recreational spot for his children. He was into soccer and there needed to be enough space to kick a soccer ball around.

I laid out the area and convinced him to plant a line of foundation plants that would complement and beautify the exterior of his house. I ran a path across the center of the property with natural rock stepping stones leading from the driveway at the right to the grassy yard on the left. On either side of the path we built the raised beds. I left room for a 3 ft. wide ground bed in the front of the vegetable garden, where I planted colorful perennials. I also allowed for a 3 ft. wide ground bed at the back end to beautify the vegetable garden from the lawn area. All sides of the raised bed were easily accessed by walks wide enough to allow him to work on his garden. On the inner side of the Arborvitae hedge there was room for a 3 ft. wide planting bed. I planted a herb garden here. Although this area had part shade, we found herbs that would thrive there. We filled the raised beds with a prepared soil according to our recommended formula and we installed a drip system on an automatic timer for the whole garden.

The project turned out great. The owner harvested more vegetables than he was able to eat; the perennials were a blaze of color that attracted rave reviews from anyone who entered his driveway; and the herb garden that he worried about, for fear of not having enough sun, turned out to be a great asset. In the winter he had a beautiful foundation planting to look at, in the summer his entryway was colorful with flowers and his family ate healthy organically grown vegetables throughout the growing season.

I discussed the project with a runner friend of mine and he told me a story about his grandfather. My friend Blase grew up in the Throggs Neck section of the Bronx. His grandfather lived in the same neighborhood. He would often visit his grandfather and they would spend time together in the vegetable garden. His grandfather was born in Italy, and when he visited Blase at his house, Grandpa would complain about the grass in the front yard. "Are you people crazy?" he would say. "What are you going to do with grass? Don't you know by planting grass you are losing money? You could be saving money by growing vegetables that would be healthy and nutritious for you. You can't eat grass and it costs money to maintain it."

Finding a place for a vegetable garden on your property makes sense. With good design the vegetable garden can be made very attractive and will serve a great function.

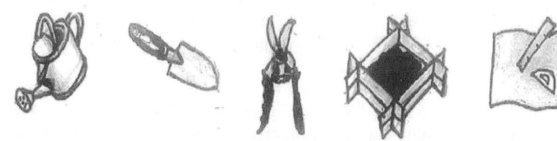

ADD YOUR GARDEN STORY HERE

19. ANNUALS

Annuals give color, beauty and warmth to our outdoor living areas. They provide color from spring to frost. They can be used in many landscaping situations and have many applications, such as in hanging baskets, window boxes, planters, front yards, back yards and rock gardens, and add additional color to perennial gardens, woodland gardens, free-flowing beds, shady areas, sunny areas or any area of your yard that needs sprucing up. They get replanted each year and they are your chance to add color, interest and style to your property.

Each year new and better varieties of annuals come on the market, making the selection greater and the combinations more exciting. New vegetative cuttings provide superior varieties that have more flower power, heat resistance and longer duration of bloom. It will pay you to research your options and to keep a record of what plants provide you with the greatest satisfaction from year to year. Each annual plant has a different role to play in the landscape that is dependent on its cultural needs, its size, its habit and its color. Any open space on your property is a space where you can add annuals. Below is a list of things you should consider when purchasing annuals.

* **LOCATION:** Sun or shade, dry or wet, foreground or background, container or in ground.
* **WATER REQUIREMENT:** Match the plant to the amount of water you will be able to provide.
* **USE:** Trailing or upright, bedding, container, vine or cut-flower, accent or filler, foliage.
* **FLOWER POWER:** Strong colors viewed from a distance, soft colors up close.
* **COLOR COMBINATION:** Complement, contrast or mass one color, mix textures.
* **TIMING:** Cool-temperature flowers for early and warm-temperature for later planting.
* **HEAT RESISTANCE:** Pick varieties that will withstand hot or cold conditions.
* **DEER RESISTANCE:** In deer country, pick plants that are deer resistant.

Varietal improvements make the difference. New varieties are selected and hybridized through vegetative propagation. New and better varieties are becoming available with stronger traits, making your garden flourish throughout the season. My list of Top 25 Annuals has been compiled from many years of growing, propagating, planting and observing the performance of these plants in the field. I love all annuals and would not limit myself to just these, but I would suggest planting as many of these as meet your needs.

MY TOP 25 ANNUALS

Vegetatively grown annuals allow us to propagate varieties with superior traits. This has changed the whole way we market plants. The following varieties—my Top 25—are grown by cuttings.

1. Ageratum houstonianum 'Patina Blue' (Hybrid Ageratum)
2. Alstroemeria hybrida 'Princess' series (Alstroemeria)
3. Angelonia angustifolia 'Angel Mist' series (Angelonia)
4. Antirrhinum majus Snapdragon 'Luminaire' series (Trailing Snapdragon)
5. Begonia Red and Pink 'Dragon Wing' (Dragon Wing Begonia)
6. Begonia richmondensis (Richmondensis Begonia)
7. Bidens ferulifolia 'Goldstar' (Bidens)
8. Calibrachoa 'Cabaret,' 'Million Bells' and 'Superbells' series (Calibrachoa)
9. Cleome hasslerana 'Senorita Rosalita' (Cleome Senorita Rosalita)
10. Coleus hybrid (Coleus)
11. Cuphea hyssopifolia 'LavenderLace' (Mexican Heather)
12. Euphorbia hypericifolia 'Diamond Frost' (Diamond Frost Euphorbia)

13. Evolvulus glomeratis 'Hawaiian Blue Eyes' (Evolvulus)
14. Fuchsia hybrida 'Gartenmeister' (Gartenmeister Fuchsia)
15. Impatiens walleriana 'New Guinea Hybrids' (New Guinea Impatiens)
16. Impatiens walleriana 'Fusion' series (Exotic Impatiens)
17. Ipomoea (Sweet Potato Vine)
18. Lantana camara 'Patriot series' (Lantana Hybrid)
19. Pelargonium hybrid 'Ivy Geranium Balcon' (Balcon Ivy Geranium)
20. Petunia x hybrida 'Tiny Tunia' (Tiny Tunia Petunia)
21. Petunia x hybrida 'Wave Petunia' (Wave Petunia)
22. Phlox x hybrida 'Intensia' (Trailing Phlox)
23. Plectranthus hybrid 'Battenberg' (Battenberg Ivy)
24. Scaevola aemula 'Bombay Dark Blue' and 'Purple Fan' (Australian Blue Fan)
25. Torenia fournieri 'Moon' series (Wishbone Flower)

Seed-grown annuals are still the most popular bedding plants used by most home owners. For use in mass plantings, the cost is much less. There are many old-time favorites that have stood up to the test of time. Seed companies continue to hybridize newer and better varieties. They can be seeded directly, started indoors or purchased in flats. Purchasing mature plants in flats will give you the longest time in the garden. Direct seeding will take the longest to come into bloom and starting your own plants indoors usually comes out somewhere in between. If you have a short season, you want to maximize your period of enjoyment. Refer to Chapter 3 PLANTING for seeding and propagation requirements.

Container plants are best planted in a rich, organic soil mix, which will supply them with the nutrients they need. At the Nursery we mixed our own soil using a large assortment of ingredients. People travel great distances to purchase it. The greater the mix, the greater the success.

Planting beds need to be prepared properly by conditioning the soil. After the first season, yearly top dressing with compost and an organic fertilizer is usually all that is needed. Take a soil sample and maintain your pH between 6 and 7.

MY FORMULA FOR THE PREPARATION OF A NEW PLANTING BED FOR ANNUALS
Per 100 sq. ft., dig and mix one foot deep:

❋ 1 bale Peat Moss (3.8 cu. ft.)
❋ 1 Coir block
❋ 3 bags Lobster Compost: (1 cu. ft.)
❋ 2 bags Penobscot Blend: (1 cu. ft.)
❋ 1 bag Dehydrated cow manure (1 cu. ft.)
❋ 1 bag Fafard Top Soil (40 lbs.)
❋ 4.5 lbs. Bone Meal

* 1 lb. Mineral Rock Dust (Azomite)
* 5 lbs. Lime
* 1.4 qt. MYKE ANNUAL AND PERENNIAL
* 8 lbs. Plant-tone (Espoma)
* Add Soil Perfector to heavy clay or sandy soils.

Whenever planting annuals, never plant too deeply. Always plant the top of the soil in your plant at the level of the existing soil. Add MYKE to the soil at planting time to increase microbes, which will help increase root development. Buy plants that are organically grown whenever you can. They will adapt more quickly to your soil when planted. Container plants should be packed as tightly as possible so that they will burst out overflowing with color. Containers have open space surrounding them where they can develop. When planting large areas in the ground, adhere to proper spacing so that plants will not crowd out. Avoid overhead watering and keep your planting beds weed free. Use a 2 in. layer of mulch to reduce weeding and conserve moisture. Corn gluten, an organic preemergent weed control, can be added prior to mulching. Release insects to reduce damage. Be vigilant and treat problems with an organic spray as they occur. Repellents may be necessary to discourage animals that feed on or harm your plants.

MONTHLY ANNUALS CALENDAR

I do not endorse any one brand and strongly believe the greater the mix of products, the greater the results. Similar brands can be substituted. For example, in place of Lobster Compost, you can use any akaline-based compost. Timing and purpose are the key ingredients to a successful program.

MARCH

* MINERAL ROCK DUST (Azomite). Purpose: Applying mineral rock dust mimics the actions of Mother Nature by replacing minerals once spread via glaciers, flooding and wind. Using mineral rock dust on your land is a sound organic practice beneficial to living soil. Application: 50 lbs./10,000 sq. ft.; 5 lbs./1,000 sq. ft.
* Plant-tone 5-3-3 (fertilizer) Purpose: To feed the soil with a total well-balanced organic fertilizer which will not injure the roots of the plant. Application: 50 lbs./ 2,500 sq. ft.

APRIL

* FEEDING. Add organic matter to your soil, including Dehydrated Cow Manure, Bone Meal, Lobster Compost and Penobscot Blend.
* CONTAINER PLANTS. The simplest solution for window boxes or small containers is to empty the boxes into garden beds, using the contents as compost and filling the containers with organic soil which has everything already in it. For larger

containers, rejuvenate your existing soil by removing 20% of the soil and adding Lobster Compost, Dehydrated Cow Manure, Bone Meal and Plant-tone. Mix the soil three times until you get a good blend. For containers with existing plant material, apply thin layers of the above additives to the soil.

❋ PLANTING BEDS. Follow instructions in "Preparation of a Planting Bed" or if you are planting whole beds, pull your mulch away, layer the above products, spade them in and reapply the mulch when you have finished planting. If your mulch has broken down, incorporate it into the soil. If you are pocketing plants into your landscape, pull mulch away from the areas where you are going to plant and prepare each hole separately.

❋ PLANT FEATURE. Pansies are your major crop at this time of the year for early spring color. Buy plants that are well hardened and will be able to go out into the garden early. We all long for spring and the thought of planting early is compelling. Here is my list of cold-tolerant annuals: Following the name is the temperature that they can take and still survive. African Daisy 25F, Bidens 25F, Bachelor Buttons 20F, Dianthus 20F, Diascia "Dark Red" 0F, Dusty Miller 25F, Felicia variegated 25F, Gloriosa Daisy 10F, Helichrysum Icicles 0F, Nemesia "Angelart" 0F, Pansies 20F, Primrose 10F, Salvia gargantica and leucantha 25F, Snapdragon 25F, Stocks 25F, Verbena "Magalena" 20F, Vinca Vines 20F, Phlox intensia 25F. A great combo for early window boxes—Pansies, trailing Snapdragon, Diascia, Verbena, Phlox for constant color, Nemesia for texture and color, Icicles for silver tones, Felicia for variegation and Vinca Vines for trailing.

MAY

❋ ESPOMA Bio-tone Starter Plus. Purpose: At planting time, use this product and MYKE to ensure microbial activity in your soil, reduce transplant shock and ensure strong plant growth. Contains natural & organic nutrients, including feather meal, steamed bone meal and sulfate of potash, inoculated with beneficial microbes for a patented biologically enhanced fertilizer. Application: Planting bed 4 lbs./100 sq. ft.

❋ JOBE'S ORGANIC ALL PURPOSE FERTILIZER SPIKES (4-4-4). Purpose: Carefully formulated fertilizer spikes listed by OMRI for use in organic production. Derived from feather meal, bone meal and sulfate of potash, Jobe's unique spike technology helps build a nourishing environment that promotes beneficial microbial action. Application: For container plants and hanging baskets, place spikes into the soil and liquid feed weekly with Daniels 10-4-3.

❋ DANIELS 10-4-3, a liquid fertilizer. Purpose: It is organic in nature, seed based, environmentally friendly and promotes microbial growth. Increases plant vigor and flowering. Promotes disease and insect resistance. Application: 1 tbs./gal. water as a thorough drench.

JUNE

* CONTAINER PLANTS. Add Jobe's Organic All-Purpose Fertilizer spikes and feed weekly with Daniels Fertilizer10-4-3, a liquid fertilizer. It is organic in nature, seed based, environmentally friendly and promotes microbial growth. Purpose: Increases plant vigor and flowering. Promotes disease and insect resistance. Application: 1 tbs./gal. water applied as a thorough drench.

* IN-GROUND PLANTS. Feed every 2 weeks with Daniels Fertilizer. Apply Kelp Booster Plus. Purpose: A natural bio-stimulate comprised of calcium and kelp. Kelp is rich in plant-growth compounds, micronutrients, amino acids and vitamins. Calcium is essential for plant growth and development. Purpose: Promote root growth, increase resistance to insects and disease, increase healthy plant growth and development, improve seed germination. Application: 35 lbs./5,000 sq. ft.

* MAINTENANCE. Keep a vigilant eye out for insects and diseases and treat early with an organic solution before it reaches epidemic proportions. Inspect your garden on a weekly basis. It is essential to eliminate weeds. Make sure plants get adequate water. Water the soil since overhead watering leads to disease. The emphasis in organic gardening is to create a healthy soil which will result in healthy, disease-and insect-free plants. Add beneficial insects to the garden.

JULY

* DANIELS 10-4-3, a liquid fertilizer. Purpose: It is organic in nature, seed based, environmentally friendly and promotes microbial growth. Increases plant vigor and flowering. Promotes disease and insect resistance. Application: 1 tbs./gal. water and apply instead of a normal watering. Feed weekly through the growing season on all plants—both in containers and in the ground.

* MAINTENANCE. Hanging baskets and containers, depending on their size, need to be checked for water daily and double-or triple-watered on a hot summer day. Plants in full sun require more water than those in shade. Heavily watered plants need additional liquid food on a weekly basis. Besides liquid feeding, add Jobe's Organic All-Purpose Fertilizer Spikes monthly. Remove spent flowers, keep your plants vigorous so that they do not heat stall. Prune back lightly if they do. Annuals planted in the ground and mulched don't need to be watered as frequently. Water thoroughly when you do water and keep the water off the flowers and foliage, particularly when watering in the evening. It is never too late to plant annuals and add more color to your garden. When adequately mulched, they require a minimum amount of care.

AUGUST

❋ NEPTUNE HARVEST FISH & SEAWEED FERTILIZER. This liquid all-natural organic fertilizer combines several species of fish, has no offensive odor, is cold processed, has no oils or proteins removed, contains no chlorine and won't clog the sprayer. Combining this with kelp makes it an incredible product. Kelp is derived from seaweed harvested from Nova Scotia and has 60 naturally occurring major and minor nutrients, carbohydrates, amino acids and naturally occurring substances that specifically promote plant growth. Purpose: Enhance crop yields, quality and vigor. Application: For all plants in containers or in ground, 1 oz./gal. water applied weekly as a thorough drench.

❋ WATER. In the heat of August, your greatest challenge is to keep your plants well watered. On extremely hot days watering hanging baskets twice a day will pay off.

❋ FEEDING. Continue to feed with Daniels and add Jobe's Organic All-Purpose Plant Spikes monthly. Cool-temperature varieties that have peaked should be removed and replaced with heat-tolerant plants.

❋ MAINTENANCE. Light haircuts can be beneficial to your plants.

❋ PLANT FEATURES. There are several annuals which thrive in the heat of summer and would be a worthwhile addition as fill-ins for your garden: Angelonia (Angel Mist Series), Begonia Red Dragon Wing, Cuphea (Mexican Heather), Euphorbia 'Diamond Frost,' Evolvulus 'Hawaiian Blue Eyes,' Lantana camara, Pentas lanceolata, Scaevola aemula, Vinca rosea.

SEPTEMBER

❋ FEEDING. Apply Daniels 10-4-3 fertilizer weekly and Jobe's Organic All-Purpose Fertilizer Spikes on a monthly basis.

❋ Fall is a new season and a new set of plants represent the season. Add color to areas that are lacking in color. Pick plants that are in strong bloom at this time of the year. There are lots of choices for you to pick from. Chrysanthemums are perennials that present fall with an array of colors. They are easy to grow, preferring a well-drained, sunny area. But they can be planted anywhere if treated as an annual. Mixed with cabbage and kale they will provide you with strong color for the fall season.

OCTOBER

❋ MAINTENANCE. Our seasons are becoming longer. Global warming may be playing a part. If we cover our plants with towels or bring our containers in for the one or two nights of frost, we can often extend our enjoyment of these plants until Thanksgiving.

NOVEMBER

❋ Once our plants have been hit by frost, plant Ornamental Cabbage, Kale and fall flowering Pansies. Pansies will rebloom in the spring. Remember at this time of the year to plant bulbs for early spring color.

DECEMBER

❋ Some of your container planters can be made very attractive by adding seasonal greens or dwarf evergreens such as dwarf Alberta spruce or Holly trees.

NOTES & OBSERVATIONS

MY GARDEN STORY

.....A LETTER TO OUR PASTOR AFTER 20 YEARS OF SERVICE TO OUR CHURCH

We would like to thank you, Jack, for becoming Pastor of our Church. And thank you and Ruth for becoming part of the Edgemont Community. Through your son John, who was in Tonja's class and who spent many days with Tor pursuing their love for music, we became enmeshed. We always looked forward to the trips that you and Ruth would make to the Nursery. Your passion for flowers and the hours of time Ruth spent planting colorful annuals that filled the church grounds with beauty were always appreciated.

We thank you for passing the passion on to your daughter who will have to take up the torch, now that you are leaving. Hopefully in this way we will be able to communicate with her and keep up with your retirement years. Ruth has always had a very close place in our hearts. Her dedication to the garden and to her children will be remembered. You have been very lucky to have her as a partner. The Nursery business is a very tough one, taking up too many hours. I always wished I could spend more time with friends and more time in Church. Somehow that was not meant to be. We will miss both of you and your loyal friendship, but next time don't leave in May.

On an informational note. The Krautters joined the Church in the 1940s. Greenville Community Church has been blessed with many great pastors. What made you special is that you had a vision and knew that the power of God could be seen not only within the Church but on the outside as well. You took a parking area, an empty lot filled with weeds and often much more and transformed it into a beautiful garden. Each tree is in memory of someone and has special meaning in the history of the church. The garden is filled with a mixture of trees, flowering shrubs, perennials and annuals. A garden that is filled with different colors, textures, tones, sizes and heights. Each living in harmony with each other. Each valued for the contribution it makes. If we look at the garden, we can see how beautiful our differences can be together. Sprainbrook plants gardens. That is what we do for a living, but the inspiration for a garden comes from people who have the vision to put them in. The church garden was on a Girl Scout Garden Tour and many people came back to me and said what a beautiful and God-loving spot it was. This was a tribute to your wisdom.

You were able to put this garden together because you believed in it and because you had Ruth, who helped carry out your vision. You were able to get all of the trees planted as memorials and when there wasn't enough money to put in a walk, you and I put it in brick by brick. You have left a great legacy for our church. Not only did you preach to us from within the church but you left us with many sermons from the plants you had planted in the Memorial Garden. You added a beauty to the grounds of the church.

We will miss you, but each time we walk out of the church we will be greeted by the miracle that beautiful flowers fill each of our hearts with. We will remember that when each of the trees come into bloom, a good friend is greeting us. We will be thankful you are still preaching to us and for the sermon that you knew would last a lifetime. I believe God communicates to us through Nature and you had the vision to make it happen.

Fondly, The Krautter Family.

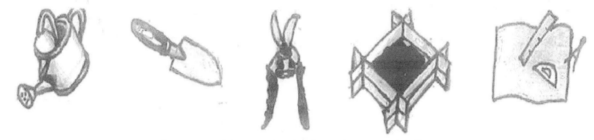

ADD YOUR GARDEN STORY HERE

20. PERENNIAL GARDEN

We define a perennial as a herbaceous plant that dies to the ground and comes back each year. Perennials come in all colors, heights, shapes, textures and scents. They add value to one's property. They are the most popular plants in the garden and we have all been living with them for centuries. Perennials are known for their beautiful flowers or colorful foliage. There are thousands of perennials with numerous varietal differences. Breeders are constantly hybridizing superior strains. Gardeners get hooked into perennials and search for something new each year. They love their perennials and become collectors of them. There is a constant desire to make changes in the garden and to introduce something new. Gardens are not static and achieving greater beauty is a constant challenge.

Perennials can be used in any part of the garden. For every location there is a pleasing plant or mixture of plants. What I love most about perennials is the charm and interest they add to any property. I love perennial gardens for the surprises that keep popping up. When they come into bloom, it is like an old friend came back to say hello. Each week there is new excitement in the garden. It is relaxing and uplifting to be among beautiful perennials. Here, a group of diverse plants live together in harmony, each one contributing to the success of the garden in its own way. We can follow suit and learn from nature to live in harmony.

When planning for a perennial garden, there are steps to consider. First you should list the plants that you love and try to make them part of the garden you plan. You can look at pictures, but it is best to get out and look at plants. Perennials are in great quantity in every neighborhood and their owners, particularly if they love their garden, will be happy to discuss their merits. Make it part of your daily exercise program to take walks through your neighborhood and exercise your power of observation as well. Each week you will find something new popping into flower. Learn to recognize and appreciate this sequence of bloom. You will find some perennials will bloom for longer periods than others. The timing and length of bloom, the color and texture of foliage and flowers contribute to the look and feel of your garden. Different heights can also add a feeling of depth. If you plan to develop a perennial garden, you need to observe. Also consider:

* Location: Sun or shade, wet or dry location.
* Height: Tall or short, upright or spreading.
* Hardiness: Make sure your plant is adaptable to your zone.
* Water requirements: Provide adequate water for its requirements.
* Sequence of bloom: Something should be in bloom at all times in your perennial garden.
* Color combinations: Blending colors can add great appeal and is soft and soothing. Contrasting colors can be dramatic.
* Mixtures: Create interest by adding different heights, mixtures, textures, tones, shapes and colors.

Find the right location for your perennials. You always want to add some color to your entryway. There may be a driveway to the side that needs some softening and a perennial bed will do the job nicely. A fence may need some color to make it look natural and beautiful. There may be a bank or slope where colorful perennials can attractively anchor the soil. Develop colorful views from your terrace, deck or windows. These focal points can be enjoyed throughout the season with perennials. Perennial gardens are very effective as part of a shrub border. You can work in bold curving lines, which will create a more natural look to your backyard and in these bold curving areas plant a mixture of flowering perennials. Areas that look stark can be softened with color and texture and interest can be created where hard structural lines dominate.

Perennials can bring life and appeal to any yard. Leave room for changes and additions. You may want to spot some annuals in for additional color. As you get addicted and your children need less area to play on, reduce your lawn and increase your plant area. Grass should be viewed as a great place for kids to play or a means to move from one area to the other. Grass as a foreground plays an important role in setting off the beauty of the garden you develop.

Once you have picked your location, then you need to find the plants that will do well in this particular area. For each location, sunny, shady, damp or dry, there are plants that will thrive. Spend some time researching cultural information. Come up with a combination of plants that you think you will be happy with. Don't be afraid to make mistakes. Plants can easily be moved and transplanted. Gardens are an ongoing challenge. This is what makes them so rewarding.

Fit your choices into your existing plot. If you are cutting into your lawn area, you need to develop an interesting curving line that will enhance your design. Lay out a garden hose to develop a line that works for you. The bolder the curve, the more dramatic the look. Spend a lot of time playing with this part of your design. You may want to do this on graph paper. Curving lines bring you back to nature, whereas straight lines are very formal.

Finally, in large areas repetition is very important. Repeating the same flower 3 to 5 times throughout a large perennial garden will have a dramatic effect. With repetition, when one specific flower is in bloom it looks like the whole garden is in bloom. Smaller areas can be treated differently and can be planted with groups of companion plants that flower at the same time to create interest and color. Location and size of the garden will help you in selecting your plants. Observe perennial gardens monthly throughout the flowering season and when they lack color or interest, buy plants currently in bloom and add them to your areas. Be critical and you will find interesting ways to improve your garden throughout the season. After preparing your garden plot, lay out your plants before planting. Spend some extra time at this stage and try to visualize your final result.

Perennial gardeners have known for years that the organic approach to gardening produces the most beautiful flowers. Organic fertilizers are nutrient rich. We feed the soil and the soil feeds the plant. If we can build up a strong, healthy plant, we can build up its resistance to insects and diseases. In an organic garden all of nature comes back to enjoy it. The birds, the bees and the butterflies all become part of the experience. As always, carefully inspect your perennials on a weekly basis and if you see a problem, treat it early with an organic control before problems reach epidemic proportions. If you get yourself involved in the organic approach, you will learn lots of tricks to help you. It is important to keep your gardens healthy for you, your children and your pets. Beneficial insects can become a great aid in your fight to avoid toxic pesticides.

Perennials are probably the most worthwhile plants we can grow. Every garden needs them. They end up giving more back than you put into them. Follow a monthly schedule of maintenance and you will find that success is fun and easy. Once you get out and work in your garden and start enjoying your perennials, you will understand why gardening is the number one pastime.

Propagation can take place through seeding, cuttings or dividing. For directions, refer to the Planting section. Your greatest success will be achieved by buying mature plants from a reputable nursery or through division in the garden.

Soil preparation is extremely important when you develop a new planting bed for your perennials. It is the best start you can give your garden to ensure success. New beds need to be properly conditioned.

MY FORMULA FOR THE PREPARATION OF A NEW PLANTING BED FOR PERENNIALS

Per 100 square feet, dig and mix into the top one foot area

✻ 1 bale Peat Moss (3.8 cu. ft.)

✻ 1 Coir block

✻ 2 bags Lobster Compost: (1 cu. ft.)*

✻ 2 bags Penobscot Blend: (1 cu. ft.)*

✻ 2 bags Dehydrated Cow Manure (1 cu. ft.)*

✻ 2 bags Fafard Top Soil (1 cu. ft.)

✻ 4.5 lbs. Bone Meal*

✻ 1 lb. Mineral Rock Dust (Azomite)

✻ 5 lbs. Lime*

✻ 1.4 qt. Myke Annual & Perennial*

✻ 8 lbs. Plant-tone (Espoma)*

✻ Add Soil Perfector to heavy clay or sandy soils

Once your plants are established and your food web has kicked in, you can maintain your plants through top dressing, using the ingredients above marked with an *. After application, apply a 2 in. layer of mulch on top.

Apply Myke at planting time. Myke contains mycorrhizae, beneficial microscopic fungi which improve root development and plant vigor. Fertilize with organic products. Top dress with compost and use nutritive mulches. Spray with Employ, a B Harpin protein, every three weeks to build up the immune system. Control weeds at all times, as they compete for food, nutrients and space. Keep an eagle eye out for insects or diseases and treat early with organic controls to minimize damage.

Deadheading (cutting off faded flower heads) might be a time-consuming chore but it keeps the plants neat and prolongs blooming time. Groom your perennials throughout the season. Staking and selective pruning may be necessary. Divide them when they get too big.

Proper watering is essential throughout the season. Avoid overhead watering if possible. Keep your plants well fed. And keep a 2 in. layer of mulch on them at all times. Perennials should be cut down in late fall and covered with salt hay or evergreen branches after the ground has frozen. If you follow these few simple steps, perennials can be the most satisfying plants in the garden. They can fill your garden with dramatic color and will be part of your life for years.

MY TOP 25 PERENNIALS

1. Achillea 'Moonshine' (Yarrow)
2. Agastache 'Blue Fountain' (Hyssop)
3. Alcea rosea plena (Hollyhock)
4. Alchemilla mollis (Lady's Mantle)
5. Aquilegia (Columbine)
6. Astilbe (Spirea)
7. Coreopsis verticillata 'Moonbeam' (Tickseed)
8. Dianthus gratianopolitanus 'Firewitch' (Pinks)
9. Dicentra 'Burning Heart' (Bleeding Heart)
10. Digitalis 'Excelsioir hybrids' (Foxglove)
11. Echinacea purpurea 'Magnus' (Coneflower)
12. Geranium 'Rozanne' (Hardy Geranium, Cranesbill)
13. Hemerocallis hybrids 'Stella d'Oro' (Daylily)
14. Heuchera micrantha 'Royal Velvet' (Coral Bells)
15. Hosta sieboldiana 'Elegans' (Hosta, Funkia)
16. Lamium maculatum 'Red Nancy' (Dead Nettles)
17. Leucanthemum 'Becky' (Shasta Daisy)
18. Liriope muscari 'Big Blue' (Lily Turf)
19. Monarda didyma Raspberry Wine' (Beebalm)
20. Nepeta faassenii 'Blue Wonder' (Catmint)
21. Paeonia lactiflora (Peony)
22. Perovskia atriplicifolia (Russian Sage)
23. Rudbeckia fulgida 'Goldsturm' (Black-eyed Susan, Coneflower)
24. Salvia nemerosa 'Ost Friesland' (Salvia)
25. Sedum spectabile x telephium 'Autumn Joy' (Autumn Joy Sedum)

Perennial gardens require maintenace. The monthly maintenance program I provide here and have followed for years has produced beautiful results. Refer to it monthly.

MONTHLY PERENNIAL CALENDAR

I do not endorse any one brand and strongly believe the greater the mix of products, the greater the results. Similar brands can be substituted. For example, in place of Lobster Compost, you can use any akaline-based compost. Timing and purpose are the key ingredients of a successful program.

MARCH

❋ Plant-tone 5-3-3 (fertilizer). Purpose: To feed the soil with a total well-balanced organic fertilizer that will not injure the roots of the plant. Application: 50 lbs./2,500 sq. ft.

* MINERAL ROCK DUST (Azomite). Purpose: Applying mineral rock dust mimics the actions of Mother Nature by replacing minerals once spread via glaciers, flooding and wind. Using mineral rock dust on your land is a sound organic practice beneficial to living soil. Application: 50 lbs./10,000 sq. ft.; 5 lbs./1,000 sq. ft.
* MAINTENANCE. Clean up any dead debris that may be lingering or lying on top of the soil or plants and make sure all perennials are adequately cut back. As the ground becomes workable, divide clumps that are too large. The preparation of new beds can take place as soon as the ground is workable. Once your plants are growing, spray with Employ every three weeks.

APRIL

* Plant-tone 5-3-3, (fertilizer). Fertilize, if you haven't done so in March, to steadily supply plants with food during their growing period. Purpose: To feed the soil with a total well-balanced organic fertilizer that will not injure the roots of the plant. Application: 50 lbs./2,500 sq. ft.
* MAINTENANCE. Top dress with compost and mulch to a depth of 2 in. Cleanliness is essential in perennial beds. All dead tissue must be removed and plants should be cut back or trimmed as necessary. The beds should be clean of any leaves. As soon as your perennials leaf out, spray with Employ. Employ is cutting-edge science boosting your plants' blooms and overall plant vigor and providing disease resistance. Before new growth takes place, it is a good time to divide existing plants that have become overgrown or transplant some to a new location in the garden. New beds should be prepared by digging deeply and mixing into the soil the ingredients recommended in PREPARATION OF A NEW PLANTING BED FOR PERENNIALS.
* April is the time to plant perennials. There are many microclimates on your property. Select the right plant for the right location. Learn the cultural requirements for all the plants you choose. If you pick the right plant, it will thrive. Ground cover can fill in bare areas. Flowers can add color to an otherwise dull view and cut flowers can add color to the interior of your home. Check out lists of new perennials and add some each year.

MAY

* DANIELS 10-4-3. A liquid fertilizer. Purpose: It is organic in nature, seed based, environmentally friendly and promotes microbial growth. Increases plant vigor and flowering. Promotes disease and insect resistance. Application: 1 tbs./gal. of water and apply instead of a normal watering. Feed weekly through the growing season

* MAINTENANCE. Do not overhead water; use drip irrigation and mulches to reduce the time needed to water. Spray Employ every three weeks. Always add Myke when planting a new perennial. Control weeds and watch out for insect damage. Pest problems should be controlled early with an organic control product before they reach epidemic proportions. Make sure you pruned and fed all of your perennials. As plants grow, deadhead and stake as necessary. Peonies need staking now. Continue to add perennials.

JUNE

* KELP BOOSTER PLUS. A natural bio-stimulate comprised of calcium and kelp. Kelp is rich in plant growth compounds, micronutrients, amino acids and vitamins. Calcium is essential for plant growth and development. Purpose: Promotes root growth, increases resistance to insects and disease, increases healthy plant growth and development and improves seed germination. Application: 35 lbs./5,000 sq. ft.
* DANIELS 10-4-3. A liquid fertilizer. Purpose: It is organic in nature, seed based, environmentally friendly and promotes microbial growth. Increases plant vigor and flowering. Promotes disease and insect resistance. Application: 1 tbs./gal. of water and apply instead of a normal watering. Feed weekly through growing season.
* MAINTENANCE. It's important to deadhead, prune, fertilize, water and mulch. Spray Employ every three weeks. Control weeds and insects. Avoid overhead watering, inspect your plants frequently for insect damage and keep a phenological calendar charting the chores you need to accomplish. Chrysanthemums should be pinched back and kept short until mid July. Asters should be cut back 1/3 in mid June. Delphiniums need staking.

JULY

* INSTANT COMPOST TEA SOIL ECOLIZER EM2. (Mother Earth Organics.) Purpose: Contains 100% organic and natural ingredients enhancing the biological activities in the soil through the introduction of beneficial soil microorganisms. Application: Apply as a thorough drench to the area.
* DANIELS 10-4-3. A liquid fertilizer. Purpose: It is organic in nature, seed based, environmentally friendly and promotes microbial growth. Increases plant vigor and flowering. Promotes disease and insect resistance. Application: 1 tbs./gal. water and apply instead of a normal watering. Feed weekly through the growing season.
* BENEFICIAL INSECTS (Ladybugs, Nematodes, Praying Mantis). Consider adding them at this time of the year for insect control.
* WATER. Water thoroughly and deeply rather than too frequently, keeping the water off the flowers and foliage. Ground covers can be overhead watered but leaves should be dry by nightfall.

❀ MAINTENANCE. Make sure your plants are mulched and keep them well watered. Spray Employ every three weeks. Asters should be cut back 1/3 in early July and Chrysanthemums should be pinched back until mid July. Keep deadheading spent flowers to ensure more flowering. Stake plants if needed. Keep your beds weed free and watch carefully for insect or disease problems. If present, control quickly.

AUGUST

❀ FEEDBACK LIQUID COMPOST. A gourmet meal for soil microbes, it's 100% organic soil food and a catalyst for soil activity. Purpose: Feed microbes, increase root bio-mass, balance soil and reduce stress on plants. Application: 1 oz./gal. water, 3 oz./1,000 sq. ft. Application: Dilute and apply as a soil drench.

❀ DANIELS 10-4-3. A liquid fertilizer. Purpose: It is organic in nature, seed based, environmentally friendly and promotes microbial growth. Increases plant vigor and flowering. Promotes disease and insect resistance. Application: 1 tbs./gal. water and apply instead of a normal weekly watering. Feed weekly through the growing season

❀ WATER. Water thoroughly and deeply rather than too frequently, keeping the water off the flowers and foliage. Ground covers can be overhead watered but leaves should be dry by nightfall.

❀ MAINTENANCE. Spray Employ every three weeks. Deadhead spent flowers to ensure more flowering. Stake plants if needed. Keep your beds weed free and watch carefully for insects and disease damage. If present, control quickly.

SEPTEMBER

❀ NEPTUNE HARVEST FISH & SEAWEED FERTILIZER. This liquid all-natural organic fertilizer combines several species of fish, has no offensive odor, is cold processed, has no oils or proteins removed, contains no chlorine and won't clog the sprayer. Combining this with kelp makes it an incredible product. Kelp is derived from seaweed harvested from Nova Scotia and has 60 naturally occurring major and minor nutrients, carbohydrates, amino acids and other naturally occurring substances that specifically promote plant growth. Purpose: Enhance crop yields, quality and vigor. Application: 1 oz./gal. water applied as a thorough drench.

❀ MAINTENANCE. This is the ideal time to divide and transplant existing perennials. Make sure you spend time cutting back, dividing, deadheading and weeding. Your perennial garden should be full of color all through the flowering season. When it is lacking color, add a perennial that will supply it. This is also a great time of the year to put in a new perennial garden. So many gardens are sterile, lacking the beauty of flowering plants. Evergreens form the foundation but perennials should form the body. Plant them now so that they get established in the fall and take off in the spring, acting like two-year old plants.

OCTOBER

❋ COAST OF MAINE LOBSTER COMPOST. Purpose: A lobster-based compost containing aged aspen bark and manure, which will feed the microbes in your soil and greatly benefit the food web. Application: Top dress at the rate of 2 bags/100 sq. ft.

❋ MAINTENANCE. Spray Employ every three weeks. Continue to plant, transplant, divide, deadhead and cut back dead tissue. Make sure your perennial beds are filled with lots of fall color. Add grasses and fall blooming perennials to your garden. Great splashes of color can be added with chrysanthemums. Increase areas for perennials.

NOVEMBER

❋ Plant-tone 5-3-3 (fertilizer). Purpose: To feed the soil with a total well-balanced organic fertilizer that will not injure the roots of the plant. Application: 50 lbs./2,500 sq. ft.

❋ MULCH. Make sure that a 2 in. layer of mulch is down before winter.

❋ MAINTENANCE. Cut perennials down and clean up dead debris. Save the plants with winter color, such as the grasses and late bloomers. Grasses can give you color all winter long. Late bloomers should be cut back at the end of their cycle.

DECEMBER

❋ MAINTENANCE. Except for grasses, most perennials should be cut back or cut down for the winter. Clean the beds and apply a 2 in. layer of mulch. A light layer of salt hay and Christmas tree branches on cut-back plants will give you additional protection.

NOTES & OBSERVATIONS

.....WRITING A BOOK ABOUT THE ORGANIC APPROACH TO GARDENING

Each week I write my e-mails full of garden tips. Rosella, Fred and Heidi read them and make corrections. Fred is very good on the technical end. He graduated from Rutgers University Horticultural Department. He also attended the Organic School. In our transition to the organic approach, he helped me write all our organic programs. Rosella and Heidi, both brought up in Europe, seemed to have the best grasp of the English language and do the editing. Weekly letters are written and corrected to meet the Friday e-mail deadline, as the work week for many is over on Friday and the weekend is when most home gardening takes place.

Customers seem to like their weekly garden tips and comment about how helpful they are. One customer told me that she forwarded them to her fellow workers who would read them on the train on the way home. One week she forgot to forward them and got scolded. Another woman said she can read me all over the world. I have a driving force to put on paper the information required to garden the natural way. I feel it is important for everyone to learn the simple steps of gardening to have a reference to go to in good times or bad times. Our survival might depend on learning these skills. My writings from over the years that were sent out as e-mails are the basis of much of what I have pieced together in this book. These writings have been tweaked and updated to respond to customer feedback. I always feel programs can be written but they need to be tested in the field. Many of my recommendations come from customer suggestions.

My written material was laid out on tables as free handouts. There were so many handouts that it was difficult to sort through and find what I was looking for. I needed to combine them into a book for easier access. I knew the information needed to reach a larger audience—so everyone would have the information at their fingertips that would allow them to switch to the organic approach. It is a simple approach with guidelines to follow. If your whole property is organic, the microbes in your soil will clean up any toxins that may still exist. Once you go organic, you will have a soil that can be amended to grow fruits, herbs and vegetables on any part of your property. Locations with proper light and access to water will have to be selected of course. It is comforting to know that we have the ability to become self-sufficient and to grow our own produce, collect our own seed and salvage our own drinking water.

Almost every landscape design I plan includes perennials. I have gotten more positive feedback on this portion of the design than on any other. Beauty and excitement take place each day in a perennial garden as a new plant pops into bloom. This makes it the most interesting area of the yard. Perennials require care, but those who are dedicated and have followed the advice in our weekly e-mails have had the greatest success. My customers have told me that when following our programs the flower power of their perennials is outstanding. Nothing will leave a greater impression on you than a beautiful flower coming into bloom.

ADD YOUR GARDEN STORY HERE

21. HERB GARDEN

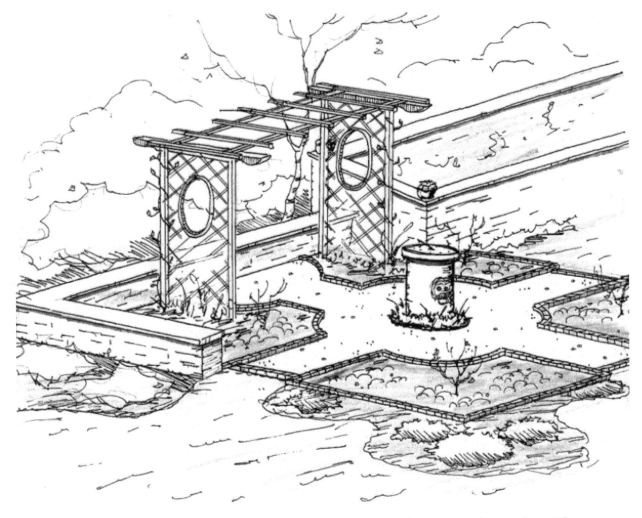

I have difficulty defining a herb. The word has such a wide range of meaning. The Encyclopedia Britannica definition is "a herbaceous plant that possesses certain aromatic properties and is used for medicinal purposes, for flavoring or garnishing in cooking and for perfumes." In addition to these qualities, many herbs actually repel insects because of their strong pungent odor. There are herbs dating way back from ancient times up to the present. The research makes fascinating winter reading. Many herbs are used as ornamentals. There is a huge selection of herbs to choose from, so you need to do the research and select the ones that are useful to you. Once you have done this, you can integrate them into a garden. Herb gardens can be not only useful but also beautiful.

There is no question that herbs need to be grown organically—free of pesticides, herbicides and fungicides. A herb garden follows the same organic program that we follow in our vegetable garden. They are used often as companion plants in the vegetable garden to ward off insects. A well-drained organic soil and a sunny location are important to a successful herb garden. Herbs like a loose friable soil and do not do well in heavy, wet soils. If the soil cannot be loosened, then it is best to build a mound or berm to plant them in.

Spend extra time to make sure your soil is weed free before planting. Weeds are the biggest problem in a herb garden and, if they are not controlled, they will take over. Mulch the soil and keep up with the weeding so that the herbs can get established and take over. Add organic matter to the soil and use an organic fertilizer like Bio-tone Starter Plus, which has mycorrhizal fungi to increase the potential for greater root mass development and thus greater success. Top dressing with organic material like Lobster Compost, Fundy Blend or Sweet Peet Mulch through the year will be beneficial.

Most herb gardens will be filled with a large mixture of plants and access to them by way of a path is necessary, especially as you will want to harvest your herbs frequently throughout the growing season. Herb gardens need to fit into the landscape design. Thought should be given to its placement and how to integrate them into your landscape. They can be very attractive and add another dimension. Locating your herb garden close to the kitchen has its advantages for those who use herbs mainly for culinary purposes.

A formal herb garden is a lot of work. Often dwarf boxwood is used to surround it. Circular or rectangular shapes are common with rectangular being used for informal settings and circular for both formal and informal. Walks are established within these areas with each herb being allocated its own space. Walks can be created out of grass or stone. The boundaries and the walks create the design. To achieve an overall look, these spaces need to be pruned frequently to confine each herb to its area and to maintain an orderly appearance. I have seen some nice herb gardens integrated into an informal foreground boundary where they randomly follow the curvatures of the landscape's lines. As a Hogarth S curve winds around a circular pattern, herbs can be easily harvested at its perimeter.

To begin, select your favorite herbs and research their growing habits. Find lists of herbs that give their cultural and growing habits. Once this is done, you can determine a plan for their balance and position in the garden. Larger areas are needed for herbs that grow aggressively and consideration should be given to the location of tall-growing varieties. Expect to make a few mistakes on your first try. Plants can easily be transplanted and their locations changed.

If you keep your garden heavily pruned, it will look good no matter what you do. Pruning will also force you to use your herbs. If you have an abundance of them, dry them and store them in a dry place. Although the traditional way to dry herbs is to allow them to hang upside down in a dry area, you can also dry certain varieties in a microwave. Many feel herbs have greater potency dried.

Mulching the garden will add a final touch. Some people will use different mulches in different areas to increase interest and to achieve a herb garden look. A lot of creativity and work go into a good-looking herb garden. It is a work of art—something a true gardener can be proud of. It is a challenge for the more experienced gardener and not a project for a novice.

Those starting out may want to plant some herbs in containers near the kitchen area. You can move and arrange your pots as the herbs grow to form an interesting look. Using an organic soil and feeding with Daniels fertilizer lets you grow and harvest your herbs as you need them. You will learn a lot about the growth habits of your favorite herbs in the first year. Familiarity with their cultural needs will become useful knowledge if you want to plant a herb garden in the future.

Herbs can be tucked into any part of a landscape. You may want to spread them out throughout your garden. Tuck some into a perennial border, a vegetable garden and your annual bed. Many herbs used this way have become important ornamentals in the garden.

Herbs do not like soaking wet soil, but since they are ideally planted in a loose, friable well-drained soil, they usually require a great deal of water—particularly on hot summer days. Many are shallow rooted and can dry out easily. Drip irrigation is your best method of watering but this can often become difficult to install, particularly in the more intricate designs, where many varieties and walks cause obstacles.

Fertilizer needs to be organic. Plant-tone, a granular organic product should be applied in early spring; and Daniels, an organic liquid fertilizer, on a monthly basis starting in June. Nutrient-rich organic mulches benefit herbs, providing them with a constant source of food.

My favorite herb is the Aloe vera plant. Every kitchen window should always have one growing on it. I eat a piece every day, picking it fresh from my greenhouse crop. It is known for curing cuts and burns but does so much more. My friends tease me saying "Your cure for everything is running and Aloe vera". Plants can teach us so much about life. Grow strong resistant plants and they will have very few insect or disease problems. Make sure you visit your plants frequently, examine them and if there is a problem, cure it immediately with an organic solution.

Herbs should be a part of every garden and everyone's life. Fit them in wherever you can. Learn about them and use them. From the beginning of time, man found uses for plants. He discovered plants that would improve his life. He passed down this information from one generation to the next. When we plant our own herbs, we will rediscover the great worth of these plants. Talk about them and pass your information on to others. This is part of the folklore and charm that they add to your garden. When you find they have done something great for you, tell others about it. For every herb you grow there is a story to be told. It is up to us gardeners to perpetuate the lore—to impress upon others the usefulness of plants in today's society.

Here is my top 25 list of perennial herbs for zones 5–6. Carefully select your perennial herbs for background, permanent structure, interest and use when planning your herb garden. Leave lots of room for the many annual herbs you will want to add each year.

When preparing beds for planting, follow the directions in Chapter 20 PERENNIAL GARDEN, Preparation of a New Planting Bed for Perennials

1.   Alchemilla mollis (Lady's Mantle)
2.   Allium schoenoprasum (Chives)
3.   Allium tuberosum (Chives, Garlic)
4.   Aloysia triphylla (Lemon Verbena)
5.   Armoracia rusticana (Horseradish)
6.   Artemesia dracunculus (French Tarragon)
7.   Artemesia stelleriana (Wormwood)
8.   Galium odoratum (Sweet Woodruff)
9.   Lavandula angustifolia (Lavender)
10. Melissa officinalis (Lemon Balm)
11. Mentha species (Mint)
12. Monarda didyma (Bee Balm)
13. Nepeta cataria (Catnip)
14. Nepeta mussini (Catmint)
15. Origanum onites aureum (Golden Oregano)
16. Origanum vulgare (True Oregano)
17. Rumex acetosella (Sorrel)
18. Ruta graveolens (Rue)
19. Salvia officinalis (Garden Sage)
20. Santolina (Lavender Cotton)
21. Satureja montana (Savory)
22. Tenacetum parthenium (Feverfew)
23. Teucrium canadensa (Germander)
24. Thymus species (Thyme)
25. Waldsteinia barrenwort (Alpine Strawberry)

.....KIM'S AND TOR'S WEDDING

Many said it was the best wedding they ever attended. A perfect day filled with excitement and interest for all. The idea was not to have a traditional wedding but a fun occasion for everyone to enjoy. My son Tor was getting married in our upstate location, which once supplied us with additional flowers. Getting married there required a lot of work and it showed that even without a lot of money you can put on a spectacular event. It all began 18 months earlier when Tor proposed to Kim. The decision was made to have a wedding on their own property, but the place needed sprucing up. The ceremony would take place outdoors and the meal would be served in the greenhouse. A stage needed to be built in the lower portion of the property where three surrounding hills led down to a flat area. The lawn needed leveling and grading and a hill of weeds needed to be landscaped with beautiful flowering shrubs and flowering perennials. The house needed to be landscaped, a greenhouse had to be emptied of its benches and a Unilock paver floor built. There was a year in which to get it done, but the task seemed overwhelming.

Topsoil was brought in and the lawn was raked and seeded in the fall. Weeds were pulled from the hill leading upto the greenhouse and the hill and the house were landscaped. The stage was built by Tor, with the help of Kim's son Zach, with trees taken down from the woods to achieve the rustic look. The area surrounding the stage was landscaped and a set of natural stone steps was designed to lead to the platform. More lawn was added under the tree. The stage was now located in the direct center of this portion of the property with grass and hills surrounding it on either side. Someone commented that it looked like a mini Woodstock in its topography. Appropriate, since Tor is a musician, writes his own music, sings vocals and plays lead guitar. His idol was Jerry Garcia from the Grateful Dead.

The plans were for a late-August wedding. The date they picked turned out to be the most beautiful Saturday of the year. Wanting to convey a very casual attire, the invitation read "shoes optional" and was beautifully done using one of Tor's computer programs.

The parking lot was a gravel field that once housed the large beds of perennials grown for sale at Sprainbrook Nursery. A labyrinth was cut into an open field. An indoor stage was built in the greenhouse and 19 round tables were set up with white tablecloths on a white paved floor. White Christmas lights were strung on the center beams. Along the outer sides of the greenhouse were white Angelwing Begonias with Helichrysum Diamond Frost between them. Throughout the greenhouse were hanging baskets. The welcome path was on the side of the greenhouse. Tor built an Arbor on either end. We placed two truckloads of flowering plants on either side, leaving a winding path. The path was breathtaking. At the end of the walk was another Arbor leading out to an open flat area where a white tent had been erected. Tables were set up and a bar was located at the far end.

As the cars arrived, the welcome path made a great impression and put everyone in a joyful mood. As guests rounded the corner, people were gathering and chatting. Mark Mercier was playing piano on the outdoor stage and with drink in hand the guests were drawn down the hill to where he was performing. He left everyone in awe as they listened to this great talent. The hill planted with perennials was ablaze with color and the grass was a rich green. Majestic views could be seen from this valley and a quiet stillness prevailed. The butterflies were out in full force; it was a picture perfect day.

Kim and Tor got married on the stage down in the valley. Bales of hay covered with colorful blankets lined the hill where the guests sat. They were surrounded by the beauty of nature and good friends. The dinner took place in the greenhouse, the music was great and the band played late into the night. I have found that the most memorable events seem to take place when nature plays an important role.

ADD YOUR GARDEN STORY HERE

22. GROUND COVERS

PACHYSANDRA TERMINALIS
(JAPANESE PACHYSANDRA)

GAULTHERIA
PROCUMENS
(CAPE JASMINE)

CALLUNA
VULGARIS
(HEATHER)

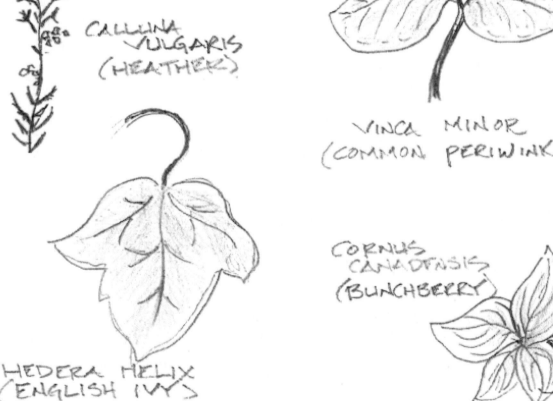

VINCA MINOR
(COMMON PERIWINKLE)

CORNUS
CANADENSIS
(BUNCHBERRY)

HEDERA HELIX
(ENGLISH IVY)

A ground cover is a tightly knit group of plants that form a blanket of vegetation which takes over an area. The purpose of planting a ground cover is to form a dense covering that no weeds can grow through, where no soil will be visible and no erosion will take place. The area can often be quite large. The trick is to select a plant that will thrive in the location, will take over and will sustain itself with a minimum amount of maintenance once it gets established. It should be relatively inexpensive to maintain but will require the purchase of many plants to cover an area. Ground cover is usually very low to the ground. Grass is the most common ground cover and the most costly to maintain. Lawns cover vast areas and are used in almost every garden. Grass plays such an important role in the garden that I have treated lawns as a separate subject. There are many areas where grass will not survive or is not practical to maintain. These are areas that are steep, rocky, heavily rooted, damp, dry, shady or difficult to mow. In each of these areas there is a plant that will survive and will cover the ground. You'll want to find that plant.

One of the most important responsibilities that we, as home owners, have is to prevent erosion. Erosion damages not only our own property because it washes away valuable soil, but it also produces ensuing environmental hazards. Every time you see muddy water washing down on the side of a road and into a sewer, it is polluting our water streams and water supply. Phosphates and nitrates are being carried into our water streams, ponds, lakes and rivers and valuable soil is being eroded away. Each of us needs to take on the task of becoming a responsible tenant of our earth. Ground covers absorb moisture and reduce runoff. In today's era of large houses, blacktop driveways, concrete terraces and impervious walks, runoff problems have greatly increased. Porous hardscape materials and ground covers absorb and trap runoff water. We need to slow the flow. Ground cover makes a difference.

Begin by recognizing problem areas. Spend some time walking your property. There are areas that may be hidden from view by banks, woods, trees or shrubs. There are places that seem not to be a problem until it rains. Larger areas are usually more visible and smaller ones tend to be hidden but are necessary in controlling runoff water and erosion. Many times exposed roots are a problem and the only solution for both safety and aesthetics is to plant a ground cover.

Find the right plant that will thrive and take over the area. This may take a little research or require expert recommendations. Many people live in deer country and this presents the additional challenge of choosing a plant that deer will not munch on. When food becomes scarce, a deer herd can devastate your ground covers, eating them down to the roots. To help you with choices, walk your neighborhood and see which ground covers predominate. Read up on the ones that appeal to you and make sure they are suitable for your specific site. Covering large areas will be a big investment, so you want to get it right the first time.

In preparation of a planting bed, it is necessary to eliminate all weeds and other invasive plant material from the site so there's no competition with the plant you have selected. In areas where you can incorporate organic matter, it will be beneficial to do so. In large, flat, tillable areas, follow the directions in Chapter 20 PERENNIAL GARDEN,

Preparation of a Perennial Planting Bed. In many cases, particularly on steep rocky slopes, it will be difficult to prepare a planting bed. Mixing organic matter into each hole as you plant is your next-best option. Use an organic fertilizer in the hole such as Bio-tone Starter Plus that contains mycorrhizae along with compost. I like incorporating Lobster Compost and MYKE, which also contain mycorrhizae, to develop a strong root system. The closer you plant your ground cover, the more costly it is but the quicker it will cover. There is usually a suggested average for spacing. Three years is a normal time frame for full coverage, with two years attainable by planting closer.

Mulch the area with a 2 in. layer. There are many choices of mulch available. On steep slopes choose a mulch that will prevent erosion until the plants develop and take over. Top dressing with a nutrient-rich mulch will aid in the organic feeding process and help promote microbial activity. Applying corn gluten prior to mulching will reduce weed germination and add nitrogen to the soil. Proper choices are important and depend on the site.

The first three years are crucial in developing ideal growing conditions so that the plant you choose will densely cover the area. The three key ingredients in this initial stage are adequate water, total weed control and a program of organic feeding.

1. Your plants should receive one inch of water per week.
2. Inspect your beds and remove any weeds that may pop through the mulch. Don't let weeds take over.
3. Follow feeding directions in Chapter 20 PERENNIAL GARDEN, Perennial Monthly Calendar.

Once your ground cover takes over, it will require very little care. Feed each spring and water in extreme periods of drought. Occasionally the ground cover may develop insect or disease problems. This is less apt to happen if you keep the plants healthy through an organic feeding program and by watering more during long dry spells. Strong, healthy plants resist insects and diseases. If you spot a problem, treat it early with an organic control. Once you have ground cover areas established, propagation through cuttings or division can take place.

Ground covers add a lot of beauty to a property. They reduce maintenance and solve difficult problems. Underplanting will protect trees and shrubs from damage. Varying ground covers on your property will add interest. There is a huge number of ground covers to choose from. If you are starting out, choose the tried and proven ones first and, as you become a better gardener, branch out to the more unusual ones. Remember, for every location on your property there is a plant that will do well.

MY TOP 25 GROUND COVERS

✳ Top three list *

✳ Top ten list **

1. Ajuga reptans (Ajuga)**
2. Asarum europaeum (European Ginger)
3. Astilbe species (Spirea)
4. Ceratostigma plumbaginoides (Plumbago)
5. Convallaria majalis (Lily of the Valley)
6. Cotoneaster dammeri (Cotoneaster)**
7. Epimedium species (Barrenwort)
8. Euonymus fortunei 'Coloratus' (Euonymus)* *
9. Fern variety & species (Fern)**
10. Geranium grandiflorum (Hardy Geranium)
11. Grass variety & species (Ornamental Grasses)
12. Hedera helix (Ivy)*
13. Hosta species (Funkia)
14. Hemerocallis species (Daylily)
15. Juniperus horizontalis (Juniper)**
16. Lamium maculatum (Lamium)
17. Liriope muscari (Lilyturf)**
18. Pachysandra terminalis (Pachysandra)*
19. Phlox subulata (Mountain Pink)
20. Rhododendron hybrid (Azalea)
21. Rosa 'Knock-out' ('Knock Out' Rose)
22. Sedum dwarf species (Sedum)**
23. Sempervivum (Hens and Chicks)
24. Thymus serphyllum (Creeping Thyme)
25. Vinca minor (Myrtle)*

There are many more to choose from. Search and you will find. Ground covers are an important part of Natural Gardening.

.....PROPAGATING PACHYSANDRA BY CUTTINGS

I worked my way through college propagating pachysandra by cuttings. It is good to have your pachysandra cut at least once every two years as it allows more light and air to circulate at the base. Pachysandra can suffer from a fungus called black rot which kills the runners. Cutting and allowing more air to circulate prevents this from developing. Trimming pachysandra beds makes them healthier.

It was always easy to find home owners who would allow us to trim their pachysandra for free because once we explained the value of doing it, they wanted it done. During the summer, I would work in the Nursery and after work I would go out three nights a week, cut pachysandra from friends' or neighbors' houses and work into the wee hours of the night sticking cuttings into a prepared soil mix while listening to country-western music. When I was away at college, my mother would sell the plants for me and save the money for my education. Carrying on the family tradition, my teen-aged daughter Tonja earned money propagating pachysandra. She was paid by the piece and made good money because she was fast.

We hired high school kids who couldn't find work for the summer. If we paid them by the hour we would lose money but if we paid them by the piece, we would get the work done quickly. Some were too slow and found it was not worth their while, but others found they could make good money. In the past 15 years, we have had to do this job with our own crew. We have a long list of customers who want their pachysandra cut. We would go out and cut for 2 hours in the morning, sending a 5-man crew and in the afternoon we would stick the cuttings. This project would take up to three weeks.

In the surrounding wooded area, there are large patches of pachysandra. At one time these must have been growing on estates, which have since been abandoned. Some of the pachysandra areas were massive, in the middle of nowhere. Pachysandra is a ground cover and takes over. When we couldn't contact a home owner, we headed for the woods. To me, the woods had always been no-man's-land that provided a place to play, to go spear fishing in its streams and to follow trails shared with horseback riders. Gathering pachysandra from this place in the wilderness seemed like it was all right. After all, trimming them benefited the plants. But no-man's-land is not "no man's" land—it is someone's land.

One day the crew called our customers but couldn't find anyone home to give us permission to cut. So they headed for a site deep in the woods, filled five bags with cuttings and were headed to the car when they were stopped by the police. We were cutting on school property even though it was deep in the woods far away from the school. School security had called the police and wanted us arrested. I was called and rushed over. The policeman told us that he didn't like where this was going and to work out a deal.

The grounds manager of the school threatened to arrest my workers and place their pictures on the front page of the newspaper. He said Sprainbrook Nursery would make the headlines and we would have to post bail to keep them out of jail. It would cost me lots of money in legal fees. After further discussion, he offered me a deal where I would have to plant up the four schools within their jurisdiction with a colorful mixture of flowering plants each fall season for three years. I argued this was harsh and unfair, that trimming benefited the plants and that the Nursery employed their students in the past. The grounds manager insisted it was stealing. He told the officer to take the men to jail. I gave in. I dreaded those years, since every fall it took two days of labor and lots of plants. We never cut pachysandra in the woods again. I felt sorry for the pachysandra plants.

ADD YOUR GARDEN STORY HERE

23. TREES, EVERGREENS AND SHRUBS

The enormity of this subject makes it impossible to cover everything in a single chapter. Instead I will try to draw upon my many years of experience to guide you with some important points to consider.

TREES: There is nothing more majestic than a tree. Trees are our hope for the future, they purify our air by turning carbon dioxide into oxygen. The big ones can reach 75–80 ft. in height, with an almost equal spread. They can provide shade for a whole back yard, including the house. They should be planted 35–40 ft. away from the house and any road that has power lines bordering the property.

There are many species to choose from. Maples are fast growers but are difficult to underplant because of their extensive surface root system. They are not the best choice if underplanting is preferred. Oaks are slow growers but are an excellent choice if you want to grow grass or other vegetation underneath. These two examples of very popular shade trees show the importance of planting the right tree in the right location for the right use.

There are many choices for trees and they need to be thoroughly researched before making a decision. Big trees should be thoughtfully selected. Care should be taken not to overplant your property with them because of concerns of them falling on your house. Follow our organic approach in planting to make sure they develop a deep root system and re-read Chapter 3 PLANTING.

Big trees that have a shallow root system can pose a danger to a house by blowing over in strong windstorms. It is important to develop deep root systems. Do not grow grass up to the trunk of your trees. Instead, provide them with their own bed. This bed will protect the trunk from mechanical lawn mower damage and provide a transition to a fungal-dominated area, which will benefit the health and growth of the tree. I like to design an interesting bed outline which will fit into and enhance the look of the property.

Small flowering trees are preferred for most residential properties and large trees should be limited in number on small properties. There are many beautiful flowering trees that will give you a sequence of bloom throughout the spring season. Walk your neighborhood and notice when they are blooming.

Below is my Top Twelve List of Small Flowering Trees. Within each of these varieties there will be many species to choose from. Research the differences to come up with a good choice. Making the right choice is a major decision. Trees, if properly planted, cared for and maintained the organic way, can outlive us and endure for future generations.

There are many more great flowering trees to choose from but these are my favorites. Within every variety there are many species, such as Dogwood, Magnolia, Crab Apple and the Prunus family. I love them all.

1. Amelanchier canadensis 'Autumn Brilliance' (Serviceberry)
2. Cercis canadensis 'Forest Pansy' (Redbud)
3. Cornus kousa (Kousa Dogwood)
4. Crataegus veridis 'Winter King' (Hawthorn)
5. Halesia carolina (Carolina Silver Bell)
6. Lagerstroemia indica (Crepe Myrtle)
7. Magnolia x loebneri 'Dr. Merrill' (Magnolia)
8. Malus species (Crab Apple)
9. Oxydendrum arboreum (Sorrel Tree, Sourwood)
10. Prunus serrulata 'Kwanzan' (Kwanzan Cherry)
11. Pyrus calleryana 'Chanticleer' (Flowering Pear)
12. Stewartia koreana (Korean Stewartia)

EVERGREENS: Evergreens are plants that hold their foliage all year long. They are a valuable part of any landscape design and are the backbone of foundation planting because they provide a cover throughout the year. They soften the rigid look of a house and provide a transition between nature and man-made structures that remains unchanged throughout the year. They come in different colors, textures and forms, adding interest to the foundation planting.

Evergreens make excellent screens, borders and hedges to create privacy for back yards and other portions of a property. Although deciduous plants can also be used for this purpose, evergreens provide screening all year round.

Evergreens can also be used as specimen plants to add an extra dimension to any landscape planting. A Blue Spruce or a grouping of Blue Spruce trees can be an impressive focal point in a landscape planting. I have a beautiful Golden Cypress located on the corner of the house as you approach the Nursery and everyone comments on its beauty. There are many beautiful Evergreen trees that can be grown into great specimen plants and, if placement is well thought out, they will add greatly to the beauty, interest and value of your property.

Upright forms are selected to soften harsh corners; spreading forms to form a natural flow between them. Pyramidal forms on either side of an entrance serve to bring the eye to the front door. Low forms like Azaleas in the same color accentuate a curving line. Intermediate forms act as fillers. Low evergreens make great ground covers and there may be no better choice than planting low Junipers on a sun-filled dry bank.

Once you have defined their location and use, maintain and train them to perform their role in your landscape design. Review chapter 8 PRUNING. Maintain them so they will thrive and become healthy additions to your landscape.

FLOWERING SHRUBS: They add color to your garden and make your property beautiful and inviting. When I was at Cornell, each day I would walk up Tower Road. The Ag campus was on the left and on the right was a long row of Lilacs acting as a hedge between the road and playing fields. In the spring when the Lilac hedge came into bloom it was the most magnificent sight and the fragrance filled the air. It was kept well pruned and acted as a great hedge throughout the playing season. It is funny how some things stick in your mind, but I can still see that hedge as if it were yesterday.

There are many variables in flowering shrubs and many uses for them. Forsythia is a perennial favorite for early spring bloom; Lilac is loved for its fragrance and beauty; summer bloomers such as Hydrangea, Hibiscus and Butterfly Bush are long-blooming favorites. But there are many more: Purple Beautyberry, Sweet Shrub, Japanese Quince, Sweet Pepperbush, Scotch Broom, Fothergilla, Witch Hazel, St. John's Wort, Kerria, Crepe Myrtle, Mock Orange, Ninebark, Potentilla, Spirea, Viburnum and Weigela are some favorites which I have used extensively in my landscape designs. People love them for they come back each year to brighten their garden. They require little maintenance.

Prune yearly, and follow our organic maintenance program and your flowering shrubs will greet you with greater vigor each year. Healthy plants have few problems.

ORGANIC PROGRAM, TREES, EVERGREENS AND SHRUBS

Our program provides you with an organic approach to maintaining strong and healthy plants on your property. The organic approach is Nature's way. Feed the soil and let the soil feed the plants. Add microbes to do the work and perform miracles in the soil. The greater the mix the greater the success.

Select the right plant for the right location. Plants that are not doing well on your property may need to be transplanted or receive remediation.

Watering is the most important factor in growing a good plant. Re-read Chapter 4 WATERING. Your soil needs to be well drained so that your plants are not sitting in water but get adequate water throughout the year.

For the installation of a new plant, follow our organic approach to planting a tree in Chapter 3 PLANTING.

MONTHLY TREES, EVERGREENS AND SHRUBS CALENDAR

I do not endorse any one brand and strongly believe the greater the mix of products, the greater the results. Similar brands can be substituted. For example, in place of Lobster compost, you can use any akaline-based compost. Timing and purpose are the key ingredients to a successful program.

JANUARY

✳ PRUNE. Weather permitting, winter months are the ideal time to do pruning. Refer to Chapter 8 PRUNING.

FEBRUARY

✳ PRUNE. An ideal time to prune before the sap starts flowing. Refer to Chapter 8 PRUNING.

MARCH

✳ Plant-tone 5-3-3 for alkaline-loving plants. Holly-tone 4-3-4 for acid-loving plants. Purpose: To feed your plants with an all-natural organic fertilizer with a diverse mixture of organic ingredients. Application: 10 lbs./100 sq. ft. For evergreens and shrubs, spread the fertilizer on the surface of the ground in accordance with directions. Do not scratch fertilizer in, for you will injure surface roots. For trees, use a crowbar to make holes in the ground throughout the root area and fill them with Plant-tone.

✳ SPRAY. Spray your yard with dormant oils when temperatures are above 50 degrees to get rid of any over-wintering eggs, which would hatch into future insect problems.

* PRUNE. Severe pruning in order to shape or lower the height of plants is best done now, before new growth takes place. If you severely prune flowering plants that set their buds in the fall, you will be sacrificing your flower crop for the year. On plants that are winter burned, scratch the bark to see if it is green beneath. If it is green, it will come back. Branches that are brittle or dead should be cut back to the green area. Once you have winter burn, you need to be patient until the new June growth has taken place before you prune.
* DEER DAMAGE. Deer do a tremendous amount of damage in late winter as food is scarce and they widen their territory, scavenging for food. Deer repellents are particularly important at this time of the year. If you affect two of their senses, both taste and smell, you will get better control.

APRIL

* Plant-tone 5-3-3 for alkaline-loving plants. Holly-tone 4-3-4 for acid-loving plants. Purpose: To feed your plants with an all-natural organic fertilizer with a diverse mixture of organic ingredients. If you did not fertilize in March, do so now. Application: 10 lbs./100 sq. ft. For evergreens and shrubs, spread the fertilizer on the surface of the ground in accordance with directions. Do not scratch in, for you will injure surface roots. For trees, use a crowbar to make holes in the ground throughout the root area and fill them with Plant-tone.
* MINERAL ROCK DUST (Azomite). Purpose: Applying mineral rock dust mimics the actions of Mother Nature by replacing minerals once spread via glaciers, flooding and wind. Using mineral rock dust on your land is a sound organic practice beneficial to living soil. Application: 50 lbs./10,000 sq. ft.; 5 lbs./1,000 sq. ft.
* WATER. Check watering of new plants at least twice a week and more frequently during the heat of summer.
* MULCH. Add a 2 in. layer of mulch.
* MAINTENANCE. Make sure your beds are clean of any leaves or dead tissue. Before new growth starts, transplant plants that you would like to move to another location. Now that the ground is workable, it is an ideal time to purchase and plant nursery stock.

MAY

* DANIELS 10-4-3. A liquid fertilizer. Purpose: It is organic in nature, seed based, environmentally friendly and promotes microbial growth. Increases plant vigor and flowering. Promotes disease and insect resistance. Application: 1 tbs./gal. water and apply as a thorough watering. Feed weekly through the growing season.
* TREE AND SHRUB THRIVE. This product contains a complex of soil bacteria and mycorrhizal fungi. Purpose: Add microbes to your soil improving soil structure, plant

growth, disease and insect resistance. Application: 2 oz./gal. water. Dilute and apply as a root drench.

❋ May is the month for planting. Prior to new growth, transplanting can also take place. There are many functional reasons to install evergreens, trees and shrubs: screening, shade, beauty, ground cover, noise reduction and, of course, the interest they add to your outdoor living. If you need help, have a landscape designer lay out a plan.

JUNE

❋ NEPTUNE HARVEST FISH & SEAWEED FERTILIZER. This liquid, all-natural organic fertilizer combines several species of fish, has no offensive odor, is cold pressed, has no oils or proteins removed, contains no chlorine and won't clog the sprayer. Combining this with kelp makes it an incredible product. Kelp is derived from seaweed harvested from Nova Scotia and has 60 naturally occurring major and minor nutrients, carbohydrates, amino acids and other naturally occurring substances that specifically promote plant growth. Purpose: Enhance crop yields, quality and vigor. Application: 1 oz./gal. water applied as a thorough drench.

❋ MAINTENANCE. As the warm weather arrives, keep your trees, evergreens and shrubs well watered and mulched. Keep a vigilant eye out for insects and control them immediately by applying an organic solution. If it appears they are suffering, prune them back. Following the organic program will help bring your plants back to health.

❋ June is a major month for planting. If your trees, evergreens or shrubs are overgrown, straggly, severely damaged from the winter or petering out, it is time to get a face-lift. Call on a landscape designer to help you if you find the task overwhelming. Professional help always pays in the long run.

JULY

❋ BENEFICIAL INSECTS (Ladybugs, Nematodes, Praying Mantis). Consider adding them at this time of the year for insect control.

❋ WATER. Remember the big guys need a lot of water. When you water, do it thoroughly. Newly installed plants need particular care, make sure their root balls get soaked close to the trunk.

❋ MULCH. Mulch your beds to a depth of 2 in. and keep a vigilant eye for any insect or disease problems. If present, control quickly.

❋ Pruning. Most nonflowering Evergreens can receive a light pruning after new growth starts hardening. This leads to fuller, more compact growth. Height needs to be controlled in foundation plantings. Selectively cut back tall branches, but allow full, shorter branches to remain for next year's flowering.

AUGUST

❀ FEEDBACK LIQUID COMPOST. A gourmet meal for soil microbes, it's 100% organic soil food and a catalyst for soil activity. Purpose: Feed microbes, increase root bio-mass, balance soil and reduce stress on plants. Application: 1 oz./gal. water, 3 oz./1,000 sq. ft.

❀ WATER. It is important to keep your plants well watered at this time of the year. Trees, Shrubs and Evergreens can suffer under hot, dry conditions. Water well and water deeply. Don't lose plants due to neglect. Cool nights can bring on powdery mildew problems. Avoid overhead watering.

SEPTEMBER

❀ If you have followed our program up to this point, you have put a lot of good things back into your soil. Sit back and let the soil web perform its magic. If any of the products have not been added yet, then add them at this time. This is the time of the year to rethink your outdoor living area. Overgrown foundation plants can be moved to the perimeter of the property and new lower plants should replace them. Open up your plantings and show off the beauty of your home. Make sure there is adequate screening for privacy and that there is enough shade for your sitting areas as well as enough sun for your growing areas. There are many microclimates on your property. Choose the right plant for the right location.

OCTOBER

❀ WATER. With cool nights and high moisture becoming prevalent, powdery mildew is a problem, so avoid overhead watering.

❀ MAINTENANCE. Evaluate your back yard to see what plants need to be replaced and what projects need to be accomplished to make your outdoor living area more functional and aesthetically pleasing. If you need help, seek out a landscape designer to plan the design and a landscape crew to do the installation. Check for insect problems. If present, control quickly. Pull mulches an inch away from the bark to allow the trunks to harden off for winter.

NOVEMBER

❀ Plant-tone 5-3-3 fertilizer. Purpose: For alkaline-loving plants to feed the roots which continue to grow in the winter by applying a complete organic alkaline plant food that contains all the essential nutrients. Application: 40 lbs./2,000 sq. ft.

❀ Holly-tone 4-3-4 fertilizer. Purpose: For acid-loving plants to feed the roots which continue to grow in the winter with an all-natural organic acid fertilizer with a diverse mixture of organic ingredients. Application: 40 lbs./1,600 sq. ft.

* WATER. Don't put your hose away. Continue watering throughout the month of November, as difficult a chore as this may be. If you stop watering too early, plants will lose moisture in their cells and when a brutal winter hits, many plants will die or suffer severe winterburn.

* PLANT. November is still a good month to plant. It is the very best month for large trees and shrubs. The inner foliage of many Evergreens will turn yellow and drop. This is a normal sequence of events. If excessive yellowing takes place, it is an indication that the plant was stressed by excessive heat or drought at sometime during the year. Some Evergreens will turn a bronzy color for the winter.

DECEMBER

* PLANT. This is an ideal time to plant deciduous material and one of the best times to transplant large trees.

* MULCH. All beds should be covered with a 2 in. layer of mulch.

* FEED. If you haven't done so yet, feed your plants–refer to November.

* All broadleaf Evergreens should be sprayed with Wilt Pruf at the rate of one part to five parts water to reduce water loss from the plant. Spray when temperatures are above freezing. When the ground freezes solid, plants can't absorb water and particularly broadleaf Evergreens continue to lose water. This causes winter injury. If broadleafed Evergreens are located in a windy location, then both burlapping and Wilt Prufing would be advisable.

* WATER. If the ground remains unfrozen but still does not get adequate rain, make sure plants receive water once a week. Plants need to be well watered to survive the winter. This can be difficult and will require attaching your hose to an inside faucet. It is well worth the time and effort.

.....MY MOTHER STILL SPEAKS TO ME

I grew up in a family business where I spent my whole life working with my parents. I lost my mother in June 2008, but she still speaks to me each day. When I get up in the morning I look over at the red brick house across the parking lot and I see through the bay window that she is no longer at the breakfast table. My mother had that large bay window built to overlook the Nursery and my house. She filled it with flowers. Customers would look up at the window overlooking the parking lot and comment at all the beautiful flowers she had.

We would see her preparing breakfast or sitting at the kitchen table. Seeing no one there, I would know she was already at work and I was late. With a guilty feeling, I would rush down to the greenhouses. She is no longer there but the guilt feeling still is. Whenever this happens I am sure she is still speaking to me. I am not sure what being enmeshed with your mother is all about. You are embarrassed at the situation and you feel a lot of pressure...it makes life complicated. I was discussing it with a restaurant owner. He was suffering from his mother constantly calling him at the restaurant when he was supposed to be working. He would drop everything he was doing and run to the phone. This was an embarrassing situation for him. Whenever his mother called, his employees would drop everything and rush to find him. So much was expected of him. He wanted to be there for a mother he loved dearly, but he also needed to live his own life. He knew my mother from his visits to the Nursery. He asked me how I handled her involvement and did her passing away ever make it go away.

It has been years since my mother passed away, but the closeness still exists. Whenever I come back from the long trip to California to visit my grandchildren, I can't wait to get home and tell my mother all about it. When I am performing my morning chores by watering my section of the plants and I see weeds, plants that are not properly arranged and areas not picked up, I feel she is upset, even though she has passed away. I can hear her ask in my heart, "How can you water here every day and not know that it needs to be cleaned up? In Germany we were not brought up this way." When my wife and I drive out to eat, we automatically look up at the red brick house to see if the light is still on and if Mother is still up. There is no light and no Mother, but we still look.

When Mother passed away early in June three years ago, the birds sang every morning as never before. I was convinced she was singing to me. Her whole life was Sprainbrook— her plants, her customers, her fellow employees and her family. I knew no matter **WHERE** she was, she would not leave Sprainbrook. Somehow it feels like she is still here looking down on us, trying to help us and telling us what to do.

A cat was dropped off at the nursery. Nobody knows where it came from. It is a beautiful cat. Our best guess it is a Russian Blue mix. We call him Streak. Every day he plops himself down in the middle of the entryway, blocking Mother's number four greenhouse that she watered on a daily basis. A customer said Streak was sent to us to guard her domain. Customers come in every day and say they miss my mother, that the place is not the same without her. She was an amazing woman and everyone bonded with her.

Working with plants, there is a lot of time you spend alone, much of it watering. It provides time to think, reflect and reminisce. I think of "the good old days," times filled with lots of hard work but also lots of fun. When I worked with my mother we would talk about business or family. Mother would regale me and the employees with lots of great stories. She would always engage in conversation, but would say the hands had to keep moving as fast as the mouth. We are a working nursery and profits are tied to production. She said that when she got married, Dad promised her a Rose Garden but she got a wheelbarrow instead. She had great sayings and would often quote them throughout the work day. She would ask my father when he was building a new greenhouse if he was going to dig down to China. "Two heads are better than one," she would often say, "even though one is a cabbage head." "Give it a good drink of water and it will perk up." "Nichts sagen, Oma fragen" (When you don't know, ask grandma). "Macht Shnell," which means "Hurry Up! "Don't walk empty-handed." "There is always something to pick up. Finish the job and clean up after yourself". Don't leave it for someone else to do." She would never ask anyone to do what she wouldn't do, but since there was very little she couldn't do, it was always difficult to keep up. Many young people got their first job while in High School at Sprainbrook. They would come back years later and say they got their work ethic from Mrs. K. She was proof you could work hard and still have fun doing it.

When you look into the sky, it is huge and you wonder where it ends. Will I meet my mother again? What is beyond? Where and when? There is more that we don't know than what we do know. When we walk on the earth's surface we don't see what is below, but there is a lot of life taking place there. The sky above us is huge and filled with great masses. We can't see very far but there is so much out there. There is much going on both below our feet and above our head that we can not comprehend. Mother Nature needs to direct us and help us find our way. Mother Nature needs to speak to us. After all, is that not what mothers are for?

\

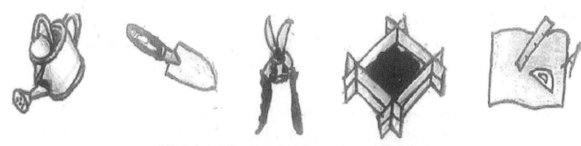

ADD YOUR GARDEN STORY HERE

24. ROSES

ROSES IN TODAY'S LANDSCAPE

A rose is one of the most beautiful plants in a garden. It is rich in heritage and lore. There are rose societies, rose collectors and rose enthusiasts throughout the world. There are great public rose gardens designed to take your breath away. The formal rose garden which was a part of many homes in the past is dwindling. Rose sale demographics have changed in the United States. Varieties used as a cut flower for the home are being replaced with roses that have landscape value. Varieties that require heavy maintenance, spraying and full sun are being replaced with varieties that are carefree. Roses are being bred for disease resistance and ability to survive in partial shade—ones that will stand up in the landscape with a minimal amount of care. Their beauty is an integral part of any landscape design.

Rose sales have plummeted in the United States as properties have become smaller and the rose garden has lost its popularity. The weekly spray programs and high-maintenance procedures recommended by rose enthusiasts, agricultural colleges and botanical gardens are not in keeping with today's lifestyles. The average home gardener loves a rose but not the work that is associated with it. The future of the industry is in developing varieties that will integrate into the landscape planting with a minimal amount of maintenance.

Many botanical gardens are moving toward growing their roses organically. They have removed varieties that are particularly disease prone and replaced them with disease-resistant varieties. It has been proven that a rose grown organically produces a more beautiful flower; a healthier, greener plant and possesses greater disease resistance and insect-repelling qualities. The move to growing roses organically will continue as the nation moves toward becoming more green. Most of us love roses and should make them an integral part of our landscape design.

Regardless of your rose preference, the following suggestions will produce the best results. Roses will thrive in a deep, rich soil and a sunny location. Plant your roses in the spring so that they will be well established before the winter. It pays to dig your holes deeply and add 1/3 rich organic matter to the soil you put back into the hole. Add and mix into the hole Rose-tone, an organic fertilizer, as well as Dehydrated Cow Manure, Bone Meal, Lobster Compost, peat moss and lime. The soil mixture should be at least 1/3 organic matter. Add Myke, rich in mycorrhizal fungi at planting time to aid in transplant shock and to increase root development.

Drip irrigation is the preferred method of watering. Prune roses back in early spring. Keep the rose bed covered with a 2 in. layer of mulch. Keep the plants well fed. We recommend a mixture of organic fertilizers throughout the year with particular emphasis on Daniels, a liquid organic fertilizer for use in the summer months. For spectacular results, spray your roses and surrounding plants with Employ every three weeks. This will significantly strengthen the immune system and help prevent black spot fungus on the leaves. Follow our MONTHLY ROSE CALENDAR.

Roses have many different uses in the garden. Climbing roses decorate walls, fences, trellises and arbors. Shrub roses are popular mixed in the garden. They are the biggest rage right now and the largest growing segment of rose sales. Roses are used for hedges and ground covers. Dwarf varieties work well in the rock garden. Many roses are used effectively for color in container plants. Roses are grown for cut flowers. Roses come in bright colors that attract the eye and give your garden flower power. Some types have a longer blooming period than any other perennial flower. They have a long history and their beauty conveys a very special sentiment to most people. There is nothing more beautiful than a rose. No garden should be without roses.

CARE OF EXISTING ROSES

Once your plants become established, avoid overhead watering. Overhead watering lowers the quality of flowers and leads to black spot, which negatively affects the health of your plant. Make sure you keep your plants well watered by giving them a good root soaking when you water. Employ a Harpin Protein complex, sprayed on your plants every three weeks, along with Foliar Ecolizer which has had tremendous beneficial results in controlling black spot and increasing flower production and quality. Spray your roses every two weeks and feed them monthly. After flowering, roses should be cut back to perpetuate their bloom. See the MONTHLY ROSE CALENDAR below for specific information on the care of roses.

PRUNING ROSES

Prune your roses when the Forsythia blooms in the spring. Follow the directions in Chapter 8 PRUNING.

My favorite major types are listed below.

* **ANTIQUE ROSES:** These have remained popular through the years. They are noted for their soft color, fragrance and free-flowering nature.
* **CLIMBING ROSES:** Fences, trellises, arbors or buildings can be covered with a profusion of color all summer long. On Climbing Roses, the main stalk is left and only the lateral branches are pruned. Keep the roses flat and prune out branches that reach too far forward. Allow in as much light as possible and you will end up with more blooms and better quality.
* **ENGLISH ROSES:** These are bred by the master rose hybridizer David Austin of Albrighton, Staffordshire. These roses are a cross between Old Shrub Roses and Hybrid Teas, Floribundas and Modern Climbers. The old roses give them their strong fragrance; full, double flowers; vigor and disease resistance. The modern roses provide their color range, glossy foliage and repeat flowering.
* **FLORIBUNDAS:** They bear clusters of flowers and give a profusion of bloom throughout the summer. This group should be used where summer color is particularly desired.

* **GROUND COVER:** These vigorous, disease-resistant, free-blooming little plants are perfect for edging and patio containers.
* **FLOWER CARPET:** An incredibly prolific bloomer, this ground cover rose is in vivid color from spring until winter. Highly disease resistant. Grows 2 -2½ ft.
* **HYBRID TEAS AND GRANDIFLORA:** The large flowered, long-stemmed Hybrid Teas have become the most popular cut flower. Grandifloras (GR) are the result of crossing hybrid teas and floribunda roses. They are generally taller and hardier than the hybrid teas, with more, but slightly smaller, flowers
* **MINI PATIO TREE ROSES:** A novelty standard. 18-24". Excellent for borders, specimen plantings and containers. Most suitable where space is limited but color is desirable. They need special winter protection.
* **SHRUB ROSES:** Selections contain both arching and upright types that are grown on their own hardy root stock. They bloom freely all season while maintaining neat growth habits, making them a low-maintenance, colorful accent for any landscape.
* **KNOCK OUT ROSES:** These shrub roses set a new standard for disease resistance. They are a carefree rose that has become the number-one seller. A full spectrum of colors has been hybridized. Their popularity is a result of their great garden performance. Knock Out Roses are known for their non-stop blooms, maintenance-free traits, exceptional hardiness, black spot resistance, drought tolerance, self-cleaning habit and beautiful flowers and foliage. They are leading the way to the rose of the future and the hope of the rose industry. There will be other hybrid groups to rival them in the future, but they have set the standard for what today's gardener wants in a rose.
* **TREE ROSES:** Three-year-old plants. These standards are especially beautiful when used as a patio plant. They blend well with other standards such as Lantana, Heliotrope and Fuchsia. They look especially striking when underplanted with low, colorful plants such as annuals, perennials or shrub roses. Protect in winter by bringing them into an unheated shed or garage or by lying them down and covering them with soil. Cut the crown portion down to 5–7 buds as you would prune a hybrid tea.

In conclusion, with the new generation of roses on the market, there is no reason to not grow a rose. There probably isn't a plant that will bloom longer, has such rich history or symbolizes such deep sentiment. Don't miss out on making this plant part of your garden. Through an organic approach to rose gardening, you will develop a healthier plant with bigger and more beautiful blooms. The most beautiful roses are those that are grown organically. Chemical fertilizers supply us with only three basics: nitrogen, phosphate and potash. Organic fertilizers are broken down into both macro- and micro-nutrients. Feed the soil and the soil will feed the plant with a well-balanced meal. A healthy, strong plant will bloom more profusely, be more resistant to insects, disease and drought and will be a darker green color.

The program we advocate addresses the microbe's role in the soil and the foliage, along with a large mixture of organic material added to the soil, which microbes can feed on. Microorganisms are the decomposers working in the soil to break down organic material, creating a function of the food web called nutrient recycling. In order for microbes to exist, they need organic material to live on, which they turn into a well-balanced meal for plants to feast on. The larger the mixture of organics, the greater the diversity of nutrients produced for plant growth and strength. Chemical fertilizers and pesticides reduce microbial activity and lead to your plants becoming nutrient dependent. My program consists of something to do each month which will benefit the soil. Once you follow an organic program, you will see the difference in your plant quality.

MONTHLY ROSE CALENDAR

I do not endorse any one brand and strongly believe the greater the mix of products the greater the results. Similar brands can be substituted. For example, in place of Lobster Compost, you can use any akaline-based compost. Timing and purpose are the key ingredients to a successful program.

MARCH

* WiINTER PROTECTION should be removed.
* Rose-tone (fertilizer) 4-3-2. A biologically enhanced fertilizer comprised of feather meal, steamed bone meal, sulfate of potash, sulfate of potash magnesia, pasteurized poultry manure, cocoa meal, green sand and humates. These organic/natural components are then inoculated with a select array of highly beneficial microorganisms. Purpose: To address soil health and nutrition. This formulation provides plants with beneficial nutrition and promotes healthy plant development through improved soil. Application: One cup of granular fertilizer per bush.
* LOBSTER COMPOST. Purpose: A lobster-based compost containing aged aspen bark and manure which will feed the microbes in your soil and greatly benefit the food web. Application: Top dress ¼ in. deep.
* MULCH. Apply a 2 in. mulch of your choice.
* PRUNE. Follow the directions in chapter 8 PRUNING.

APRIL

* Rose-tone (fertilizer) 4-3-2. A biologically enhanced fertilizer comprised of feather meal, steamed bone meal, sulfate of potash, sulfate of potash magnesia, pasteurized poultry manure, cocoa meal, green sand and humates. These organic/natural components are then inoculated with a select array of highly beneficial microorganisms. Purpose: To address soil health and nutrition. This formulation

provides plants with beneficial nutrition and promotes healthy plant development through improved soil. Application: One cup of granular fertilizer per bush.

* MINERAL ROCK DUST (Azomite). Purpose: Applying mineral rock dust mimics the actions of Mother Nature by replacing minerals once spread via glaciers, flooding and wind. Using mineral rock dust on your land is a sound organic practice beneficial to living soil. Application: Once every 3 years, 10 lbs./1,000 sq. ft.
* FOLIAR ECOLIZER IB2 (Mother Earth Organics). Beneficial bacteria and fungi species. Purpose: To apply beneficial microbes to the surface of the leaf, thus fighting black spot and other fungus problems. Application: 1 tsp./gal. water sprayed on the foliage of the plants every two weeks. Combine with Employ.
* EMPLOY. A B Harpin protein. Purpose: To control black spot and build up the immunity of the plant. Application: ¼ tsp./gal. water sprayed every 2–3 weeks on the foliage of the plants. Mix in the same gallon of water as Foliar Ecolizer IB2.
* PLANT. Time to select and plant new roses.

MAY

* DANIELS 10-4-3. A liquid fertilizer. Purpose: It is organic in nature, seed based, environmentally friendly and promotes microbial growth. Increases plant vigor and flowering. Promotes disease and insect resistance. Application: 1 tbs./gal. water and apply instead of a normal watering. Feed weekly through the growing season.
* FOLIAR ECOLIZER IB2 (Mother Earth Organics). Beneficial bacteria and fungi species. Purpose: To apply beneficial microbes to the surface of the leaf thus fighting black spot and other fungus problems. Application: 1 tsp./gal. water sprayed on the foliage of the plants every two weeks. Combine with Employ.
* EMPLOY. A B Harpin protein. Purpose: To control black spot and build up the immunity of the plant. Application: ¼ tsp./gal. water sprayed every 2–3 weeks on the foliage of the plants. Mix in the same gallon of water as Foliar Ecolizer IB2.

JUNE

* KELP BOOSTER PLUS. A natural bio-stimulant composed of calcium lime and kelp. Purpose: Kelp is rich in plant growth compounds, micro-nutrients, amino acids and vitamins all of which are essential to plant growth and development. Application: one cup per bush.
* DANIELS 10-4-3. A liquid fertilizer. Purpose: It is organic in nature, seed based, environmentally friendly and promotes microbial growth. Increases plant vigor and flowering. Promotes disease and insect resistance. Application: 1 tbs./gal. water and apply instead of normal watering. Feed weekly through the growing season. Water thoroughly but avoid overhead watering.

* FOLIAR ECOLIZER IB2 (Mother Earth Organics). Beneficial bacteria and fungi species. Purpose: To apply beneficial microbes to the surface of the leaf thus fighting black spot and other fungus problems. Application: 1 tsp./gal. water sprayed on the foliage of the plants every two weeks. Combine with Employ.
* EMPLOY. A B Harpin protein. Purpose: To control black spot and build up the immunity of the plant. Application: ¼ tsp./gal. water sprayed every 2–3 weeks on the foliage of the plants. Mix in the same gallon of water as Foliar Ecolizer IB2.
* MULCH. Maintain a 2 in. layer of mulch throughout the season.
* PLANT and select new roses. Keep your beds weed free.

JULY

* ALPHA BIOSYSTEMS FLOWER THRIVE. Contains 100% organic and natural ingredients with a large mixture of soil microbes. Purpose: To add microbes to the soil and increase microbial activity. Application: One cup per bush.
* BENEFICIAL INSECTS. Release Ladybugs to help control aphids.
* DANIELS 10-4-3. A liquid fertilizer. Purpose: It is organic in nature, seed based, environmentally friendly and promotes microbial growth. Increases plant vigor and flowering. Promotes disease and insect resistance. Application: 1 tbs./gal. water and apply instead of a normal watering. Feed weekly through the growing season. .
* FOLIAR ECOLIZER IB2 (Mother Earth Organics). Beneficial bacteria and fungi species. Purpose: To apply beneficial microbes to the surface of the leaf thus fighting black spot and other fungus problems. Application: 1 tsp./gal. water sprayed on the foliage of the plants every two weeks. Combine with Employ.
* EMPLOY. A B Harpin protein. Purpose: to control black spot and build up the immunity of the plant. Application: ¼ tsp./gal. water sprayed every 2–3 weeks on the foliage of the plants. Mix in the same gallon of water as Foliar Ecolizer IB2.
* WATER. Keep the water off the flowers and the foliage. Water thoroughly and deeply rather than too frequently.
* MAINTENANCE. Keep deadheading to ensure more flowering. Reduce excessive growth and clean up any fallen leaves. Keep beds weed free and watch carefully for insect or disease problems. If present, control quickly.

AUGUST

* FEEDBACK LIQUID COMPOST. A gourmet meal for soil microbes, it's 100% organic soil food and a catalyst for soil activity. Purpose: Feed microbes, increase root bio-mass, balance soil and reduce stress on plants. Application: 1 tsp./gal. water; one qt. per bush.
* BENEFICIAL INSECTS: Add Ladybugs to help control aphids.

* DANIELS 10-4-3. A liquid fertilizer. Purpose: It is organic in nature, seed based, environmentally friendly and promotes microbial growth. Increases plant vigor and flowering. Promotes disease and insect resistance. Application: 1 tbs./gal. water and apply instead of normal watering. Feed weekly through the growing season.
* FOLIAR ECOLIZER IB2 (Mother Earth Organics). Beneficial bacteria and fungi species. Purpose: To apply beneficial microbes to the surface of the leaf thus fighting black spot and other fungus problems. Application: 1 tsp./gal. water sprayed on the foliage of the plants every two weeks. Combine with Employ.
* EMPLOY. A B Harpin protein. Purpose: To control black spot and build up the immunity of the plant. Application: ¼ tsp./gal. water sprayed every 2–3 weeks on the foliage of the plants. Mix in the same gallon of water as Foliar Ecolizer IB2.
* WATER. Keep the water off the flowers and the foliage. Water thoroughly and deeply rather than too frequently.
* MAINTENANCE. After your first flush of flowers in early August, cut back your roses to obtain a greater display of flowers in September. Landscape roses, which bloom constantly, should be deadheaded instead. Make sure your plants are mulched and keep them well watered. Keep deadheading to ensure more flowering. Reduce excessive growth and clean up any fallen leaves. Keep your beds weed free and watch carefully for insect or disease problems. If present, control quickly.

SEPTEMBER

* Rose-tone (fertilizer) 4-3-2. A biologically enhanced fertilizer comprised of feather meal, steamed bone meal, sulfate of potash, sulfate of potash magnesia, pasteurized poultry manure, cocoa meal, green sand and humates. These organic/natural components are then inoculated with a select array of highly beneficial microorganisms. Purpose: To address soil health and nutrition. This formulation provides plants with beneficial nutrition and promotes healthy plant development through improved soil. Application: One cup of granular fertilizer per bush.
* DANIELS 10-4-3. A liquid fertilizer. Purpose: It is organic in nature, environmentally friendly and promotes microbial growth. Increases plant vigor and flowering. Promotes disease and insect resistance. Application: 1 tbs./gal. water and apply instead of normal watering. Feed weekly through the growing season.
* FOLIAR ECOLIZER IB2 (Mother Earth Organics). Beneficial bacteria and fungi species. Purpose: To apply beneficial microbes to the surface of the leaf thus fighting black spot and other fungus problems. Application: 1 tsp./gal. water sprayed on the foliage of the plants every two weeks. Combine with Employ.
* EMPLOY. A B Harpin protein. Purpose: To control black spot and build up the immunity of the plant. Application: ¼ tsp./gal. water sprayed every 2–3 weeks on the foliage of the plants. Mix in the same gallon of water as Foliar Ecolizer IB2.

* MAINTENANCE. You have added a great many good organics to the soil and your plants should be strong and healthy. Continue with the good work and you should be blessed with a floriferous display of flowers. Continue to keep your roses watered and weed free, maintain a 2 in. layer of mulch and clean up any fallen leaves.

OCTOBER

* COAST OF MAINE LOBSTER COMPOST. Purpose: A lobster-based compost containing aged aspen bark and manure, which will feed the microbes in your soil and greatly benefit the food web. Application: Top dress ¼ in. deep
* MAINTENANCE. Continue to keep your roses watered and weed free, maintain a 2 in. layer of mulch and clean fallen leaves.

NOVEMBER

* MULCH. Add mulch to your beds making sure that a 2 in. layer of mulch is down before winter.
* RAKE. As the leaves fall, make sure they are raked and removed as they are a breeding ground for insects and diseases.
* HILL. In the latter part of November, as the plants approach dormancy, roses that are grafted need to be hilled. Hilling requires that you cover the crown with shredded bark or soil topped with a layer of salt hay. These mulches insulate from the effects of alternate freezing and thawing weather. Many of the newer landscape roses, such as the Knock Outs, are on their own root stock and do not need hilling.

DECEMBER

* Roses need to be put to bed for the winter. Remove all fallen leaves so that they will not recontaminate the area next spring. Each bush that is grafted needs to be hilled. The simplest hilling method is to use pine bark mini nuggets and mound them over the crown of the rose plant. This protects the base of the plant from severe cold and wind in winter. In the spring, the mini chips can be pulled away from the base of the plant and used as additional mulch. Another hilling method is to cover the crown of the plant with soil and apply a heavy layer of salt hay on top of it. Tree roses should be brought to a protected area such as a tool shed or unheated garage. Water these plants once a month. If this is not feasible, lay them down and bury them in the soil. When the ground thaws in the spring, uncover them. Except for long branches that might break in the snow, roses should be pruned in the spring.

NOTES & OBSERVATIONS

MY GARDEN STORY

.....THE CHINESE CONNECTION

My high school friend and college roommate's wife works in the administrative office at Scarsdale High School. Through the years we have remained close friends. She was looking for a home for three teachers who were visiting from China. Desperate to find a place, she asked if we knew of any apartments for rent. Mother's house was empty, it had three bedrooms, it was furnished and it seemed like the perfect fit. The Chinese teachers, Zhao, Toto and Zhi, were taking part in an exchange program where they were to observe our way of learning and we would send teachers to observe their system. The idea behind this is that both could learn valuable lessons.

It is interesting how fate shapes our lives. How one day a new person appears and bonds are developed with someone you never knew existed. How it is possible to bond with someone totally different from a totally different culture. How in the end we found that similarities were greater than differences. The Chinese teachers lived a half a world away from us. They taught us and we taught them. They helped us and we helped them. We were concerned about them and they were concerned about us. We became a family. Each of the teachers came from a different part of China, each was prominent in their own right and each was their own person. In that red brick house where I grew up and where my mother lived for over 70 years on this little speck of the earth, fate brought us together. They bonded with us and we bonded with them.

Three years ago my mother passed away but the house still had her character. Nothing within it was changed. Instead of making changes they lived in it and embraced it. The house furniture remained the same. The pictures were left on the wall. A strong European influence prevailed and they became part of it and the warmth it exuded. We each were proud of our heritage and we learned to love each other. For every two people there is a bond if we spend the time to find it. We need to unlock it and learn to live together in harmony. We need to open our hearts to this bond and let each other in. When we do this, we gain so much more than if we shut each other out. As Zhao would say, "We need to be open. We need to be innovative and we need tenacity to get it done." From concern comes love with no place for hate. Positive actions lead to positive feelings. The world needs to learn to coexist. Understanding is better than bullets.

Zhao learned that it is necessary to be open, to be innovative and to be tenacious. Toto learned that high-quality courses, good management and teaching that is focused on creative thinking is necessary. Zhi said he was going to change the curriculum in his school system. He wanted to get people to think more rather than just to learn by the book.

All three are great men and can have a great influence in their country. They have the opportunity to shape the learning process in their schools. The learning process is the future and is what will shape the new world we all will live in. China is but one country in a world economy that needs to coexist. China is a great power and we need to live side by side with her for the betterment of all our people. We cannot fight wars anymore with bullets, we need to find solutions through love. If we learn about each other and bond with each other, we will not want to kill each other, for we will love each other too much. We all need to coexist. We need to be open in our solutions. We need to direct power to benefit all. The universal language that we all understand is Nature. If we listen, she will talk to us and guide us. Different religions divide us but Nature speaks to all of us and can unite us. In the end we all believe in the same thing, we just interpret it differently. When we observe the miracle that from a little acorn can grow a huge Oak tree, we have got to believe. The Oak is a powerful tree. It is a slow grower and we need to be patient for it to become majestic. Power needs to be earned and directed in the right direction. Each branch reaches out with wisdom. The new generation will need to learn to be open, innovative and will need to be tenacious.

As the school van pulled in at 6:00 in the morning, a group of us gathered with handkerchiefs in hand. We wanted to say goodbye. I brought my guitar out and we sang "Country Roads" one more time and said our farewells. We waved good-bye with tears in our eyes. I knew we might never meet again, but I also knew the memory would survive. They brought us through a tough winter—heating fuel prices were soaring, our business was failing and we were depressed. We brought them through a new experience. We were different but we were the same. They lived in my mother's house. At dinner time we would look across to the window in Mother's house and see Zhao with Mother's apron on cooking dinner and Heidi and I felt a tickle in our hearts. When we would drive home at night we would see if Mother's light was on and if she was in her bedroom. The light was on but it was occupied by Toto. At night I would be working into the wee hours, trying to finish my landscape plans and then work on my book. I would go to bed after 1:00 in the morning and Zhi would still be working in my old room—sitting at my old desk, trying to finish his manuscript. It reminded me of old times and a silent bond developed.

Zhao, Toto and Zhi would come down to the Nursery and they felt the warmth and beauty of the flowers. They took walks and saw trees in their dormant state break out into leaf and bloom. They marveled at the sunset each evening over the greenhouse. In this foreign place they felt like they belonged even though everything was strange. Nature has a universal meaning. We loved them and felt they were our family. We never wanted to interfere but we always wanted to embrace. And if one of the three was left behind alone, we invited him to be with us and have an even better time.

I am not sure what the future holds and if we will ever see each other again. We were invited to their homes in China and we have a strong desire to meet their families and see the places where they live. Our hope is that they will come back to America, bring their families and stay with us. We do not know what road each of us will travel or where the future will take us. We are glad they came and we will remember them as being a great force in creating happiness for six months of our lives. For getting us through tough times with a smile on our faces and warmth in our hearts, we want to say thanks.

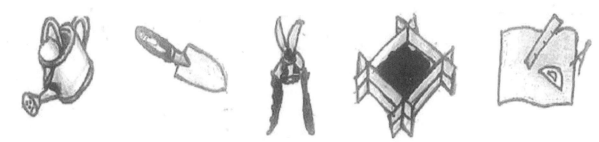

ADD YOUR GARDEN STORY HERE

25. PLANTS THAT ATTRACT BUTTERFLIES

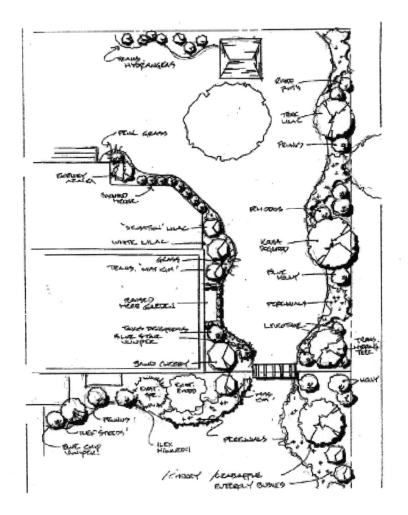

A grandfather once told me he needed plants that attract butterflies in his garden because not only do they attract butterflies, he claimed, but they attract grandchildren. His grandchildren loved to come to his house and search for butterflies. It was a unique experience that they shared together. There is nothing more exciting than to see the eyes of a child looking in awe at the beauty of a butterfly. A butterfly garden is an attraction that draws children into the miracle of a garden. If we can teach our youth the tender beauties of life, they will grow into better people. Find a sunny, easily visible area for plantings that attract butterflies.

NECTAR

Butterflies need nectar plants whose sweet fluids are used as foods. They also require plants in which to lay their eggs and where caterpillars can feed. Flowering plants that produce the nectar should be of closely related colors and clustered together. Host plants, where eggs are laid and where caterpillars feed, should be located a short distance from the flowering nectar-producing plants. Caterpillars can do great damage. Do not use insecticides on the host plant as it will kill the caterpillars. In the pages ahead you will find lists of nectar-producing and host plants. Both are necessary to create a successful Butterfly Garden.

NECTAR PLANTS

These are plants that, when flowering, produce the sweet nectar substance that attracts butterflies. It is necessary to have flowers in bloom throughout the season. I have compiled one list for annuals and one for perennials. Annuals are particularly useful as they are always in bloom in season. Avoid double flowers, stick to short, tubular flowers or flowers with large flat petals. Mass your colors.

ANNUAL NECTAR PLANTS

- ❋ Ageratum houstonianum (Ageratum)
- ❋ Callistephus chinensis (Aster)
- ❋ Cosmos bipinnatus (Cosmos)
- ❋ Helianthus annus (Sunflower)
- ❋ Heliotropium arborescens (Heliotrope)
- ❋ Impatiens walleriana (Impatiens)
- ❋ Lantana camara (Lantana)
- ❋ Salvia species (Salvia)
- ❋ Tagetes species (Marigold)
- ❋ Tropaeolum majus (Nasturtium)
- ❋ Verbena species (Verbena)
- ❋ Zinnia angustifolia (Zinnia)

PERENNIAL NECTAR PLANTS

- ❋ Aesculus parviflora (Buckeye)
- ❋ Ajuga reptans (Bugleweed)
- ❋ Alcea rosea (Hollyhock)
- ❋ Allium schoenoprasum (Chives)
- ❋ Asclepias species (Milkweed)
- ❋ Asclepias tuberosa (Butterfly Weed)
- ❋ Aster species (Aster)

* Baptisia australis (False Indigo)
* Boltonia asteroides (Boltonia)
* Buddleia davidii (Butterfly Bush)
* Cercis species (Redbud)
* Chrysanthemum maximum (Shasta Daisy)
* Cirsium species (Thistle)
* Clethra alnifolia (Summersweet Clethra)
* Coreopsis species (Coreopsis)
* Crataegus species (Hawthorn)
* Echinacea purpurea (Coneflower)
* Eupatorium fistulosum (Joe Pye Weed)
* Hemerocallis species (Daylily)
* Hibiscus species (Hibiscus)
* Hibiscus syriacus (Rose of Sharon)
* Liatris species (Gayfeather)
* Lobelia cardinalis (Lobelia)
* Monarda didyma (Bee Balm)
* Philadelphus species (Hawthorn)
* Phlox paniculata (Phlox)
* Prunus species (Plum)
* Pyrus communis (Pear)
* Rudbeckia species (Black-eyed Susan)
* Sedum species (Sedum)
* Solidago species (Goldenrod)
* Spirea species (Spirea)
* Trees and shrubs
* Vaccinium species (Blueberry)
* Veronica species (Veronica)
* Viburnum species (Viburnum)

HOST PLANTS (SUGGESTED LARVAE FOOD PLANTS)

* Anaphalis margaritica (Pearly Everlasting)
* Anethumum graveolens (Dill)
* Antirrhinum majus (Snapdragon)
* Asclepias species (Milkweed)
* Asimina species (Paw Paw)
* Aster species (Aster)
* Brassica species (Mustard family)
* Celtis species (Hackberry)

- Cornus species (Dogwood)
- Daucus carota (Carrot)
- Daucus carota sativa (Queen Anne's Lace)
- Foeniculum species (Fennel)
- Gnaphalium leontopodium (Gnaphalium)
- Grasses species (native grasses)
- Liriodendron tulipifera (Tulip Tree)
- Passiflora species (Passion Flower)
- Petroselinum hortensis (Parsley)
- Plantago species (Plantain)
- Prunus laurocerasus (Cherry Laurel)
- Pyrus species (Wild Plum)
- Quercus species (Oak)
- Sassafras albidum (Common Sassafras)
- Trifolium species (Clovers and other legumes)
- Viburnum species (Viburnum)

by Brody Krautter Pearson
Age 6

You may be lucky enough to have host plants in your neighborhood or surrounding wood area. Add some of the herbaceous ones recommended for larvae food to the back of your garden. This is a simple and inexpensive addition to any garden. Different caterpillars feed on different host plants, producing differently colored butterflies. You may be able to attract butterflies to your area from surrounding trees. Try planting a Butterfly Bush in a very sunny area, underplanting with a large display of nectar-producing annuals in strong colors. See what happens and take it from there. Adding water in a dish and a rotten piece of fruit nearby can maximize the attraction.

As you become more intrigued by this subject, you can become creative in your garden design. The butterfly life cycle is from adult to egg to caterpillar to chrysalis to butterfly. The butterfly lays the egg and the egg hatches and becomes a caterpillar—a ferocious eater—and then moves to the chrysalis stage. Here the caterpillar pupates into a butterfly, which breaks through the hard outer shell that had encased it.

There are hundreds of species of butterflies and a large variety could be found on your property. Buy binoculars and identification picture books to find their names. One of the most popular is the monarch butterfly. With its large wings garbed in orange and black, it is hard to miss as it migrates south in the fall. Butterflies like it sunny and warm and many will migrate as the weather turns cold. The average life span of a butterfly is short—from two to four weeks. Some live only a week, while the monarchs can live nine months. Butterflies are a very beautiful part of nature. Attracting them to your back yard creates interest and adds beauty. However, the caterpillar stage can do a great deal of damage to your plants, so you need to perform a careful balancing act between feeding them and having your plants destroyed.

NOTES & OBSERVATIONS

MY GARDEN STORY

.....AN E-MAIL TO MY CUSTOMERS WHEN A MAN-MADE DISASTER STRUCK

When Con Ed or your utility company comes knocking at your door or drops you a card that they will be coming by to do some pruning and selective tree removal, be aware. In the past they have followed a pruning program that would cut back limbs interfering with power lines. They have changed their attitude in our area and are eliminating whole trees rather than spending time and money in pruning them. Westchester County is known as the "green" county because of the lush foliage that inhabits our soils. Con Ed is not working with nature, they are out to control it.

They took down a large swath of trees that lined both sides of their New York Aqueduct property in the town of Greenburgh. In dismay, neighboring property owners saw their tree barriers, which blocked the view of unsightly power lines, removed. Property values along the Aqueduct fell overnight. In desperation, the property owners tried to counter this decision, but in an act of seemingly deliberate deception, the tree felling was timed to coincide with a long holiday weekend, when Con Ed worked long hours and through the weekend to beat the clock of consumer reaction.

For the home owner, there was no one to call and no one to rally and by the time a response could be assembled, the damage was done. Con Edison had a 14-man crew—climbing trees, attaching lines high in the trees to be held by personnel on the ground pulling the trees to the direction they wanted them to fall, cutting with chain saws and landing trees on the ground where they fell and remained. Within one week a 6.2-mi. stretch with up to 120 ft. on each side of the Aqueduct, within their boundaries, was cleared. Any limbs crossing over from a homeowner's property to Con Ed's property were eliminated, sometimes by cutting the tree in half vertically. This left their overbearing weight to eventually fall back toward private homes.

So when Con Ed comes knocking at your door, get the neighborhood to respond before they arrive equipped to do the job. Get your town involved and work out a deal to save the trees long before the workers arrive. When they do arrive, make sure you are out there in force to try to prevent them from taking down or mangling your favorite specimens. Your presence at the time of removal is your best chance to work out a deal. We all need to take part in saving our trees.

There is a connection between man and plants—one much deeper than we may realize. Everything in the universe is connected. We need to learn to work with nature rather than try to control her. Trees are important to us in preserving our life on this earth. They are our longest lived plants. They protect us from the sun and wind and soften the rain. They prevent erosion. They provide food and beauty. They buffer sound and screen ugly sights. They purify our air and give us back oxygen to breathe. They provide us with shade and shelter. They provide a home for nature's animal life. They provide a place for birds to perch and build nests in.

When we go on a rampage to kill trees for whatever reason, we are killing a little bit of each of us who has lived in harmony with them. These trees were our neighbors and we loved them. They were our friends. The birds they housed provided cheerfulness and the squirrels that climbed them provided entertainment. The trees provide psychological benefits and soothe us with their being. In a stressful world they were our companions in life. All things in nature are related. We are killing nature's ecosystem, one we all need to live in harmony with. Many of us have grown up with these trees and to see their brutal death is killing a part of us. Stop Con Edison and other power companies from rationalizing that we are better served without them. They will argue it is for our safety and convenience. They claim they are following an aggressive program to protect our power lines. We need to let them know that eliminating beautiful trees are terrible acts they have committed against us. We are all in this struggle together and we need to work out compromises that will benefit all.

ADD YOUR GARDEN STORY HERE

26. PLANTS THAT ATTRACT BIRDS

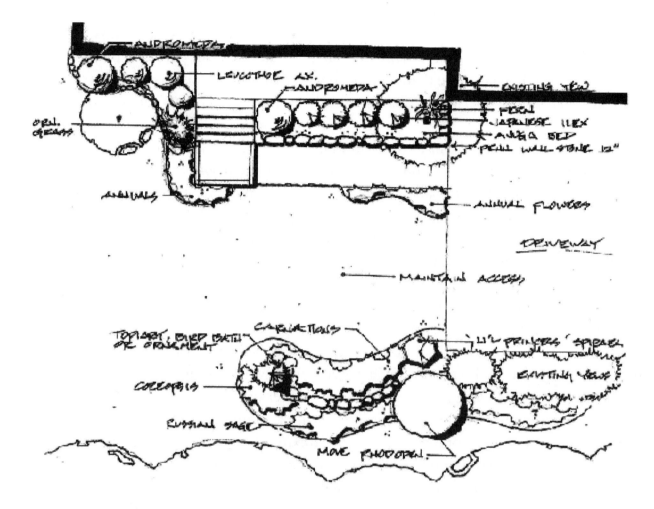

IVORY-BILLED WOODPECKER
by: Tyler Krautter Pearson, age 9

Birds are gardener's best friend. They are not only beautiful and fascinating, but they also play an important part in the natural garden by controlling harmful insect populations. As organic gardeners, we want to do everything we can to increase the bird population on our properties.

The natural garden is the ideal habitat for birds. Free of toxic substances and full of organically grown produce, berry plants and plants that go to seed assure birds a healthy food source. Every organic plant that you add to your property will pay dividends in insect control. A house wren can snatch up hundreds of insect eggs, beetles and grubs. A Baltimore oriole will wolf down harmful pests. Chickadees' winter diet is aphid eggs. And the swallow lives up to its name by consuming massive amounts of flying insects. Birds play an integral part in any natural approach to gardening.

The key to attracting birds is to plant enough vegetation to attract a large diversity of birds and supplement their food in the winter, when natural sources are scarce. Once birds find a great location they will flock to it.

Birds like a water source and this should be available to them at all times of the year. Adding a simple birdbath to your property is a great attraction. Set your birdbath 3 ft. off the ground in an open area, preferably near shrubs that birds can perch on or escape to. The water should be no more than 2 in. deep with some small rocks or pebbles for footing. There are a variety of birdbaths, some with heating elements that can prevent freezing.

Bird feeders are important during the winter months. Use a variety of feeders and seed to attract as many types of birds as possible. Vary the heights of the feeders. Locate your bird feeders where you can enjoy the show but do not have to walk too far to fill them. Birds provide great winter entertainment and will help educate your children to the wonders of nature. Feeding birds during the winter will assure you that they will be there for you in the spring. Once natural food is available, stop feeding and let them do their job keeping your plants insect free.

Birds love the berry crops that you are growing for your own consumption. Protect these crops with bird netting as they come close to the crops harvest time. Birds however need plants that will supply them with a succession of available food throughout the year. They also need plants that will provide them with shelter from other wildlife and a place to perch on. Dense trees around the perimeter of your property will attract birds and evergreens will afford them shelter in the winter. Many of the plants that attract birds may already be on your property. Add to your mixture to attract a greater variety of birds.

Below is a list of commonly recommended plants that attract birds and are also valuable additions to any garden. Some are recommended for their berries, others for flowers that provide nectar and seed; some provide winter protection and others provide cover and places to perch on.

FLOWERS (NECTAR AND SEED)

* Ageratum houstonianum (Ageratum)
* Aquilegia species (Columbine)
* Aster species (Aster)
* Centaurea cyanus (Bachelor's Button)
* Chrysanthemum species (Chrysanthemum)
* Coreopsis species (Coreopsis)
* Cosmos bipinnatus (Cosmos)
* Echinacea purpurea (Purple Coneflower)
* Helianthus annus (Sunflower)
* Monarda species (Bee Balm)

* Penstemon species (Penstemon)
* Rudbeckia fulgida (Black-eyed Susan)
* Tagetes species (Marigold)

SHRUBS (BERRIES AND FOOD)

* Buxus sempervirens (Boxwood)
* Cornus sericea (Red Osier Dogwood)
* Cotoneaster species (Cotoneaster)
* Hamamelis virginiana (Witch Hazel)
* Ilex crenata species (Japanese Holly)
* Ilex species (Holly)
* Ilex verticillata (Winterberry)
* Mahonia aquifolium (Oregon Grape Holly)
* Myrica pensylvanica (Bayberry)
* Prunus cistena (Sand Cherry)
* Pyracantha angustifolia (Firethorn)
* Rubus occidentalis (Blackberry)
* Sambucus canadensis (American Elder)
* Taxus cuspidata (Japanese Yew)
* Vaccinium species (Blueberry)
* Viburnum species (Viburnum)

DECIDUOUS TREES (SHELTER AND FRUIT)

* Acer palmatum (Japanese Maple)
* Amelanchier species (Serviceberry)
* Cornus florida (Dogwood)
* Crataegus veridis (Hawthorn)
* Fagus grandifolia (American Beech)
* Malus species (Crabapple)
* Prunus species (Cherry)
* Quercus species (Oak)

EVERGREEN TREES (WINTER SHELTER)

* Abies concolor (White Fir)
* Ilex opaca (American Holly)
* Juniperus species (Juniper)
* Picea species (Spruce)
* Pinus species (Pine)
* Pseudotsuga menziesii (Douglas Fir)
* Tsuga canadensis (Canadian Hemlock)

GROUND COVERS AND VINES (FOOD AND COVER)

* Hedera helix (English Ivy)
* Lonicera species (Honeysuckle)
* Parthenocissus tricuspidata (Virginia Creeper)
* Vinca minor (Myrtle)

NOTES & OBSERVATIONS

.....LANDSCAPING MY DAUGHTER'S HOUSE

My daughter decided to buy a house in Silicon Valley, ten minutes away from her practice. She invited me out to draw a landscape plan. Heidi and I went to visit. I measured the property and mapped the location of everything on graph paper. I spent time drawing detailed plans for her. Much of the plant material commonly used there is similar to that in the New York Metropolitan area. They have a hard freeze once a year and replace annuals, but as temperatures rarely drop into the twenties, I had a more varied plant list to choose from.

The plots in her neighborhood are rectangular, each has a high redwood fence separating the lots, which are about ¼ acre in size. Tonja's house is a ranch style with an attached garage, rectangular in shape, and takes up nearly the full width of the lot with a small walkway on either side. Twenty-five percent of the remaining land is in the front of the house with about seventy-five percent in the back.

Outdoor living is a big part of the California lifestyle. For the back yard, I designed a large terrace that ties into the family room. The lot in the back is rectangular and I planned to break the straight lines and add curves, while preserving as much grass area as possible for recreational activity. My plan included a berm in the left back corner. In the right back corner was a playhouse (later changed out with a water feature). The right corner of the terrace was softened with a curving bed and incorporated a shade tree as protection from the heat of the sun. Planters were located on the terrace to provide color and to soften the exterior of the house. I recommended a new organic lawn and a drip system on an automatic timer. The yard was designed to have lots of color, nice gentle curving lines to break the monotony and enough grass for a large play area. The back yard plan looked great.

The front yard presented a challenge as everything was squared off, creating a boxy look. The front of the house and the front of the property ran as parallel lines. The driveway approached the house on the right side, running perpendicular to it as did the boundary lines. The road was parallel to the house. The driveway usually had a car parked in it and I wanted to hide the car. The front yard needed lots of color to attract attention. I came up with a design that featured curving lines and planting beds on all of the perimeters. The bed bordering the front street was to be filled with colorful eye-catching annuals, which would be a showstopper for anyone passing by. The planting bed bordering the driveway would be a mixture of ornamental grasses to partially screen the parked cars. The foundation planting would be evergreens with bays of color arching out into a lush lawn of green that would set off the colorful plantings. It was a good plan.

Implementation would offer another challenge. I shipped annuals and perennials out by FedEx, bought the shrubbery from my West Coast vendors and had it delivered to the site, while Tonja ordered the blocks for the terrace and other hardscape material to be delivered to her driveway. Jason, her husband, was overwhelmed by the challenge and rounded up family and friends to help. We worked for over two days, from early morning into late night, building the large patio. On Friday, all the soil was prepped in the yard and I marked out all the planting beds. On the weekend, Tonja hired a six-man landscape crew who, along with friends and neighbors, did all the planting. It was a busy and hard day placing the plants in their proper location. Tonja also wanted me to add plants that would attract birds to add interest to her back yard.

When the job was finished we put down mulch and installed a drip system. Everyone commented on the beauty and functionality of the design. A great deal of money was saved by doing most of the work ourselves. At the end of the last day, late into the evening, dirty and muddy and too tired to change, we all went to the Outback Steakhouse to have a glass of beer and a large steak. We were tired but proud of the job we had done. I went back to the house and showered and Heidi and I took the red-eye home to New York.

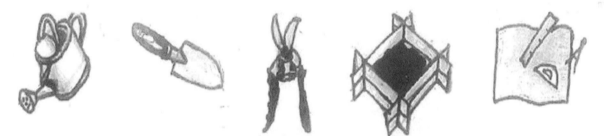

ADD YOUR GARDEN STORY HERE

27. PLANTS THAT ATTRACT HUMMINGBIRDS

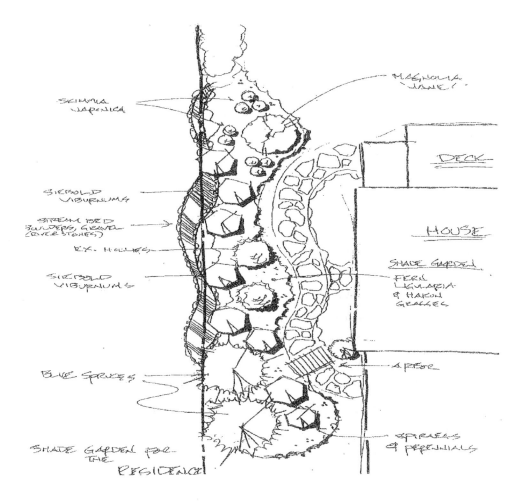

A hummingbird is a new world bird, chiefly tropical of the family Trochilidae. Usually very small in size, it has a long slender bill and often brilliant colored plumage. The humming sound is produced by the rapidly  vibrating wings. These tiny, brightly colored birds have narrow  wings, a long bill and a lengthy extensile tongue. Hummingbirds are known for their acrobatic flight capabilities. There are 20-plus species recorded in North America that will migrate south during the winter.

Hummingbirds need a protected area to perch on, a source of water to bathe in and drink, sweet nectar to sip and tiny insects for protein. Shade trees, shrubs and evergreens will provide protection, shade and a place to perch. Some of these, which I will list, also provide flowers as a source of nectar. Adding water features to your garden may be necessary. Birdbaths, garden ponds, waterfall displays are all good sources for hummers to drink and bathe in. They prefer areas with shallow water. Add two or three hummingbird feeders to an area that you can view and photograph from. Hummingbird feeders require sugar-water solutions that are regularly replaced. Boil water and make a solution of four parts water and one part sugar. Do not use honey, molasses or artificial sweeteners. Clean weekly to keep water and feeders clear.

Hummingbirds are attracted to flowers by sight. Hot colors in red, orange, yellow and pink work best. Tubular flowers with high-nectar production are the ones hummingbirds seek out. Try not to use insect sprays in this area, but if you need to, limit your spray to safe organic controls. Below is a list of plants that will attract hummingbirds to your garden.

TREES AND SHRUBS

* Buddleia davidii (Butterfly Bush)
* Chaenomeles species (Flowering Quince)
* Forsythia x intermedia (Forsythia)
* Hamamelis virginiana (Common Witch Hazel)
* Hibiscus syriacus (Rose of Sharon)
* Kolkwitzia amabilis (Beauty Bush)
* Malus species (Crabapple)
* Rhododendron species (Azalea, Rhododendron)
* Syringa vulgaris (Lilac)
* Weigela florida (Weigela)

VINES

* Campsis radicans (Trumpet Creeper)
* Ipomoea purpurea (Morning Glory)
* Lonicera japonica (Japanese Honeysuckle)
* Phaseolus coccineus (Scarlet Runner Bean)

PERENNIALS

* Aquilegia (Red Columbine)
* Asclepias tuberosa (Butterfly Weed)
* Campanula rotundifolia (Bluebells)
* Castilleja affinis (Indian Paintbrush)
* Dicentra spectabilis (Bleeding Heart)

* Digitalis (Foxglove)
* Hemerocallis species (Daylilies)
* Heuchera species (Coral Bells)
* Lobelia cardinalis (Lobelia)
* Lupinus species (Lupine)
* Malva species (Hollyhock)
* Monarda species (Bee Balm)
* Penstemon species (Penstemon)
* Phlox paniculata (Phlox)
* Yucca filamentosa (Yucca)

ANNUALS

* Agapanthus africanas (Lily of the Nile)
* Cuphea ignea (Little Cigar)
* Fuchsia x hybrida (Fuchsia)
* Gladiolus communis (Gladiola)
* Impatiens wallereriana (Impatiens)
* Lobelia erinus (Blue Lobelia)
* Mirabilis jalapa (Four-O'Clocks)
* Petunia x hybrida (Petunia)
* Salvia elegans (Pineapple Sage)
* Salvia species (Salvia)
* Tropaeolum majus (Nasturtium)

NOTES & OBSERVATIONS

.....THE TREE WHISPERER

I invited the Tree Whisperer to come to Sprainbrook Nursery to give a presentation. Both Fred, our greenhouse manager and I had met him and listened to his lecture at the Nature Lyceum's organic class. The Tree Whisperer, Dr. Jim Conroy, is a teacher at the Nature Lyceum. I had wanted to bring him to the Nursery but wondered how he would be received. Change was coming, but change is slow. People not only have to understand a concept but they need time to experience the result. The bond with nature comes from experiencing it. I knew I was taking a chance in inviting him but I wanted my customers to meet him.

Dr. Conroy is a plant pathologist from Purdue University. He heals trees through a Green Centric system. His method directs you through a hands-on, bioenergy-based, tree-healing session. His goal is to reconnect your love of nature by stepping "inside" the tree's or plant's world through a tactile- and sensory-guided visualization. He teaches you to recognize signs of tree decline. He gives you a list of 12 tree/plant stressors and tips to alleviate stressors. If your tree has three or more of these, it is usually in decline. Dr. Conroy works with Ms. Basia Alexander, who is the chief "listener." She is the founder of the Institute for Cooperation with Nature.

My concern was that this lecture would be too cutting edge for my customers. I had a terrible feeling that I would be bringing in someone of this stature only to have 2 to 3 people sitting, chairs apart, in the audience. The group of people that I was trying to bring in were the recipients of my weekly newsletter, KRAUTTER'S KORNER. I had spent three years converting my customers from the chemical to the organic approach by way of gardening tips and organic programs. Our only advertising for this event was through our e-mail newsletter and word of mouth.

We cleared out a 40 x 40 ft. area in our foliage house, power washed the red brick pavers floor, brought railroad ties in to build sitting areas on our surrounding benches, placed indoor foliage trees behind them and on the perimeter of this area and filled the overhead pipes that run throughout our greenhouses with a hundred hanging baskets to make it a truly beautiful setting. We had parties before in this area, including my daughter's wedding and knew how to decorate. It was a beautiful space and we were able to seat over a hundred people.

The night before, I couldn't sleep. I was thinking how naive I was to think that others would feel as passionate about this subject as I did. In the 60s there was a lot written about our ability to communicate with plants, but not much has been written about it since. I knew one should live in the present and not fret about the past. When the day arrived, I felt at ease. I had prepared the best I could for this event and I was excited and looking forward to being a part of it. About 60 enthusiastic people arrived.

When the lecture was over, Dr. Jim took us all out to a large shade tree. He put his hands around the tree and held it tight. He had each of us do the same. Then he tapped the tree to get the energy moving. We now had the energy from the tree, the energy from the earth on which we were grounded and our own energy all working to help circulation within the tree. He communicated with the tree, found out what the tree needed and he redirected the energy to correct the tree's problems. It is amazing that this process works. I have always said there is more in life that we don't know than we do know. He boasts a cure rate of over 95 percent. I brought a neighbor's tree back to life following this technique.

ADD YOUR GARDEN STORY HERE

28. INDOOR GARDENING

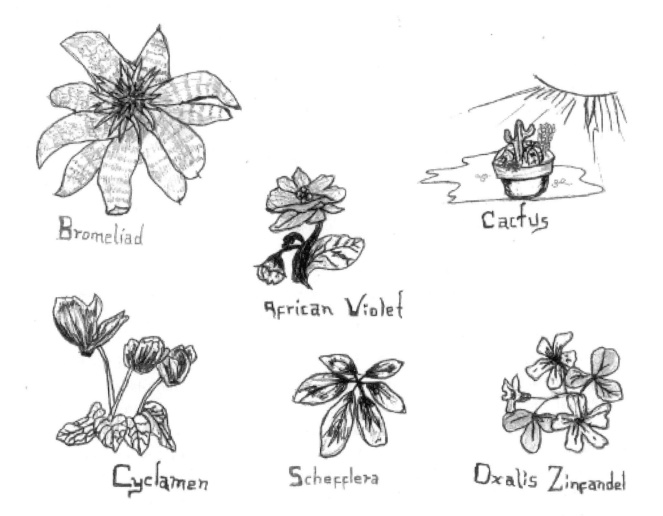

Bromeliad

African Violet

Cactus

Cyclamen

Schefflera

Oxalis Zinfandel

There are many reasons why houseplants should become part of our lives. When we erect a building, we close nature out. When we fill it with houseplants, we bring nature back in. The benefits of having plants are many.

Plants add to the beauty and decor of any indoor environment. Nature is brought into the home and the harsh lines of man-made structures are softened with the natural lines of large, strategically placed foliage plants. Flowering plants are welcoming and add a colorful warmth to a home. Hanging plants add yet another dimension, as do foliage plants of various sizes and shapes. When decorating, consider both the plants you choose and the pots you place them in. The greater the mixture of plants the more interesting your collection becomes. Plants can be grouped together for effect or stand individually to soften a corner or add color to a dull area.

Plants link us to nature and their presence becomes important to our lives. We learn to appreciate each one for its uniqueness and we become caregivers, bonding with its needs and receiving its rewards. Each new flower and each new leaf provides us with satisfaction. A green thumb is a thumb of knowledge and a thumb of love. Living plants add fresh beauty and living charm to our daily lives. We respond by doing our best to keep our plants happy. By decorating our house with plants we are creating an atmosphere which benefits the whole family.

Plants have a very soothing psychological effect. Flowers smile at us and make us happy. Foliage plants become part of the family and we bond with them. Many people name their foliage plants, talk to them and enjoy an even deeper relationship. This type of communication is beneficial to both you and the plant. A caretaker personality thrives when caring for plants. Children who grow up taking care of their own plants learn responsibility and benefit psychologically from a pleasant environment. Bringing nature into the home helps build harmony in the home. Plants purify the air and make life indoors healthier. We will examine in more detail the reasons for making plants part of every home, classroom, workplace and restaurant.

When you plan a vacation, plan to have someone go to your house once or twice a week to water your plants. You can return that service when they take their vacation. If you have built up a relationship with someone at a garden center or a plant shop, you could hire that person to perform this task.

There are several watering methods that will help your plants survive through this time if you are on your own. You can fill your bath tub with water and place your plants on crates just above the water line. Soak towels and place them on the crates with both ends submerged in the water. Place your plants pot to pot on the towels and water them thoroughly before you leave. The plants will take up water by capillary action as they need it. This works best with clay pots. Also there are tubes that you can purchase which will slowly drip water into the plant while you are gone. You can double pot your containers to conserve moisture or use plastic to create enclosures. Perhaps the best device is a product called Hydro Spike. It provides even, continuous and automatic watering to any plant. It siphons water up from any water reservoir and by capillary action draws it into the soil of the plant.

GROW FRESH AIR

Growing fresh air in the home and workplace by adding houseplants is an important step to take. An alarming health problem is developing in homes and workplaces. In our desire to conserve energy, we have developed tightly sealed buildings which trap toxic gases from synthetic materials and other sources in the air we breathe. Long-time exposure to these chemicals is causing health problems. Indoor air pollution is considered by many health professionals to be one of the major threats to health. Eyes, nose and throat irritations and sneezing are common initial problems. Allergies, asthma, respiratory problems and cancer are associated with these indoor toxins.

Perspiration and other body fluids from large gatherings of people in classrooms, the workplace or meeting areas contribute to impure air. All of these cause low-toxin exposure that builds up in our system over time and which can cause devastating problems later. Infants and small children are particularly vulnerable to indoor air pollution as their bodies are not fully developed. And we all know the effect secondhand smoke can have on us.

Breathing fresh air is important for our lungs. Many people spend more than 90% of their time indoors. The adverse effect of indoor air pollution is referred to as "sick building syndrome." This is a growing health problem which can be solved by adding plants to purify the air. The more plants you add, the healthier the air you breathe. If you spend a good portion of your day in front of a computer, place a plant in your breathing area. It is amazing how much better you will feel and how much better you will function. Plants purify air. It is nature's way of preserving our earth. The plants provide added oxygen and moisture to a room. Through tiny openings in the leaves called stomata, plants absorb carbon dioxide and convert it into oxygen. Along with this process they absorb chemicals from the air. These toxic chemicals can be utilized by the plant or translocated to the roots, where microbes will ingest them and break them down. Plants release phytochemicals that suppress mold spores and bacteria found in the air. Plants organically grown have lots of microbial activity taking place in the soil which is the key to toxin removal. Growing fresh air is a challenge we can easily meet. Houseplants are the answer to healthier living. With a little bit of cultural knowledge, you will find caring for them a pleasant task.

Flowering plants add color throughout your home, make great decorations for the holidays or memorable centerpieces for special occasions. They are less expensive than cut flowers and last longer. Flowers add joy to your day. Europeans have learned this and won't live without flowering plants in their homes. With our stressful lives, Americans should also learn this simple lesson. Foliage plants add color to dull areas and come in all sizes, shapes, textures and colors.

In the 80s, as the hippie generation matured, Americans fell in love with houseplants. People would block their indoors from view by placing large foliage plants in front of windows rather than curtains. Apartments were filled with foliage, flowering plants, hanging baskets and terrariums were the craze. Once the indoor areas were filled with the common selections, the search was on to find something new and different.

In those days many articles were written, backed by scientific data, about communication between people and plants. Cleve Backster (born 1924) is best known for his 1960s polygraph experiments in biocommunication in plant and animal cells. Backster did polygraph tests in New York City that indicated that plants can actually feel emotions and read our minds, responding favorably to affection and even music but also detecting threats or ill intent. Plants, through this connection, may develop our taste for music. Everything in the universe is connected and that connection may be stronger than we understand. Plants teach us many lessons; all we need to do is listen.

Houseplants have been selected for their ability to adapt to the home. When choosing a plant, read the required light conditions for the plant to determine where its needs will best be met. Many flowering plants will require full sunlight and need to be placed directly in front of windows that receive direct sunlight. Many foliage plants can burn in full sun and these will thrive with less light. Light is also a growth inhibitor producing compact full plants. Where light is lacking, a plant can become tall and leggy. A plant placed on a windowsill may form a curvature toward the light. We say it is turning toward the light but actually there is less growth on the sunny side and greater growth on the dark side. When germinating seedlings, we need to get them in full sun as soon as possible so that they do not become leggy. Light requirements differ with each plant. Even though many plants can tolerate and even thrive in poor light, all plants require light to survive. My mother grew her best flowering plants in her bay window but had foliage plants throughout her house.

❋ **BASIC PLANT FUNCTIONS:** Plants perform a complex set of functions. Understanding some basic plant functions will help us care for our indoor plants. The roots of a plant are their strength. I have always considered the roots of a plant to be the brains of a plant. Roots need oxygen to breathe. Without oxygen a root can't survive. More plants are killed by overwatering than in any other way. Roots carry water and nutrients up to the plant. In light, photosynthesis takes place within the plant. Through small stomata openings, plants absorb CO_2, which is converted into sugar when combined with hydrogen. This provides the plant with energy. Oxygen is released as a byproduct into the surrounding air. Good growth requires that the photosynthesis process takes place.

Transpiration is a process where moisture is released into the atmosphere through stomata openings. Excessive moisture loss can lead to wilting. Caught in the early stages, temporary wilting can be corrected by watering. Permanent wilting can cause death. The xylem moves water and nutrients up the plant and the phloem moves sugars down. Respiration is a process where sugars combine with oxygen to produce energy for the manufacture of other substances required for growth and survival. Microbes are in an organic soil and are the key to toxic chemical removal as translocation takes place and photochemicals are released from leaves.

❋ **POTTING SOIL:** My father always said growing a good plant starts with a good soil. A good soil produces a great root system. I put a great deal of effort into the production of my soil. My soil has always been organic, with its base starting from a mixture of rich leaf mold and compost. I add rice hulls, aged bark, peat moss, coconut fiber and perlite. I also add organic fertilizers, microbes, humates and lime to the mix. My father was fond of saying that we put everything in our soil but the kitchen sink. People would come from great distances just to purchase it.

* **WATERING:** A simple rule to follow when you are watering your plants is to water them thoroughly rather than too frequently. Fill your pot to the rim with water and then let the soil become dry or dry to the touch before watering again. If a plant becomes too dry, water may run through the soil like a sieve. There is no moisture in the soil to create capillary action. When this happens, soak your plant in a bucket of water or rewater your plant slowly until the moisture can be retained in the soil. Always make sure your pot has a hole in the bottom where water can drain out. There is no general rule I can give you on how often to water because environmental conditions will vary at different times of the year and from home to home. If I had to give a general rule, I would say water large plants thoroughly once a week but check on them in between. Water smaller plants more frequently. Big plants in small pots require more water and small plants in big pots less water. Plants in warm houses need more water than those in cool houses and plants near hot air ducts will need heavy watering. I always consider your finger to be the best indicator, but there are water meters that can be used to do the measuring for you. In the old days, my father would tap each clay pot with his wand before watering. He could tell by the tone if it needed water.

* **HUMIDITY:** Dry, warm houses can be harsh on plants and the acclimation process will be more difficult on new plants. This process may cause temporary leaf drop. Anything you can do to increase the humidity will help. Foliage plants that first come from a greenhouse into a home will benefit from misting for the first three weeks. The more plants you have, the higher the humidity and the better your plants will do. Placing plants on oversized saucers filled with gravel with the bottom half filled with water will increase humidity around your plants. Keep plants away from hot air ducts. As the heat goes on, the humidity in a house goes down. If your plants are suffering, misting at this time of the year will help. Plants that have taken a beating during the winter can usually be revived by placing them outside in the summer in a shady area. Bay windows, window greenhouses and greenhouse-like extensions tend to contain high humidity when filled with plants. As you increase your collection, humidity will increase due to transpiration from the surrounding plants.

* **FEEDING:** I grow plants in a rich organic soil that is filled with microbes. Microbes are a plant's best friend. Chemical fertilizers can kill microbes in the soil while organic fertilizers will aid them. Daniels is my favorite indoor fertilizer. It is a seed-based fertilizer derived from rap seed. All the nutrients go into the seed so that it can reproduce itself. The seed is squeezed and a fertilizer is made out of it. As a result, this fertilizer is filled with nutrients and micronutrients that yield fantastic results. During

the winter, feed once a month; during spring and fall, every two weeks; and during the summer every week.

❊ **PRUNING:** Houseplants need to be trimmed to keep them full and compact. Trailing plants need to be cut back when they get too long; floor and table plants need their shape maintained. Every time you make a terminal cut, it stops growth and forces branching. These cuts can help maintain a compact, full plant and are of particular value in restraining your foliage plants. Sometimes plants just get too big and may need lateral pruning where a whole branch is removed to the stem. The question often arises "What do I do with my floor plant that has hit the ceiling?" Many floor plants have two or three plants in a pot and you want to cut the tallest one back severely. Dracanea is a good example of this. Other good examples of plants that profit from severe pruning are Schefflera and Yucca. Remember that where you make the cut you will develop two to three new branches. Make the cut low enough so that it does not develop a top-heavy look. Ficus trees usually have a crown and branches should be trimmed back individually as they get too long. Pruning is an art that can help maintain the vigor and height of plants.

❊ **LIGHTING:** Light is essential in growing plants. Light is a required ingredient in carrying out the photosynthesis process. Some plants require full sunlight while others will tolerate low light and will even burn in too strong a light. Light intensity varies throughout the year, as does day length. Plants receive the most light on a bright summer day. The intensity of light is higher and the duration of light is longer. Plants receive the least amount of light during the winter months, but they can be helped by additional light sources, such as fluorescent light and plant light bulbs. The longer the lights are left on, the greater the value to the plant. Also spotlighting can highlight the beauty of a plant and provide additional light for the plant.

❊ **REPOTTING:** You can keep a plant growing in a small pot for a long time by feeding and pruning. Ideally, keep your plant in the same size pot for three years or more if you can. Move it up one size at a time. Do not overpot. You do not want your pots to become too large or your plant too big for the space. Plants will usually tell you when they need repotting. New leaves will become smaller, lower leaves will drop and the general vigor of the plant will be gone. Pot-bound plants have a heavily netted root system that should be cut vertically with a knife to stimulate lateral rooting. Use rich organic potting soil and place a pot shard over the drainage hole and then place soil on top of the shard. Place the root ball at a height that will allow for watering and pack the soil on the sides with a narrow piece of wood to prevent air pockets.

DOUBLE POTTING: This is a method used by many to reduce the number of times you need to water a plant. A plant already in a pot is placed inside a decorative pot and packed with wet sphagnum moss between the two pots. As the plant dries, the clay pot pulls moisture from the wet moss. This works best with clay pots. When your plant needs watering, so will the sphagnum moss.

PROPAGATION: Propagation is the reproduction of existing plants. Many of your favorite plants are easy to propagate and make great gifts to friends. Some homeowners will stick cuttings into water and wait for roots to form, then plant the cuttings in soil. Growers prefer starting plants in soil and then transplanting them when they root. Use a sterile organic soil and have a system that provides bottom heat and keeps the foliage moist. Below are some common methods of propagating with an example:

* **STEM CUTTING.** Coleus: Cut a 2 in. tip with a sharp knife below a leaf, remove leaf dip into rooting hormone and place in a rooting medium.
* **LEAF-PETIOLE CUTTING.** African Violet: Take leaf, cut petiole ½ in., place in sand.
* **PLANTLETS.** Spider Plant: Cut plantlet off to form a small plant and plant it.
* **DIVISION.** Bromeliad: Remove the pups and replant.
* **LEAF CUTTINGS.** Rex Begonia: Dissect the leaf following the veins, crop the leaf size and place in a very well drained rooting media.
* **AIR LAYERING.** Corn Stalk Dracaena: Cut a rim in the outer phloem tissue, pack with sphagnum moss, tie plastic around and keep moist. The stem will root into the moss.
* **CANE CUTTINGS.** Dracaena, Yucca: Cut cane in sections and lay on side in soil.
* **ROOT CUTTINGS.** Plumbago, Clerodendrum: Cut roots, divide and set in soil.
* **JOINT CUTTINGS.** Christmas Cactus: Cut joints leaving a small portion of the stem and place in a rooting soil medium.
* **SEEDS.** Cineraria: Start seeds and keep transplanting until plant is mature.
* **FERNS.** Spore and spore cases: Place on an agar solution, germinate and root.

INSECT AND DISEASE PROBLEMS

Insect and disease problems can plague your plants. Keep a vigilant eye open and treat as soon as you discover any symptoms. Healthy plants resist insect invasion. Grow plants in rich organic soil and feed regularly with Daniels organic plant food.

* **APHIDS:** These usually occur in clusters on tender growing shoots or flowers. They are sucking insects that exude a sugar-based sticky substance called honeydew and cause distorted foliage. They multiply rapidly, are soft-bodied, come in green or black, are winged or wingless, are about 1/8 in. long and have six legs. Control with sprays containing combinations of natural pyrethrins and canola oil.

❋ **CYCLAMEN MITES:** These are small microscopic eight-legged pests related to the spider. They thrive in hot conditions, multiply rapidly and prefer sucking in newly formed leaves or buds. They cause distorted and crippled foliage and flower buds. Control with natural pyrethrins and canola oil combination.

❋ **MEALYBUGS:** These are pinkish-white soft-bodied crawlers with many legs. They're covered with a waxy, white fluffy substance that prevents insecticides from entering them. They live by siphoning sap and are found in the axils or ribs of leaves. The young emerge from cottony masses. Control with insecticidal soaps.

❋ **SCALES:** They are like leathery plants. They are sucking insects that have hard shells to protect them from insecticides. They come in tan, brown, black or white. Their shape is oval, oblong or circular. They exude a substance sticky to the touch. Control with super fine horticultural oil or soap.

❋ **SLUGS:** These are slimy snails without shells which come up at night to chew tender leaves and flowers. They live in damp places such as pebble trays. Sprinkle iron shavings into the moist pebble tray.

❋ **SPIDER MITES:** These are microscopic red mites which thrive in hot, dry conditions. They usually occur on the underside of leaves where they puncture plant tissue, causing speckling and discoloration of the leaf surface. These tiny eight-legged creatures multiply rapidly. Control by misting daily and spraying with insecticidal soap.

❋ **WHITE FLY:** A tropical insect that loves the heat. They are 1/16 in. long, covered with a white waxy substance and take flight when disturbed. They lay their eggs usually on the underside of a leaf. Vacuum around the plants and spray with a insecticidal soap.

Diseases are not a major problem in the dry atmosphere of a house. Listed below are the most common diseases that attack indoor plants.

❋ **POWDERY MILDEW:** A fungus that may occur with sudden changes in temperature, cold drafts or dampness. Leaves develop a powdery film. Avoid overhead watering. Control by applying a fungicide recommended for powdery mildew.

❋ **ROOT ROT:** A condition that occurs from overwatering.

❋ **CROWN ROT:** Usually occurs in the crown of African Violet or Cyclamen when dead tissue from the stem of the flowers is not removed to the base.

FLOWERING PLANTS

Flowering plants add color and warmth to your house. They greet you with a smile each day and make you and your family feel better. These are some of the most popular houseplants and their requirements. I am listing them by common name first.

❋ **AFRICAN VIOLET** (Saintpaulia ionantha): African Violets prefer good light but not direct sun, except in the winter. They bloom all year. Keep out of cold drafts. Water with lukewarm water. Cyclamen mites will deform their flowers and cause hard stunted growth on their inner foliage. Flower thrips are microscopic insects that stunt flowers. Keep to a single crown and prevent bunching, which will reduce flowering. Give the plant's a good drink of water and let them run on the dry side before watering again. They belong to the Gesneriad family. When they develop elongated stems below their whorl of leaves, re-pot them and set them lower. The buildup of salts on clay pots can cause leaf-petiole damage. Scrape the salts off or change the pot. African violets are propagated by a leaf petiole cutting. They come in all colors and are very rewarding plants.

❋ **AMARYLLIS** (Hippeastrum species): A colorful, exotic plant that is easy to care for. Needs filtered light. Water well and let it become slightly dry. It usually sends up several stalks. Remove the first stalk when it has finished blooming. After flowering, keep allowing the plant to grow until summer and then dry off and keep dormant for several months. It will start up again in the fall.

❋ **AZALEA** (Rhododendron cultivars): Can be placed in any location as long as it is kept well watered. Hardy varieties can be planted in the garden. Non-hardy ones are grown outdoors, then brought inside in the late fall and forced into flower.

❋ **BEGONIA** (Begoniaceae species): This is a large group of plants with many varieties. Popular are the Wax Begonia, Angel Wing, Red Dragon, Rex, Reiger, Richmondensis, Stem Begonia and many more. They all like filtered light to full sun in winter. Keep water off leaves. Water well and let run dry between waterings. They like it warm.

❋ **BROMELIA** (Bromeliaceae species): These belong to the pineapple family. They enjoy filtered light. Keep water in the cup formed by the leaves. A very hardy plant. Transplant pups for next year's flowers. Place a green apple along with the plant in a plastic bag with holes to initiate the flower bud.

❋ **BULB PLANTS:** Tulip (Tulipa), Daffodil (Narcissus), Hyacinth (Hyacinthus), Grape Hyacinth (Muscari) and Crocus (Crocus) all like a sunny, cool location to extend their bloom. They naturalize well when planted in the garden, producing blooms the following spring.

❋ **CINERARIA** (Senecio cruentus): A colorful plant that will last 4 to 6 weeks if placed in a cool location. Keep constantly moist but not waterlogged.

❋ **CYCLAMEN** (Cyclamen persicum): These come in miniature and large flower types. They are a European favorite. Cyclamen bloom all winter and well into the spring. They prefer full sun in the winter and like being close to a cool window. Water them well and let them go on the dry side before watering again. When they run too dry, they will collapse but will perk up again after a good watering. They bloom profusely but require weekly cleaning. Remove spent flowers by pulling the stem slightly to the side to remove it all the way to the base. This stimulates new buds to form. Feed weekly during the growing season reducing to twice a month in the winter. Cyclamen mite and a fungus called botrytis are the main problems.

* **GARDENIA** (Gardenia jasminoides 'Veitchii'): Sunny, warm area. They require lots of water and high humidity. Use a pan with 2 in. of gravel and 1 in. of water to increase humidity and to avoid bud drop. Fragrant flowers will fill a room with a sweet scent.

* **GLOXINIA** (Sinningia speciosa): These large-leaf, exotic flowering plants belong to the Gesneriad family. They make for a very colorful fall flowering plant. Water well with lukewarm water and allow to dry. Provide good light but not strong light. After flowering they can be cut back to rebloom or allowed to dry, forcing it into a dormant state and starting up again the following year. They make great centerpieces for any occasion. They are also a great gift plant.

* **HIBISCUS** (Hibiscus rosa): Give liberal water, sun and warmth. Constant bloomer but bloom lasts only one day. A favorite for planting in the garden for the summer. Cut back when it gets too leggy.

* **HYDRANGEA** (Hydrangea macrophylla): Provide filtered light, keep cool and well watered. Dramatic large flowers. Can be planted in the garden. Feed weekly.

* **JASMINE** (Jasminum species): Flowers filling a room with fragrance. Provide a sunny, cool and moist spot.

* **KALANCHOE** (Kalanchoe blossfeldiana): An easy-to-grow plant that sets buds during long nights. Water and allow to dry. Keep in filtered light and keep water off the foliage. Can bloom a second time if cut back after blooming.

* **ORCHID** (Phalaenopsis): These prefer filtered light and are easy to take care of. Water well once a week. Bringing the plant to the sink is a good method of watering. The biggest problem people have with Orchids is watering them too frequently, which allows them to stay wet. Water with a half a cup of water once a week. Feed every two weeks. After blooming, cut the stem back to the third node. Everyone enjoys the elegance of an Orchid.

* **OXALIS** (Oxalis species): Water well and allow to dry. Provide filtered light. It is a good indoor plant and a good combination plant for outside containers during the summer. Colorful foliage and colorful flowers.

* **MARTHA WASHINGTON GERANIUM** (Pelargonium x domesticum): Sunny window, cool location, water well and run slightly dry before rewatering.

* **POINSETTIA** (Euphorbia pulcherrima): Poinsettia require long nights to flower and therefore are difficult to carry over in the house. They are a traditional Christmas plant, but if you purchase a well-grown organic plant, it will last for months in the house. Feed every two weeks and water well, then let run dry. They can take full sun but will do well in any well-lit location. Their strong colors brighten up any house.

Red colors are traditional for Christmas, but other colors were bred to just make them a great flowering houseplant.

* **PRIMROSE** (Primula species): Keep cool in bright light and keep well watered. They can be planted in the yard in a shady, moist location as a perennial.

* **RIEGERBEGONIA** (Begonia hiemalis): A great houseplant that will bloom from the early fall into most of the winter. They bloom off new shoots, so the more breaks you have the longer you can keep them blooming. They like good light to full sun in the winter months. Give them a good drink of water and let them run dry before you water them again. Keep moisture off the leaves as they are susceptible to powdery mildew. Feed weekly during the growing season. Rieger Begonias come in a mixture of vivid colors.

* **STREPTOCARPUS – CAPE PRIMROSE** (Streptocarpus x hybridus): It belongs to the Gesneriad family and flowers throughout the year. Water with lukewarm water. Keep at room temperature in filtered light. Take off dead flowers after they bloom.

* **ZYGOCACTUS** (Zygocactus truncatus), Christmas Cactus (Schlumbergera bridgesii): This plant can live for years and thrives on neglect. Run on the dry side and increase watering when in flower. It needs cool, long nights to initiate buds. If kept in a warm house with lights that are turned on, it probably will not set buds. Our recommendation is to leave it outside until mid November, bringing it in on nights frost could be a problem. Feed every two weeks.

FOLIAGE PLANTS

Foliage plants are chosen for their ability to survive the indoor climate. In most cases they can tolerate lower light conditions than flowering plants. They come in a mixture of sizes, shapes, textures and colors and tones. They soften awkward areas and brighten up dull corners; they remove toxins from the air and add humidity to a dry house. They bring nature inside and make your home more comfortable to live in. I am listing them by their Latin name first.

* **ADIANTUM PEDATUM** (Maidenhair Fern): Dainty clouds of scalloped, wedge-shaped leaflets makes this a sought-after plant. It is more difficult to grow than many other houseplants because it requires high humidity, so add a pan with 2 in. of gravel and 1 in. of water to set it on. It likes the light of a north window. Keep it moist.

* **AGLAONEMA COMMUTATUM** (Chinese Evergreen): This is a dark green to silver plant that is hardy and can survive under poor lighting. It requires warm temperatures and moderate watering. It can also be grown in water. Basal branching remains relatively low.

* **ALOE VERA** (Indian Medicine Plant): It has great medicinal value for cuts, burns and internal problems. Give it filtered to good light, water well and allow to dry. Releasing

oxygen at night makes it a good bedroom plant. Every house should have an Aloe vera plant on a windowsill.

❋ **ANTHURIUM ANDRAEANUM:** This is one of the most eye catching of all foliage plants, having lovely pink, red or white flowers. It is shade tolerant and requires good humidity. Place a gravel pan with water beneath.

❋ **BEAUCARNEA RECURVATA** (Pony Tail Palm): This is a curiosity plant with a large swollen bulb at base and long strap-like leaves that arch. It requires warm, filtered light. Water well and then allow to dry.

❋ **BOUGAINVILLEA SPECIES** (Bougainvillea): This is a colorful plant that has large clusters of colorful flowers. Because it requires full sun and warmth, it can be kept outdoors in the summer.

❋ **BRASSIA ARBORICOLA** (Small-leaf Schefflera, Arboricola): This is a smaller leaf, shorter, more compact form of Schefflera. Keep warm and dry, never cold and wet. Water well and allow to dry between waterings. Needs filtered light, avoid dark locations. Easy to grow and thrives on neglect. Can be cut back when it gets too large. Scale and overwatering are its main problems.

❋ **CACTI SPECIES** (Cactus): Miniature cactus thrives on neglect. It requires good light. Do not overwater, keep on the dry side.

❋ **CALATHEASPECIES**, Maranta leuconeura kerchoveana (Prayer Plant): These come in a variety of colors and patterns. They all are noted for their large leaves that close up at night. Give them filtered light, warm temperatures and keep moist.

❋ **CHAMAEDOREA ELEGANS** (Neanthe Bella Palm, Parlor): This dwarf palm has been valued as a houseplant since Victorian times. It can tolerate low humidity and low to filtered light. Keep moist but don't allow it to sit in water.

❋ **CHAMAEDOREA SEIFRIZII** (Bamboo Palm): This is one of my favorite palms, adding a tropical look to any interior. It has a tall, narrow growth habit that fits nicely into corners and reaches about 6 ft. It's a hardy plant for low light. Keep it constantly moist but not waterlogged.

❋ **CHLOROPHYTUM COMOSUM VITTATUM** (Spider plant): This is a hardy plant that's good in hot or cool temperatures, sun or shade and doesn't mind dry air. It received worldwide attention in 1984 when NASA released findings showing that it removed pollutants from the air. Since then we have found most plants play an important role in this process. Water well and allow to slightly dry.

❋ **CISSUS RHOMBIFOLIA** (Grape Ivy): This is popular as a hanging basket or a 4 in. potted table plant. A hardy plant that tolerates low light. Water well and allow to dry.

❋ **CITRUS:** Keep in a sunny but cool and humid location. Keep moist but not wet.

* **CODIAEUM SPECIES** (Croton): This is a colorful foliage plant that will brighten up any dull room. It prefers good light and warm temperatures. Keep it well watered and away from hot air ducts.

* **COLEUS HYBRIDUS** (Coleus): This is an indoor or outdoor plant producing colorful and often intricate patterns on its leaves. It prefers a warm sunny location in the winter. Keep it well watered. It is also easy to propagate to build up your summer collection for shady locations.

* **CRASSULA ARBORESCENS** (Jade Plant): This is a very hardy plant that you can have for years. Repot it as it becomes larger. Prune it to keep shaped and within bounds. Stands up to abuse. Needs at least filtered light. Water it well and than allow to dry before watering again.

* **CYCAS REVOLUTA** (Sago Palm): Known for its hulky trunk topped by palm-like leaves. Needs filtered light, Let the soil become moderately dry between watering.

* **CYPERUS ALTERNIFOLIUS** (Umbrella Plant): This is a plant that can be grown in water or kept in a pot on a saucer of water. Very hardy if given the proper amount of moisture. Requires filtered light.

* **DIEFFENBACHIA AMOENA** (Dumbcane, Mother-in-law plant): Comes in many different varieties. Tolerates low humidity. Water well and then let run dry. Prefers filtered light. The stems and leaves are poisonous. If eaten, causes speechlessness and swelling.

* **DIONAEA MUSCIPULA** (Venus Fly Trap): Carnivorous plant. Catches and digests insects, requiring a damp mossy location.

* **DIZGOTHECA ELEGANTISSIMA** (Aralia elegantissima) False Aralia: These do best in indirect light and like it warm. Water well and allow to run slightly dry. A floor plant with slender jagged leaflets of coppery color that turn darker with age.

* **DRACAENA DEREMENSIS** 'Warneckei' (Striped Dracaena): Comes in yellow or white stripes. Likes it warm. Will tolerate low light and low humidity. Water well and allow to become slightly dry before watering. A favorite among designers, can be kept contained through pruning.

* **DRACAENA DEREMENSIS FRAGRANS** 'Janet Craig': One of the best low-light plants. Dark green foliage. Keep well watered but allow to become slightly dry. Likes it warm.

* **DRACAENA FRAGRANS MASSANGEANA** (Cornstalk Dracaena): A good low-light plant that will withstand low humidity. Keep moist but not waterlogged. Likes it warm. A hardy plant used in difficult corners. Usually grown as a cane with three stalks in a pot.

* **DRACAENA MARGINATA** (Madagascar Dragon Tree): A decorator's delight because of its irregular branching habit. A very hardy plant that can tolerate low light

and low humidity. Water well and allow to become slightly dry before watering. Leggy side shots can be pruned back. An excellent floor plant.

❊ **FICUS BENJAMINA** (Ficus Tree): Needs good light and warmth. Water well and allow to become slightly dry. Will drop leaves in its acclimation period. Mist for the first 2 weeks. Once acclimated it will thrive for years. Branches can be trimmed if they become too long or too high. The tree-like look is quite dramatic in any house setting. They come in bush form with multiple stems, tree or braided tree form.

❊ **FICUS ELASTICA** 'Decora' (Rubber Tree): It likes a warm, sunny location but will tolerate dim light and cool temperatures. . Water well and allow to become slightly dry. Its large, glossy leaves make a dramatic statement.

❊ **FICUS LYRATA** (Fiddleleaf Fig): Filtered to low light. Avoid full sun. Water well and then allow to dry. Large fiddle-shaped leaves with a leathery texture that always looks waxed.

❊ **FITTONIA VERSCHAFFELTII** (Fittonia): A very colorful oval leaf prominently veined in white that can be effectively used as a table decoration, on a desk or on shelves. It can take low light, likes it warm and needs lots of water. Keep pinched to maintain it as compact and full. It also has a sister variety with olive-green leaves veined with deep pink. Fertilize monthly.

❊ **HEDERA HELIX SPECIES** (Ivy): Indoor Ivy varieties come in various leaf shapes and colors. Grow in bright or indirect light but not in dark locations. Keep the soil moist but not waterlogged. Feed regularly. Grown as topiaries, hanging baskets or tabletop decorations. Keep trimmed to keep contained. Feed regularly.

❊ **HELXINE SOLEIROLII & PILEA DEPRESSA** (Baby's Tears): Low, moss-like plants with tiny green leaves. Filtered light, cool, moist and humid. Used in terrariums.

❊ **HOWEIA FORSTERIANA** (Kentia Palm): Warm, partial shade. Keep moist but not waterlogged; never let it sit in water. Avoid drafts and hot air ducts. A hardy plant that can last for years. Slow growing. An elegant palm with a cast-iron constitution.

❊ **HOYA CARNOSA** (Wax plant): Bright light, humid air, water heavily in summer and sparingly in winter. Likes to be pot bound, don't remove flowers.

❊ **MARANTA LEUCONEURA KERCHOVEANA** (Prayer Plant): This plant closes its leaves at night in prayer. Likes filtered light. Keep warm and run drier in winter. Small- leafed relatives of Calathea.

❊ **MARANTA LEUCONEURA MASSANGEANA** (Red veined prayer plant): Related to the prayer plant and requires the same conditions as above.

❊ **NEPHROLEPIS EXALTATA** (Fern as in Boston, Dallas, Fluffy Ruffles): Does well in filtered light. Keep constantly moist but not waterlogged. One of the oldest plants known to man. Stiff fronds arching out make for a good hanging basket, pedestal plant or table plant. Feed weekly.

- ✳ **NERIUM OLEANDER** 'Carneum florepleno' (Oleander): Needs a very sunny location, water sparingly in the winter.
- ✳ **OSMANTHUS FRAGRANS** (Sweet olive): Fills a room with fragrance. Keep cool, water well and then run slightly dry. Needs good light.
- ✳ **PHILODENDRON CORDATUM** (Philodendron): One of the most popular plants because of its hardiness and ability to survive in poor conditions. Can tolerate low light. Keep out of bright sun. Can withstand dryness. Frequent pinching keeps it bushy and compact. Excellent for a bookshelf, desktop, mantel or tabletop.
- ✳ **PHILODENDRON HYBRIDS** (Hybrid philodendron): There are many philodendron hybrids with large and unusual leaves. They make good floor plants and survive in poor to indirect light. Water well and let dry before watering again. Keep out of direct sun.
- ✳ **PHILODENDRON SELLOUM** (Selloum philodendron): Filtered light, but will adapt to poor light. Likes it warm. Water well and allow to dry between watering. It can tolerate drier atmosphere and lower light than most other Philodendrons. Can have a dramatic effect in a large room when used as a floor plant.
- ✳ **PHOENIX ROEBELENII** (Dwarf date palm): Filtered light, keep moist but not waterlogged. Keep warm. Slow growing but reaching 5 ft. Graceful fronds on an interesting trunk. Can adapt to low light levels.
- ✳ **PILEA CADIEREI** (Aluminum plant): Easy to grow in bright light. Water well and allow to dry. Short tabletop or dish garden plant.
- ✳ **PLECTRANTHUS AUSTRALIS:** (Swedish ivy): Trailing plant with roundish, thick dark leaves. One of the easiest trailing plants to grow. Does best in bright or indirect sunlight. Water well and let become dry between watering. Pinch back to keep full and bushy. Tolerates low humidity.
- ✳ **PLECTRANTHUS COLEOIDES** 'Marginatus' (Battenberg ivy): Bright light, allow to go dry between watering. Keep pinched to keep compact. A colorful green and white trailing foliage.
- ✳ **POLYSCIAS FRUITICOSA** (Ming Aralia): This plant can give you heart failure as it drops its leaves every time you change its location. Once it acclimates, it thrives. It is one of the most interesting plants. It likes it warm with indirect to low light and moderate watering. A decorator's delight with its artistic feel. Twisting slender brown branches with beautiful fern-like, lacy, light-green foliage.
- ✳ **PTERIS CRETICA AND PTERIS ENSIFORMIS** 'Victoria' (Pteris Fern): Warm and humid, gravel pan, filtered light, keep well watered. A low 'table fern' often used in dish gardens or terrariums.

❋ **RADERMACHERA SINICA** (China Doll): A hardy plant with large, compound leaves that tolerate low humidity. Bright filtered light. Keep moist but allow to become slightly dry between watering.

❋ **RHAPIS EXCELSA** (Lady palm): It is one of the easiest houseplants to care for. A large palm that has fans 6–12 in. long. A great floor plant that thrives in the house and grows to 6 ft. and over. Water well and allow to become slightly dry. Prefers it warm with filtered light.

❋ **ROSMARINUS OFFICINALIS** (Rosemary): Place in a sunny location with good humidity. Water well and allow to become slightly dry. Plant outside in the summer. Keep trimmed for a full and bushy plant. Used in cooking.

❋ **SANSEVIERIA TRIFASCIATA** (Snake plant): This is the most resistant houseplant in difficult situations. Tolerates poor light, drafts and dryness. Thick fleshy, mostly erect sword-shaped leaves, often variegated.

❋ **SAXIFRAGA SARMENTOSA** (Strawberry geranium): Easy to care for. Prefers good light but tolerates poor light. Water well and allow to dry before watering. A small plant that spreads along the soil with thread-like runners.

❋ **SCHEFFLERA ACTINOPHYLLA** 'Brassaia actinophylla' (Umbrella tree): Keep warm and dry, never cold and wet. Water well and allow to dry between waterings. Needs filtered light, avoid dark locations. Large leaves, easy to grow and thrives on neglect. Can be cut back when it gets too large. Scale and overwatering are its main problems. A great floor plant.

❋ **SCINDAPSUS AUREUS** (Epipremnum aureum) (Pothos): One of your best low-light plants with variegated golden foliage. It can withstand neglect. Keeps its color in dark locations. Grown as a hanging plant, or for tabletop, mantel or shelf. Can withstand low humidity. Water well and run dry before watering.

❋ **SEDUM MORGANIANUM** (Burros tail): Filtered light. Water well and let dry out. A lovely hanging succulent plant, with tassels of short spindle-shaped leaves. Beautiful sight when grown long.

❋ **SETCREASEA PURPUREA** (Purple heart): Trailing plant with a very striking purple color. Keep pinched to contain. A very attractive hardy hanging plant. Prefers good light and will tolerate low humidity. A great plant to set out in the summer. Water well and allow to dry.

❋ **SOLANUM PSEUDO-CAPSICUM** (Jerusalem cherry): Bright light. Keep cool and well watered. A popular old house plant loaded with large, globular, lustrous orange-scarlet, cherry-like fruits.

❋ **SPATHIPHYLLUM WALLISII** (Peace lily): Filtered light but can tolerate low light. Keep warm and out of cold drafts. Water well and let become slightly dry. An outstanding foliage plant that also produces white flower-like spathes. Feed regularly.

❋ **STRELITZIA REGINAE** (Bird of Paradise): For flowering, keep root bound and run dry and cool in spring. Known for its exotic flowers. Likes sun in the winter and bright, filtered light in summer.

❋ **SYNGONIUM PODOPHYLLUM** (Nephthytis): Warm, semi-shade. Keep moist. In juvenile stage a small plant with arrow-shaped, thin green leaves, on slender petioles.

❋ **TOLMIEA MENZIESII** (Piggyback Plant): Filtered light, cool temperatures, keep moist. It looks like one plant piggybacks on the other. Is hardy outside and makes an interesting ground cover.

❋ **TRADESCANTIA FLUMINENSIS** (Wandering Jew): Hardy plant that tolerates low humidity, filtered light. Water well and let run dry. Keep pinched to keep contained. Creeping or hanging branches. Easily grown on any window shelf, or in baskets.

❋ **YUCCA ELEPHANTIPES** (Yucca): A hardy plant that can withstand low humidity, Prefers good light and can take it cool. Water well and let dry between watering. A floor plant grown on canes—usually 3 plants in a pot.

❋ **ZAMIOCULCAS ZAMIIFOLIA** (ZiZi): The ZiZi plant thrives on neglect and survives in almost any location. A terrific, slow-growing upright.

NOTES & OBSERVATIONS

.....HOUSEPLANTS

My wife runs the office at the Nursery. She was trained in business in Germany. She keeps us all on our toes. Being brought up in Europe, she was raised with flowering and foliage houseplants all of her life. Our home is always filled with colorful potted plants and without them, we feel a void. My daughter and son carry on the same tradition by filling their houses with plants. Once you have made this bond with nature, the special joy you feel in the presence of flowering and foliage plants remains with you for life.

Once, when I was doing a houseplant lecture for two garden clubs, I was approached by one of the hosts who introduced herself as a former employee of mine. She asked how my mother was doing and I informed her that my mother had passed away two years earlier. She was very sad to hear that. She told me of the time she couldn't stop hiccupping. Everyone had a suggestion to stop it but nothing worked. My mother went up to her in front of everyone and said "I am very upset with you." When asked why, she said, "You owe me money and you still haven't paid me." She said she was so mortified and shaken up that her hiccuping stopped immediately and that she has used this shock treatment many times since. She then shared with me that she enjoyed working in the greenhouse more than any other job she had and thought of it as one of her best times. There is something about working among plants that enriches your life.

One customer told me about a large house plant he was taking care of for his sister. She was very attached to this plant and when she was transferred for a year to the West Coast, she did not want to move the plant that far. She told her brother that he could live in her Manhattan apartment if he would take care of the plant. He was taking good care of it when it started not doing well. He called his sister and she was not feeling well. He tried harder to bring the plant back but it was looking worse. He again spoke to his sister and she had become very ill. The whole family was worried about her. He worried about her and her plant. After a while the plant began to get better and he called his sister to tell her the good news. She also was getting better. When she completely recovered the plant looked great. He said it was the weirdest thing he had ever witnessed. I told him about Cleve Backster's experiments in the 60s showing the bond between plants and people. Baxter concluded that plants can sense human intentions and can feel their pain. My customer had no doubt that there was a strong bond between the plant and his sister.

ADD YOUR GARDEN STORY HERE

276

29. PART THREE: PROBLEM SOLVING

THREE IMPORTANT TOPICS

The last section of my book covers three important topics that are all connected to nature. The first topic covers plants that possess great healing powers. They are nature's medicinal gifts to us that both aid prevention and provide cures. We need to spend more time researching the plant world to find the many benefits plants provide. I will focus on two of them in this book—Wheatgrass, grown through sprouting and Aloe vera, the Indian Medicine Plant.

My second topic will be the huge problem gardeners in deer country are facing. There are methods we can employ to deter deer rather than kill them. I have compiled a large list of deer-resistant plants and methods to deter deer. I have struggled with this problem on many landscape jobs I have designed and installed over the years and am passing on what I have learned.

Drought, the third topic, is always a potential problem. We continue to over-use our water, leaving it in short supply. The DROUGHT SURVIVAL MANUAL will get you through a drought and allow your plants to survive. I, along with the Sprainbrook Nursery staff, wrote the DROUGHT SURVIVAL MANUAL in the 1980s, when the New York Metropolitan area was suffering terrible droughts. It was distributed throughout the state and was used widely. I have rewritten and updated the information. The concepts are applicable to any location and are as important today as they were then.

MY GARDEN STORY

.....WE BOUGHT THE PROPERTY ACROSS THE STREET

After Heidi and I bought the property across the street where Mr. Young and then Miss Lasher lived, we rented out the small cottage to some interesting people. For many it was a great starter house. Our first tenant after Miss Lasher was a Sprainbrook employee who headed our perennial department. When she left for sunny California, we rented it to a lawyer who got married and left to join his father's firm in upstate New York.

My daughter, Tonja, went to college at the University of San Diego and when she returned to get her Master's at Columbia University, Jason, her fiance, followed her to New York and worked in the World Trade Center. When the small house became available, they moved in and got themselves a Shar-Pei puppy. Later they got married in our greenhouses between Christmas and New Year's Day. A huge dance floor was created by moving away all of the foliage plants that were placed on a floor built out of pavers. The acoustics in the greenhouse were terrific. A "King Arthur" table, to seat over 200 people, was created in the adjoining greenhouse. The center of the table was decorated with Christmas greens and white lights. I worked every night up to the wedding to finish the decorating. Tonja and Jason living next door to their wedding hall made planning much easier. Many people said it was the best wedding they ever attended.

Jason couldn't take the cold New York winters, so he and Tonja moved back to the Bay Area in California where he was brought up. Tonja got her Doctorate in psychology in California and Jason was very glad he made the move when he heard the devastating news that the World Trade Center, where he had worked, was attacked and collapsed.

Maryanne, who had previously worked for us, had a very high-pressure job in the City. Long hours were taking a toll, so she decided to take a cut in salary, live across the street and become our office manager. When she bought her own house and left the Nursery, her very best friend married Brian Cashman. They needed to rent a place to live in and they became our next tenant. Brian had joined the New York Yankees with an entry job in management. He later became general manager. In his first year with the Yankees, he had to travel to spring training and left his wife at home. Not feeling comfortable living alone, his wife stayed with her family in Scarsdale, leaving the cottage empty until Brian's return.

One day Brian called from Florida and said "I am embarrassed to ask you this, but my wife called and was totally freaked out. She is living with her parents while I am away but went back to the cottage and there is a mushroom that grew in the middle of the bathroom floor. She is afraid to go into the house. Could you go over and have someone remove it?" We said "No problem," wondering why anyone would get freaked out about a mushroom. Heidi and I walked into the house and opened up the bathroom door. Heidi let out a screech and I backed away at the sight of a huge mushroom the size of a large loaf of bread with a rainbow of colors that matched the bathroom tiles. We should have taken a picture, but in our fear, dismay and haste we didn't. I whipped out my pruning knife and cut the small stem off at its base and threw it into the garden. It was the most unbelievable sight. Mushrooms are saprophytes and feed on dead organic matter. They develop in a moist, dark location. Through a little pore in the grout between the floor tiles this monstrosity of a mushroom sprang from an old floor beam.

Up until then rentals were by word of mouth. We finally needed to put an ad in the paper and were flocked with people. Deciding who to pick was tough. We got good vibes from a person named Charlotte. Charlotte later became a good friend. She rescued a cute dog called Ginger, who originally was shy but is now happy to greet us. Charlotte is an editor and when I started to put this book together I knew destiny had brought her to Happy Valley.

ADD YOUR GARDEN STORY HERE

30. FOCUS ON PREVENTION RATHER THAN CURE

There are lessons that Mother Nature teaches us. Lessons that come from the earth and the plants we grow. These are lessons that we too often neglect to observe. My switch to organic growing techniques has brought me revelations that seem so simple to understand and yet eluded me for most of my life.

Most of us in the horticultural business were taught how to grow plants by our agricultural colleges. We were taught to accelerate growth through the use of chemical fertilizers, to solve problems by developing cures and to find ways to increase production through mechanization, thus reducing human involvement. For each crop we grew there was a suggested program to follow. Our medical profession has followed a similar path.

My switch to organic growing taught me many lessons and the one that probably was the most important was that prevention is more important than cure. I found that if I concentrate on building up the immune system of a plant, I don't have to go through the painful process of curing it. Mother Nature provides us with lots of help and we need to work with her not against her in order to utilize what she has to offer. We don't need a different fertilizer for every plant; what we need is a soil filled with microbes and a mixture of organic products on which they can feed. A strong, healthy plant will resist most insects and diseases. Organic fertilizers feed the soil and the soil feeds the microbes and the microbes in an organic soil work in conjunction with the roots to supply the plant with the nutrients it needs.

Man is an integral part of this relationship. When he works with nature, he becomes a facilitator. He works to come up with ways to increase a plant's resistance and to help nature develop the ecosystem to solve problems on her own. Everything in nature is connected and has a purpose. In growing plants organically, I have had amazing results. It has changed my whole philosophical outlook.

I am making this analytical case about plants again because I believe it provides a parallel to follow for our own health. I am convinced that human beings need to concentrate more on prevention than on cure. Cures are often painful and debilitating. I believe the path to healthy living is the building up of our immune system, as is the case in plants. Prevention is not an easy road to follow and it takes work, discipline and knowledge. To build up one's immune system requires know-how and good doctoring. It requires a concentrated effort, a good work ethic and a relationship with the many plants that provide us with their secrets to life. Nature provides us with plants that have great medicinal value. We have moved our attention and focus away from them and have developed drugs and synthetic products to solve our health problems. The side effects are many and our use of these synthetic products often comes back to haunt us. The use of chemicals and drugs in medicine parallels the agricultural community's recommendations to use chemical and synthetic products to grow plants. Following these recommendations has led to all kinds of problems for our soils and our environment. Understanding this parallel validates my switch to organic solutions.

I am sure there are many ways to build up one's immune system and it probably requires a mixture of things to become successful. In the organic world, we say the greater the mix the greater the results. I am also convinced that nature has provided us with the plants that can treat and cure most of our problems. We need to concentrate more on learning about these plants and what they can do for us. Each human body is different and we need to research the positive affects and possible side affects of anything we ingest. Not all foods agree with all people. Nature has supplied us with natural solutions that have been handed down from one generation to the next by word of mouth. In the modern age much of this folklore has been lost as we gravitate to tested results produced by the big and powerful chemical and drug companies, whose driving interest is to create more products for greater profit.

Doctors have been taught through many hard years of schooling that the use of recommended drugs is the way to heal. I have to cringe when my doctor friends tell me about the lavish dinners they are invited to attend as the drug companies explain the benefits of the new drugs they have developed. Many doctors, highly schooled in medicine, consider natural cures as voodoo medicine and the people who prescribe them as witch doctors. Nature is a great force that has given us plants that can heal. Medicine has lost its connection with nature; we need to get it back. We need to look to her for health and help.

Two plants with which I have had personal, medicinal experience are discussed below. My hope is that by visiting these two examples, you might realize the value that plants play in our well-being. We have not devoted enough time, research or money into this part of health care. Each of the two plants that I am covering have had many personal claims made on their behalf. I cannot validate any of the claims, but these claims exist and many people believe strongly in their medicinal benefits.

ALOE VERA (INDIAN MEDICINE PLANT)

We need to familiarize ourselves with herbs and other plants that we can grow and that will benefit our well-being. My favorite herb is Aloe vera (Indian Medicine Plant, Ancient Egyptian Medicine Plant). For centuries people have heralded this plant for its great healing powers. Mother Nature provides us with a great many plants of therapeutic value. When you can grow them yourself they become an economical option to prescription medicine. They are safer to use and in many cases more effective than the drugs our medical profession is recommending. The chemical and pharmaceutical companies have become very powerful and rich while the cost to our country and to us as individuals has soared. By focusing on cures rather than prevention, we are driving our health insurance costs to unsustainable levels. We need to change the tide and find economical and healthy solutions.

I am in the plant business and I know there are many plants with healing secrets. We need to dig into the past and search them out. We can grow them. There is a relationship between man and plants. Everything is connected and we need to develop this relationship. I have had a long-time relationship with Aloe vera and this relationship has influenced my way of thinking.

Aloe vera is an herb with great medicinal value. In the New York Metropolitan area, Aloe vera is not winter hardy and we grow it as a house plant. It is a plant that no household should be without. Accounts of the miraculous healing powers of Aloe vera have been handed down for more than 3,500 years. Scientists have found that the Aloe vera plant is a diverse mixture of antibiotics, astringents, coagulating agents, pain-inhibitors and growth stimulators. It appears to contain a "wound hormone" that accelerates the rate of healing of injured surfaces. The healing properties of Aloe vera are attributed partly to its 96% water content, which provides water to the injured tissue without closing off the air necessary for tissue repair. The remaining 4% of the pulp contains complex carbohydrate molecules believed to be essential to the Aloe's natural value as a moisturizer.

I have had a great deal of personal experience with Aloe vera and eat a piece of it every day. For over 50 years I've grown it and my customers have brought me their stories and experiences of its benefits. I have read a great deal about its healing powers and its uses and suggest you research the subject on your own. I am a strong believer in natural cures and very skeptical of the many drugs that have flooded our market, and I am a strong believer that there are many herbs that can do the job better with fewer side effects. I have used Aloe vera for most of my life and have found it to be an amazing plant with amazing results. Here are some of the uses that my family, friends and I have discovered.

* **BURNS.** I strongly feel there should be an Aloe vera plant on every kitchen windowsill. The quickest cure, from my experience, for a burn or a scald is to cut the leaf off the Aloe vera plant and apply it directly to the injured area. for severe burns, it is particularly important to keep the Aloe vera gel applied to the wound for the critical first 48 hours.

  On many occasions my family, friends or employees have had burns or scalds, some severe. By immediate application of Aloe vera taken directly from a live plant, there was quick relief and no scarring. It is particularly important to have a plant close at hand in case of a third degree burn, where by the time you get to the hospital for treatment most of the damage is already done. The cures I have witnessed have been amazing.

* **SUNBURN.**

  My family has used Aloe vera for sunburn for as long as I can remember with fantastic results. A friend of mine goes to Aruba, every winter. On the beach a man comes around calling himself The Aloe Man. He wears a big, bright-yellow hat, an oversized pair of sunglasses and a matching yellow suit with contrasting tie loosely knotted at his chest. He carries a bag slung over his neck filled with bottles of Aloe vera juice, his pockets are filled with bottles of Aloe vera juice and he carries a bottle in each hand…all to attract the attention and conversation of tourists. You see, in Aruba Aloe vera is a local crop, and he makes a living selling them his fresh Aloe vera.

  He attracts groups that listen to the cures and health benefits that this plant provides. He ends up his pitch by saying, "And for the men in this audience, it is better than Viagra." My friend has no fear of a sunburn on the beaches of Aruba for he knows the Aloe man is nearby.

Being an outdoor family, our clan has had its share of sunburns. We apply Aloe vera immediately. It is important to keep the skin moist through frequent application so the burns will heal quickly.

* **CUTS AND WOUNDS.** Our neighbor, and at the time of this incident our bookkeeper, had the deepest wound I ever saw cured by Aloe vera. She had such a deep gash that we couldn't stop the bleeding. It desperately needed many stitches. The wound was caused by an ax that landed on her leg rather than on the tree that she was trying to chop down. She refused to go to the doctor so we bound the wound and made her apply Aloe vera from a large plant I gave her. She applied it constantly for a week and continued to make applications for a month. It was the most incredible recovery I have ever seen. There was no infection and the healing took place within a month without any scars.

My wife had a deep cut on her finger which should have also required stitches. We were leaving for a trip to Germany and there was no time for treatment. My wife treated herself by keeping Aloe vera on the wound. Again incredible healing without any scarring. My daughter ran into a glass window and severely cut up her face as a young child. We pulled out the Aloe vera plant for application 3 times a day. There are no signs of scars on her face. A former employee of mine had a hole in her intestine and conventional treatments couldn't close it. I told her to try ingesting Aloe vera, which she did, and the hole healed.

There have been countless stories about Aloe's healing power throughout history. Take some time to research and read about them, it is a fascinating subject.

* **DIGESTIVE PROBLEMS.** My wife suffers from Irritable Bowel Syndrome and takes Aloe vera daily. It has helped tremendously and keeps her away from traditional medicines with side effects that scare her. Aloe vera heals the digestive tract, keeps the colon wall clean of excessive mucus and slows down food reaction. She tells her friends with similar problems to use it.

* **INFECTION.** Since I am a grower who uses his knife constantly to make cuttings, I end up with many cuts of varying degrees. Whenever I have a cut and fear infection, I apply Aloe vera gel from a fresh leaf. The results have been excellent. As of yet no infection has set in and healing takes place quickly.

* **ACNE.** In the 1970s a doctor had us grow Aloe vera plants for his two teenage daughters who suffered from a severe case of acne. They got a total cure from the Aloe vera plant. Aloe vera gel was applied directly from the leaf of the Aloe vera plant. Antiseptic action treats infection in oil-clogged pores. Aloe vera does a remarkable job of counteracting infection, stimulating tissue and healing without scarring.

❋ **POISON IVY.** For those in the landscape installation business, poison ivy is an occupational hazard. My men constantly raid my Aloe vera plants. For them it inhibits the pain, greatly reduces the problem of itching and enhances healing.

❋ **SHINGLES.** Blase, a fellow marathon runner friend of mine, suffered from an attack of shingles. He was in excruciating pain. We are both marathon runners and don't give into pain very easily; however, with the onset of shingles, the pain was so intense that he was not able to run. He went to doctors and tried everything they recommended but nothing helped. I told him to try applying Aloe vera. He thought I was crazy and ignored me. I had given him an Aloe vera plant and one day the pain was so unbearable he was willing to try anything. It ended up being the only thing that helped him.

Whenever I rave to my running group about Aloe vera's healing powers, they make fun of me. They say "Krautter, your cure for everything is running and Aloe vera." Blase joins in the mockery, but says, "There is one thing I have to admit, it worked on my shingles."

❋ **SCRAPES AND ABRASIONS.** Treated with Aloe vera were the many scrapes my children and grandchildren have had over the years. Their pain was greatly relieved and the healing process was quick. From the Aloe vera plant apply a split leaf, sliding it gently over the area. As it is being applied it feels very soothing. Reapplication should be done frequently in the first 24 hours.

❋ **SKIN CANCER.** Being in the sun constantly and having a bald head I have developed early stages of skin cancer. I apply Aloe vera from the leaf to my bald scalp. Skin cancer is a serious medical problem and should have medical attention. Along with sunscreen, I feel Aloe vera has helped me and I now have no precancerous cells.

❋ **SKIN CARE.** Once a week I take a leaf from the Aloe vera plant and at night before going to bed apply it over my whole body. At one time I was doing it daily, but doing it too frequently, I found, dries out the skin. I feel it is important to rejuvenate tissue, particularly as you get older.

❋ **INSECT BITES AND STINGS.** Whenever we get a sting at the Nursery, we run for the Aloe vera plant. When bitten by a bee, ant, wasp, yellow jacket, centipede or other insect, time is very important. Split a leaf immediately and lay the leaf filled with sap over the area.

❋ **ULCERS.** It was in the early 60s when we first got into growing Aloe vera. It was for a neighbor of my sister who had ulcers. My sister called him Grandpa Duff. He wanted us to grow Aloe vera for him on a regular basis for treatment of his bleeding ulcers. He would eat chunks from the leaf 4 times a day. He claimed it was the only thing that worked to heal his inside wound. I have always been thankful to him for getting me involved with this incredible healing plant. It heals not only from the outside but also from the inside.

* **ARTHRITIS.** Coming from a family that is prone to arthritis, I eat my piece of Aloe vera every day. This is not the only thing I do to reduce arthritis but I am a firm believer the juice from the Aloe vera plant is an important ingredient in helping to reduce inflammation and other debilitating effects.

* **RADIATION BURNS.** I had prostate cancer and underwent radiation without side effects, while my friends who had similar radiation treatments did. I attribute my success to my daily ingestion of part of an Aloe vera leaf. I chew Wheatgrass and eat Aloe vera every day and have been cancer free for over 10 years. Radiation kills cells and Aloe vera regenerates cells. I hope with my new preventive program I will never have to undergo this treatment again. So far so good.

* **ANIMAL FIRST AID.** When my dog and my children's dog got old and were ailing with internal problems, we would squeeze liquid Aloe vera into their drinking water. It helped them live healthier, happier and longer lives. I often said we should have started this procedure long before they developed their problems. Prevention is always better than cure.

Aloe vera has been called the Indian Medicine Plant. I can understand why it got this name. I have personally experienced many of the healing wonders of Aloe vera. There have been many claims made through history about its healing abilities. Some of my frieds say I have become brainwashed, having read so much on the subject. I believed in Aloe vera before it became fashionable. Now many healing and skin care products have Aloe vera in them. You can find it in many forms, but I believe it is best when taken directly from the plant. It can be grown at a minimal cost. This is a point that will drive the pharmaceutical companies crazy. Much of the lore about Aloe vera has been handed down by word of mouth. Research this subject on your own and learn more about the Aloe vera plant. It is a fascinating subject about a fascinating plant. I will list some additional areas where Aloe vera has been used successfully by others.

* Hair and Scalp Care
* Hemorrhoids and Bleeding Piles
* Psoriasis and Eczematous Rashes
* Stretch Marks from Pregnancy
* Varicose Veins
* Brown Skin Spots
* Blood Clotting
* Chronic Nose Congestion
* Asthma
* Sore Throat

Aloe vera is a succulent and great care should be taken to not overwater it. We grow all our Aloe vera in clay pots which provide them with greater drainage. We use our organic soil, which we feel affords it greater nutritional value. We feed it with a liquid organic fertilizer.

Place the plant in a well-lit location, water it well and then let the soil become dry to the touch before watering again. The plant likes to be pot-bound and can be grown in a small pot as long as it does not become top heavy. It can be divided when it gets too full. Harvest your outer larger leaves and cut sections to the bottom. Cutting sections does not injure the leaf as it quickly heals itself. It is a plant you don't want to be without. Buy a plant now. Grow it in your house so it will be there when you need it.

WHEATGRASS

I added sprouting Wheatgrass to my mix for healthy living. Sprouting Wheatgrass is intriguing, and I got involved in it because of my interest in it as an aid in curing cancer. Since I'd had prostate cancer and was desirous of preventing a recurrence, I thought to myself, "I have the soil and the know-how to sprout seeds, so why not see what it can do for me." I started chewing Wheatgrass over a year ago and I'm amazed at the difference it has made in my energy level and in the reduction of my allergies. As an extra bonus, it has encouraged healthy gums. I am sprouting Wheatgrass in 4 in. pots and end up chewing it three to four times a day. I usually go through three 4 in. pots a week. If you germinate it yourself it will cost you less than a $1 a week. Printed instructions are found at the end of this section.

The secret of Wheatgrass' success is its high content of chlorophyll. Chlorophyll. Chlorophyll is often referred to as "the life blood of plant life." As it closely resembles the molecules of human red blood cells, it is absorbed quickly through our digestive system and quickly begins rebuilding our blood cells. Wheatgrass offers the healing benefits of a primary "sun food," converting the sun's rays into chlorophyll as well as vitamins, minerals, amino acids and enzymes. Chlorophyll helps to regenerate the liver, detoxify and invigorate the body and energize the immune system, which is our natural means of prevention and healing from illnesses. It is not advisable to try Wheatgrass after surgery as it could stimulate the blood flow to this area.

As a plant person, my hope is to broaden your knowledge of the part that plants can play in our health. Here are some of the many virtues of Wheatgrass I have personally witnessed and read about and wish to share with you.

❋ **ANTIBACTERIAL.** My dentist warned me that my gums were in bad shape and suggested I work harder to keep them healthy. After this I started chewing Wheatgrass. When I went back for my three-month cleaning my dentist couldn't believe the change. My gums became stronger and healthier and had very little bleeding. Chlorophyll increases tissue-cell activity and is effective for healing bleeding gums, pyorrhea, gingivitis and infected ulcerated wounds. My dentist, a running friend of mine, said I was trying to put him out of business.

❋ **ANTIBIOTIC.** Chlorophyll builds up the immune system.

❋ **ANTI-INFLAMMATORY.** Chlorophyll helps reduce inflammation. Wheatgrass will break down the mucus and allow it to drain.

❋ **ANTIOXIDANT.** Wheatgrass contains powerful antioxidants. Wheatgrass juice will drain the lymph system which carries away many toxins from the body.

❋ **BUILDS RED BLOOD CELLS.** Because chlorophyll is nearly identical to the hemoglobin in red blood cells, Wheatgrass encourages red blood cell development, speeds up circulation, cleanses the blood, lowers high blood pressure and stimulates tissue growth. My wife has high blood pressure and will not use drugs to control it. She uses alternative natural products, including chewing Wheatgrass and taking Aloe vera juice. Her blood pressure has gone down dramatically.

❋ **CANCER.** Many customers have told me they purchase Wheatgrass in the hope of a cancer cure. A customer told me how the medical profession had given up on his sister. She has cured herself with Wheatgrass and is now cancer free. I had prostate cancer and have been cancer free for ten years. I chew Wheatgrass three times a day. For me Wheatgrass is a powerful and safe healing aid.

❋ **DEODORANT.** Chlorophyll is an effective deodorizer. It neutralizes body odors. It is added to deodorants, chewing gum and breath fresheners.

❋ **ENERGY BOOSTER.** I have found my energy level has tremendously increased by eating Wheatgrass. Wheatgrass is an energizer for the mind and the body. I encouraged a close friend to start chewing Wheatgrass. To our amazement, she was able to swim extra laps in the pool. When she stopped chewing Wheatgrass, she was not able to keep up to her newly achieved distance. She came back to tell me of her experience and to purchase more Wheatgrass.

❋ **IMMUNE SYSTEM.** The high chlorophyll content builds up and energizes the immune system.

❋ **IRRITABLE BOWEL SYNDROME.** Chlorophyll is beneficial in controlling irritable bowel syndrome. My wife suffers from this and has benefited from chewing Wheatgrass.

❋ **LAXATIVE.** It is a natural laxative.

❋ **NUTRITION.** Wheatgrass is a healthy source of minerals and vitamins.

❋ **OSTEOPOROSIS.** Wheatgrass is rich in vitamin K, which is essential in bone formation.

❋ **TONIC.** Wheatgrass is an economical tonic to improve general health. It is loaded with antioxidants which protect us in many ways.

There are many books and articles written about the great benefits of taking Wheatgrass on a regular basis. Spend some time reading and researching this subject. My grandchildren live in California and we travel frequently across the country to visit them.

My daughter arranged, on several visits, for me to present to their classroom a horticultural project for their classmates to complete. The first project I chose was showing them how to grow Wheatgrass. I was addressing a second grade class and a kindergarten class. I asked the second grade class if anyone had heard about the benefits of Wheatgrass. A pretty blond-haired girl raised her hand and said she drinks a small glass of Wheatgrass every morning before coming to school. She looked so healthy and had so much energy that I was even more excited with my choice of presenting a great project for them to learn about.

Below is my set of directions for growing Wheatgrass. I grow three 4 in. pots on a weekly basis for myself and cut the grass directly from the pot, harvesting it whenever I pass by. I put the Wheatgrass in my mouth and chew. I wash and reuse all my pots and add new organic soil before reseeding it for the next crop. By following this procedure, I am always chewing Wheatgrass, at its greatest point of nutritional value. I multitask, never lose time and keep my body tuned up. Below is my formula for growing and germinating Wheatgrass. Once you develop a routine, you will find how easy and rewarding this process can be.

DIRECTIONS FOR WHEATGRASS GERMINATION:

1. Soak enough seed overnight in cheese cloth or other porous cloth, tying it together in a knot. Hang out to drip dry in a shower for about 1 hour. Use roughly 2 tbs. of Wheatgrass seed per 4 in. pot. Soaking seed is optional and can be skipped if you water your seed well two times a day.
2. Fill 4 in. pots 4/5 full with organic soil.
3. Place seed on the surface of the soil thick enough to completely fill in all bare spots with no soil showing.
4. Lightly cover the seed with organic soil.
5. Water containers well to completely wet soil and seed. Place in dark or light at normal house temperature.
6. Cover seed with white paper.
7. Water seed daily and uncover after about 3-4 days when germination has taken place.
8. Place in sun and harvest in about ten days. Cut to within one inch of soil level and harvest about three cuts per pot. One to two pots should be enough for one person for a week. Repeat this procedure on a weekly basis to keep yourself and your family stocked.

CONCLUSION:

I have gone over in detail two plants and the benefits they have afforded me through the years. Wheatgrass is a medicinal herb that has been used since ancient times. In our own home and on our own property, we can grow plants that will benefit our health. The organic vegetable garden can grow produce far superior to any that we can buy. The herb garden can provide us with plants of medicinal value. Fruit trees and small fruits can add more health to our diet. Edible landscaping can become part of our back yard beauty.

We have explored Natural Gardening and it has shown us that if we build up the immune system of a plant, it is less likely to be prone to insect or disease problems. A Natural Approach to gardening makes our plants thrive. Our back yard will come alive and we will live through lessons our plants teach us. Everything in nature is connected and when we are in harmony with her she will support us. When we understand how beautifully a plant can grow using the natural approach, we will understand how important it is to follow a natural approach to solving our health problems. This parallel is an important lesson for us to learn. Resistance is better than cure. Acquiring knowledge that gardening the natural way can produce plants that not only beautify our garden, but also can keep us in healthy living, is a gift that will last us a lifetime.

NOTES & OBSERVATIONS

.....GRATEFUL DEAD KEYBOARD PLAYER TOM CONSTANTEN COMES TO SPRAINBROOK

It is 8:00 p.m. and the doors are opening at the celebration of the Rev. Tor Band's 15th Anniversary Show in Pittsfield, Massachusetts. I was looking forward to going but snow started at 5:00 p.m. and was continuing into the following day. It is a 2½ hour drive over hilly, winding roads. Heidi and I decided not to take the chance. My sister also decided not to go because of the weather.

Tom Constanten, the keyboard player from the Grateful Dead, had toured with my son Tor and played on one of his CDs. Due to icy conditions in Albany, he was detoured into Michigan and then flew into Hartford the following day to make the show just in time. This was going to be a big event for Tor with lots of big names and musicians from the past coming to play music and celebrate. Lots of thoughts were going through my mind—the saddest that I was not attending. This was a milestone for Tor and I was missing it.

My thoughts wandered to the past. My son would have been the logical person to take over the Nursery. I followed in my parents' footsteps and joined the family business. Tor grew up in the Nursery. I always felt it was a great place to bring up children. Both of my children grew up to be very kind and thoughtful people, but Tor's passion was music not flowers. On spring weekends, when the parking lot which our house overlooked was full of customers, Tor and his high school band would open the windows and play to the crowd. He idolized Jerry Garcia and now plays a mean guitar like he did. He writes and composes his own songs, sings vocals and has produced over six records. He studied at the Hollywood Institute for Music in California. He is well known in the Berkshires. Once, when I took my grandchildren on a ride at Jiminy Peak, my son-in-law asked the attendant if he ever heard of Tor from the Rev. Tor Band. "Tor is a legend in these parts," the attendant said.

As I sit in my office on the computer writing this story now, to get my mind off the great concert now in full swing, my mind flashes back to when Tom Constanten came to Sprainbrook. (Tom studied classical music in Germany and enjoyed speaking German to my wife.) Tom Constanten was on tour with Tor and they were going to play Hell's Kitchen the following night in New York City. Tor drove his bus down early with the rest of the band to set up and Tom was going to ride down with us to arrive later. We took the West Side Highway and traffic came to a standstill. Showtime was nearing. It was nerve-racking. We suggested that Tom get out of the car and take the subway. "That," Tom said, "would be more nerve-racking." He got there for the second set.

For a number of years, Tor ran the Sprainbrook Farm in upstate New York. It was his belief in the natural approach that influenced my move to organics. Due to the economy, we had to close our upstate operation. Since then Tor has immersed himself deeper into performing with lots of solo gigs to supplement the income from playing with the band. I was thinking of all the options both of us had on this journey. Did we make the right choices? Tonight is a highlight moment for Tor and I'm missing it.

I closed my eyes and then I could hear Tor singing "Mystic Wolf." I could see the crowd dancing and singing along, his guitar licks were creating a new level of frenzy, the band members were playing off each other in a wild jam. What a show! What a night! I was proud my son was able to follow his passion and that we supported his dream. The Rev. Tor Band played through the night.

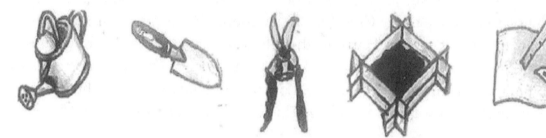

ADD YOUR GARDEN STORY HERE

31. DEER-RESISTANT PLANTS

As the sun goes down, the deer come out, roam through the night and browse on delicious well-maintained plants. They seem to particularly like the lush growth in suburban gardens. They are creatures of habit and have developed familiar trails they like to follow, revisiting them daily. When food gets scarce, they will venture into more unfamiliar territory. Blocking their entry or changing their course can greatly reduce the number of deer visiting your property. Keeping deer out of your back yard and play areas reduces the potential for deer ticks and Lyme disease and allows you to plant anything you want.

The best solution for controlling deer is to fence in your area. Deer can easily jump any fence below 8 ft. and an 8 ft. permanent fence surrounding your property can be unattractive, impractical, very costly and may not be allowed by your local code. I have spent a lot of time designing gardens in deer country and my favorite solution is simple. Fence in your back yard with a 6 ft. fence. This allows you to have a safe back yard for children and pets and meets most local codes. Plant attractive hedges on the inner side of the fence for screening and privacy. Once these hedges reach 8 ft. or higher, deer will not be able to jump the fence. Another good solution is to use UV-treated polypropylene mesh 8 ft. high. From a distance, the black mesh is nearly invisible, as it blends into the objects and shadows in the background. Installation is easy and cost is much less than metal or wood fences. Attach the lightweight mesh to trees and posts. This method is ideal for enclosing large areas. Call a local installer for pricing or do it yourself.

There are motion detector devices on the market which scare deer by sound, water or lights. Initially they are scared away but eventually they become used to this. I prefer a more natural approach using physical barriers, deer-resistant plants and natural organic repellents. Nothing is a sure thing in Deer Country. You need to experiment and develop your own testing ground. The plants we list are some of your best choices to make.

Install deer-resistant plants in the front of your house and use deer repellents to further discourage them. Another trick I have used, particularly in shady areas, is to plant Native Rhododendron with Andromeda or Boxwood in the foreground. Deer will eat Rhododendron but can only reach to a certain height. Above that height Native Rhododendron forms a good screen. Deer do not eat Boxwood and rarely eat Andromeda. The same principle can be followed in the foundation planting when a greater mixture is desired. If you have no other good choice, use plants for height that deer eat and put plants that deer do not eat in the foreground.

Fertilize your plants with Milorganite, which acts not only as a good fertilizer but also as a deer repellent. The aromatic smell of certain herbs such as basil, lavender and thyme keeps deer away. Deer do not like fuzzy foliage or prickly plants but they do eat the soft flowers off the tops of rose bushes. Blue does not seem to be their favorite color. Large dogs that love to live outdoors can provide good deer control.

Each situation in areas where deer exist is different; you need to watch the browsing pattern for your particular area as there are many variables. Educate yourself as much as possible regarding your choices. Through trial and error, your diligence will pay off with the best plan to combat deer. A customer told me that she planted Taxus to the right and left of the front of her property. Deer love Taxus and they eat them leaving the other plants in her garden alone. So each person needs to find his or her own way. There are good books out that explore the problem in greater depth. There are also pamphlets put out by various agricultural universities that offer some good advice.

In summation, living in deer country poses problems that each gardener will have to deal with on an individual basis. A plan of action needs to be developed for each particular situation. If you love gardening, you should not deny yourself the plants you love but you may need to make compromises. There are enough selections and options for you to have a beautiful garden.

Below is my list of Deer-Resistant Plants. My lists are compiled from personal experience and published data. They have been refined throughout the years. All plants do not always work and some plants work better than others. There is tremendous variability within the plants that deer do not like since they will eat less desirable plants to survive when food gets scarce. I had Rolf Svensson, a landscape architect who grew up in deer country, rate the evergreen and woody plants for me. He rated them on a scale from 1 to 10, with 10 being the best. His rating is shown in parentheses after the entry. On perennials and annuals, I have come up with my top 25 list. The star beside a plant means it is one of the top 25 Annuals or Perennials that I have rated in their respective sections. Therefore, a star rating means that it is not only deer resistant but a great plant. I hope this will help you make informed choices. I prefer using deer-resistant plants along with deer repellents for maximum control.

Most deer-resistant plants affect taste, so make sure to use deer repellents that affect smell as well. If you affect two or more of the deer's senses, you get better control. If the deer doesn't like the taste and doesn't like the smell, he figures this is not a great place to hang out. Deer repellents keep changing. Go to your local garden center for recommendations of what best suits your needs. Be diligent and change your "taste products" so deer don't get used to the taste. Discourage them from your property in the hope they will find a different route. Again, through educated choices, "trial and error" and diligence you will prevail.

SHRUBS

* Abelia grandiflora (Glossy Abelia) (6)
* Berberis thunbergii (Japanese Barberry) (8)
* Buddleia davidii (Butterfly Bush) (9)
* Calycanthus floridus (Common Sweetbush) (7)
* Caryopteris x clandonensis (Bluebeard) (9)
* Cornus sericea (Red Osier Dogwood) (3)
* Deutzia gracilis (Slender Deutzia) (8)
* Elaeagnus angustifolia (Russian Olive) (9)
* Enkianthus campanulatus (Redvein Enkianthus) (4)
* Forsythia x intermedia (Forsythia) (5)
* Fothergilla gardenii (Dwarf Fothergilla) (5)
* Hamamelis x intermedia (Hybrid Witch Hazel) (5)
* Kerria japonica (Japanese Kerria) (8)
* Kolkwitzia amabilis (Beautybush) (8)
* Potentilla fruticosa (Bush Cinquefoil) (9)
* Spiraea species (Spirea) (9)
* Symphoricarpus albus (Snowberry) (5)
* Syringa vulgaris (Common Lilac) (7)
* Viburnum sieboldii (Siebold Viburnum) (9)

✽ Weigela florida (Old Fashioned Weigela) (4)

EVERGREENS

✽ Aucuba japonica (Japanese Aucuba) (5)

✽ Berberis x gladwynensis 'William Penn' (Barberry) (7)

✽ Buxus microphylla (Little Leaf Boxwood) (10)

✽ Buxus sempervirens (Common Boxwood) (10)

✽ Cedrus atlantica (Atlas Cedar) (8)

✽ Cedrus deodara (Deodar Cedar) (8)

✽ Chamaecyparis obtusa (Hinoki Falsecypress) (5)

✽ Cotoneaster dammeri (Bearberry Cotoneaster) (6)

✽ Cryptomeria japonica (Japanese Cryptomeria) (8)

✽ Cupressocyparis leylandii (Leyland Cypress) (6)

✽ Ilex aquifolium (English Holly) (6)

✽ Ilex x aquipernyi (Dragon Lady, San Jose) (7)

✽ Ilex glabra (Inkberry) (7)

✽ Ilex hybrid 'Nellie Stevens' (Nellie Stevens Holly) (5)

✽ Ilex opaca (American Holly) (9)

✽ Juniperus chinensis (Chinese Juniper) (6)

✽ Kalmia latifolia (Mountain-laurel) (4)

✽ Leucothoe axillaris (Leucothoe) (6)

✽ Magnolia grandiflora (Southern Magnolia) (8)

✽ Mahonia aquifolium (Oregon Grapeholly) (5)

✽ Microbiota decussata (Siberian Carpet) (7)

✽ Myrica pensylvanica (Northern Bayberry) (9)

✽ Phyllostachys species (Bamboo) (9)

✽ Picea abies (Norway Spruce) (9)

✽ Picea glauca 'Conica' (Dwarf Alberta Spruce) (9)

✽ Picea pungens (Blue Spruce) (9)

✽ Pieris japonica (Andromeda) (9)

✽ Pinus mugo (Mugo Pine) (6)

✽ Pinus nigra (Austrian Pine) (7)

✽ Pinus thunbergiana (Japanese Black Pine) (9)

✽ Prunus laurocerasus (English & Skip Laurel) (6)

✽ Pyracantha coccinea (Firethorn) (6)

✽ Rhododendron Hybrid 'P.J.M.' (P.J.M. Rhododendron) (6)

✽ Skimmia japonica (Japanese Skimmia) (6)

✽ Viburnum rhytidophyllum (Leatherleaf Viburnum) (7)

TREES

Any flowering or shade tree is deer-resistant if the branches are kept above the reach of a deer. In deer country, buy large-size trees and prune them up above browsing level. Or choose from the list below.

* Acer negundo (Box Elder, Ash-leaved Maple)
* Betula nigra (River Birch)
* Carpinus betulus (European Hornbeam)
* Catalpa speciosa (Northern Catalpa)
* Cercidiphyllum japonicum (Katsura Tree)
* Chionanthus virginicus (White Fringetree)
* Cornus kousa (Kousa Dogwood)
* Cotinus coggygria (Common Smoketree or Smokebush)
* Crataegus oxyacantha (English Hawthorn)
* Fagus sylvatica (European Beech)
* Ginkgo biloba (Ginkgo)
* Gleditsia tricanthos (Common Honey Locust)
* Halesia carolina (Carolina Silverbell)
* Laburnum anagyroides (Common Laburnum, Golden Chain)
* Liquidambar styraciflua (American Sweetgum)
* Magnolia species (Magnolia)
* Oxydendrum arboreum (Sourwood, Sorrel Tree or Lily of the Valley Tree)
* Salix matsudana (Hankow Willow)

PERENNIAL PLANTS

Perennials with a * are from my Top 25 List of Perennials, making them not only deer-resistant but outstanding perennials as well.

* Achillea species (Yarrow)
* Aconitum napellus (Monkshood) *
* Agastache foeniculum (Anise Hyssop)
* Allium species (Ornamental Chives)
* Amsonia tabernaemontana (Eastern Blue Star)
* Anemone species (Japanese Anemone)
* Anthemis tinctoria (Golden Marguerite)
* Aquilegia canadensis (Columbine) *
* Arabis caucasica (Rock Cress) *
* Arisaema triphyllum (Jack-in-the-Pulpit)
* Armeria maritima (Sea Thrift)
* Artemisia species (Wormwood) *

* Aruncus dioicus (Goat's Beard)
* Asarum europaeum (European Wild Ginger) *
* Asclepias tuberosa (Butterfly Weed)
* Astilbe species (Spirea) *
* Aubretia deltoides (Purple Rock Cress)
* Aurinia saxatilis (Basket of Gold)
* Baptisia species (Wild Blue Indigo)
* Bergenia species (Bergenia) *
* Boltonia asteroides (Boltonia)
* Calluna species (Heather)
* Camassia species (Camas)
* Campanula persicifolia (Bellflower)
* Carex species (Sedge) *
* Centaurea montana (Cornflower)
* Centranthus ruber (Red Valerian)
* Cerastium tomentosum (Snow in Summer)
* Ceratostigma plumbaginoides (Plumbago)
* Chelone species (Turtle Head)
* Chrysanthemum coccineum (Painted Daisy)
* Chrysanthemum morifolium (Mum)
* Chrysanthemum morifolium 'Dendranthema' (Hardy Garden Mum)
* Chrysanthemum nipponicum (Montauk Daisy)
* Chrysanthemum parthenium (Feverfew, Tansy) *
* Cimicifuga racemosa (Snakeroot, Fairy Candles)
* Convallaria majalis (Lily of the Valley)
* Cordydalis lutea (Fumewort) *
* Coreopsis species (Tickseed) *
* Delphinium species (Delphinium)
* Dianthus species (Dianthus)
* Dicentra eximia, spectabilis (Bleeding Heart) *
* Dictamnus albus (White Gas Plant)
* Digitalis grandiflora, purpurea (Foxglove) *
* Echinacea purpurea (Purple Coneflower) *
* Echinops species (Globe Thistle)
* Erica species (Heath)
* Eryngium species (Sea Holly)
* Eupatorium species (Hardy Ageratum)
* Euphorbia species (Spurge, Milkwort)
* Fern species (Fern) *

- Filipendula species (Meadowsweet)
- Gaillardia species (Gaillardia)
- Geranium Cranesbill (Hardy Geranium) *
- Geum species (Geum) *
- Grasses species (Ornamental Grasses) *
- Gypsophila paniculata (Baby's Breath)
- Helenium species (Helen's flower) *
- Helleborus species (Lenten Rose) *
- Hesperis matronalis (Dame's Rocket)
- Heuchera sanguinea (Coral bells)
- Hibiscus moscheutos (Rose Mallow)
- Iberis sempervirens (Candytuft)
- Iris ensata (Japanese Iris)
- Iris siberica (Siberian Iris)
- Lamium maculatum (Dead Nettle)
- Lavandula species (Lavender) *
- Leucanthemum x superbum (Shasta Daisy)
- Liatris species (Gayfeather)
- Lilium lancefolium (Lily)
- Linaria species (Toadflax)
- Linum perenne (Perennial Flax)
- Lupinus species (Lupine)
- Lychnis (Maltese Cross)
- Lysimachia clethroides (Japanese Loosestrife)
- Lythrum (Purple Loosestrife)
- Macleaya cordata (Plume Poppy)
- Melissa officinalis (Lemon Balm)
- Mentha species (Mint)
- Monarda didyma (Bee Balm) *
- Myosotis palustris (Forget-Me-Not)
- Nepeta species (Catmint) *
- Oenothera species (Evening Primrose)
- Paeonia species (Hybrid Peony) *
- Papaver orientalis (Oriental Poppy)
- Perovskia atriplicifolia (Russian Sage) *
- Physostegia virginiana (Obedient Plant)
- Platycodon grandiflora (Balloon Flower)
- Polemonium grandiflora (Jacob's Ladder)
- Polygonatum species (Solomon's Seal)

* Primula species (Primrose)
* Pulmonaria species (Lungwort)
* Salvia species (Perennial Salvia) *
* Santolina chamaecyparissus (Lavender Cotton)
* Saponaria ocymoides (Rock Soapwort)
* Scabiosa caucasica (Pincushion Flower)
* Sedum species–creeping types (Sedum)
* Sempervivum species (spiny varieties) (Hens and Chicks)
* Senecio aureus(Golden Ragwort, Groundsel)
* Solidago species and hybrids (Goldenrod)
* Stachys byzantina (Lamb's Ear)
* Teucrium species (Germander)
* Thalictrum flavum (Meadow-Rue)
* Thermopsis caroliniana (False Lupine)
* Thymus species (Thyme)
* Tiarella cordifolia (Foamflower) *
* Trillium undulatum (Painted Trillium) *
* Verbascum species (Mullein)
* Veronica species (Speedwell)
* Viola labradorica (Violets and Johnny-Jump-Ups)
* Yucca filamentosa (Yucca)

ANNUALS

Annuals with a * made my top 25 list. They were evaluated not only for their deer resistance but for their overall ornamental value as well.

* Agapanthus africanus (Lily of the Nile)
* Ageratum houstonianum (Ageratum) *
* Alternanthera amoena (Joseph's Coat)
* Angelonia angustifolia (Angelonia) *
* Antirrhinum majus (Snapdragon) *
* Begonia semperflorens (Wax Begonia) *
* Begonia tuberhybrida (Tuberous Begonia)
* Bidens ferulifolia (Bidens) *
* Brachycome angustifolia (Swan River Daisy)
* Calibrachoa species (Million Bells) *
* Consolida ambigua (Annual Larkspur)
* Cuphea hyssopifolia (Mexican Heather)
* Datura meteloides (Downy Thornapple)
* Emila javanica (Tassel Flower)

❈ Eustoma grandiflorum (Lisianthus)

❈ Evolvulus glomeratus (Hawaiian Blue Eyes) *

❈ Felicia amelloides (Blue Marguerite) *

❈ Gaillardia pulchella (Blanket Flower) *

❈ Gomphrena globosa (Globe Amaranth)

❈ Helianthus maximiliani (Sunflower)

❈ Helichrysum bracteatum (Strawflower)

❈ Heliotropium arborescens (Heliotrope)

❈ Hunnemania fumarifolia (Mexican Tulip Poppy)

❈ Hypoestes phyllostachya (Polka-Dot Plant)

❈ Ipomoea alba (Moonflower)

❈ Ipomoea purpurea (Morning Glory) *

❈ Lantana camara (Lantana)*

❈ Lobelia erinus (Lobelia) *

❈ Lobularia maritima (Sweet Alyssum) *

❈ Matthiola incana (Common Stock)

❈ Melampodium paludosum (Butter Daisy)

❈ Mimulus cupreus (Monkey Flower)

❈ Mirabilis jalapa (Four-O'Clock)

❈ Nemesia fruticosa (Carnival Flower)

❈ Nierembergia caerulea (Cup Flower)

❈ Nigella damascena (Love-In-A-Mist)

❈ Osteospermum hybrid (African Daisy)

❈ Oxypetalum caeruleum (Southern Star)

❈ Pelargonium x hortorium (Geranium) *

❈ Pennisetum rubrum (Annual Fountain Grass) *

❈ Penstemon x gloxinoides (Hybrid Penstemon)

❈ Pentas lanceolata (Pentas, Egyptian Star Flower) *

❈ Perilla frutescens (Perilla)

❈ Petunia x hybrida (Petunia) *

❈ Phlox drummondii (Annual Phlox)

❈ Polygonium capitatum (Pinkhead)

❈ Rudbeckia hirta (Annual Black-Eyed Susan)

❈ Salvia species (Sage) *

❈ Scaevola aemula (Australian Blue Fan Flower) *

❈ Senecio cineraria (Dusty Miller) *

❈ Tagetes species (Marigold) *

❈ Thymophylla tenuiloba (Dahlberg Daisy)

❈ Tithonia rotundifolia (Mexican Sunflower)

✳ Tropaeolum majus (Nasturtium) *
✳ Verbena bonariensis (Upright Verbena) *
✳ Vinca rosea (Periwinkle-Flowering Vinca) *
✳ Xeranthemum annum (Everlasting)
✳ Zinnia angustifolia (Star Zinnia)
✳ Zinnia haageana (Mexican Zinnia)
✳ Zinnia linearis (Narrow-leaf Zinnia)

BULBS

✳ Allium species (Ornamental Chives)
✳ Chionodoxa luciliae (Glory of Snow)
✳ Colchicum autumnale (Autumn Crocus)
✳ Crocus species (Crocus)
✳ Eranthis hyemalis (Winter Aconite)
✳ Fritillaria species (Fritillary)
✳ Galanthus elwesii (Giant Snowdrop)
✳ Galanthus nivalis (Common Snowdrop)
✳ Leucojum vernum (Spring Snowflake)
✳ Muscaria botryoides (Grape Hyacinth)
✳ Narcissus species (Daffodil)
✳ Puschskinia scilloides (Striped Squill)
✳ Scilla siberica (Siberian Squill)

GROUND COVERS

✳ Ajuga reptans (Bugleweed) (5)
✳ Alchemilla vulgaris (Lady's Mantle) (7)
✳ Arctostaphyllos uva ursi (Bearberry) (6)
✳ Asarum europaeum (European Wild Ginger) (8)
✳ Bergenia crassifolia (Bergenia) (7)
✳ Cerastium tomentosum (Snow-in-Summer) (8)
✳ Convallaria majus (Lily of the Valley) (8)
✳ Cotoneaster horizontalis (Rockspray Cotoneaster) (6)
✳ Epimedium grandiflorum (Barrenwort) (8)
✳ Fern species (Fern) (9)
✳ Galium odoratum (Sweet Woodruff) (7)
✳ Juniper procumbens nana (Creeping Juniper) (8)
✳ Lamium maculatum (Dead Nettle) (8)
✳ Pachysandra terminalis (Pachysandra) (8)

* Potentilla species (Cinquefoil) (7)
* Pulmonaria officinalis (Lungwort) (8)
* Santolina chamaecyparissus (Santolina) (7)
* Sempervirens tectorum (Hens and Chicks) (7)
* Vinca minor (Myrtle, Periwinkle) (9)

VINES

* Campsis radicans (Trumpet Vine)
* Celastrus scandens (Bittersweet)
* Clematis species (Clematis)
* Lonicera x heckrotti (Goldflame Honeysuckle)
* Parthenocissus quinquefolia (Virginia Creeper)
* Parthenocissus tricuspidata (Boston Ivy)
* Polygonum aubertii (Silver Lace Vine)
* Wisteria floribunda (Japanese Wisteria)

HERBS

* Angelica archangelica (Angelica)
* Allium shoenoprasum (Chives)
* Anethum graveolens (Dill)
* Artemisia species (Tarragon) (Wormwood)
* Borago officinalis (Borage)
* Chamaemelum nobile (Chamomile)
* Foeniculum vulgare (Fennel)
* Hyssopus officinalis (Hyssop Agastache)
* Lavandula species (Lavender)
* Levisticum officinale (Lovage)
* Marrubium vulgare (Horehound)
* Melissa officinalis (Lemon Balm)
* Mentha species (Mint)
* Nepeta cataria (Catnip)
* Ocimum species (Basil)
* Origanum species (Oregano, Marjoram)
* Petroselinum hortensis (Parsley)
* Pimpinella anisum (Anise)
* Rosmarinus officinalis (Rosemary)
* Ruta graveolens (Rue)
* Salvia officinalis (Sage)
* Satureja montana (Winter Savory)

* Symphytum (Comfrey)
* Tanacetum parthenium (Feverfew)
* Tanacetum vulgare (Tansy)
* Teucrium chamaedrys (Germander)
* Thymus vulgaris (Thyme)
* Verbascum thapsus (Great Mullein)

SUMMATION

In summation, I would like to repeat some important points. Living in deer country poses problems that each gardener will have to deal with on an individual basis. A plan of action needs to be developed for your particular situation. If you love gardening, you should not deny yourself the plants you love. Compromises may need to be made in many situations. Try to fence in a portion of your property so you can enjoy those things you really want and block the entryways to your property that deer use. This can be done in many ways—through plantings or by simply stringing 3 levels of fishing line at deer height from tree to tree. In the areas that are not fenced in, fill with plants from our Deer-Resistant Plants list. Add deer repellents religiously to these areas. I prefer using both granular applications with organic products like Deer Scram, which repels by smell and foliar applications with a product like Deer Stopper, which repels by taste. If you develop an area where the deer do not like the smell and do not like the taste, they will choose another area.

Observe the deer pattern in your area, change tactics when necessary and don't lose focus on winning the battle. In the end, you are smarter and more capable of winning. Don't let that pretty little deer win the fight.

NOTES & OBSERVATIONS

.....ROLF SVENSSON'S WORST NIGHTMARE

I can't write this book without telling you about Rolf Svensson. Rolf's mother shopped at Sprainbrook Nursery. Rolf graduated from high school in Dobbs Ferry, New York and went off to Penn State, one of the leading colleges in the horticultural field, to study Landscape Architecture. Prior to his senior year, Rolf's mother suggested that he apply for a summer job at Sprainbrook Nursery. Rolf applied and landed a job in the Design Department. He was a very talented individual and his sketching ability blew us away.

Each summer we held a company picnic when things slowed down. The first year Rolf was with us we had just built our large, modern greenhouse, which replaced two plastic greenhouses and three sash greenhouses. It put everything under one roof, giving us easy access from one house to another without having to go outside—a distinct advantage in winter. One portion of the greenhouse was the foliage house, which had benches only on the perimeter with heated Unilock pavers for flooring where we displayed the large foliage plants. To celebrate the opening of our new greenhouse, we cleared away the foliage plants opening up a large area where we could party. We had a big party, inviting Sprainbrook Nursery's friends and employees. Everyone attended with their family. We ended up eating too much and drinking too much, making it important to find a safe ride home for everyone.

When everyone had left, Rolf was still hanging out and talking to Tor and his band. It was late, the party was over and we wouldn't let Rolf drive home, so we had him stay in our guest room. The next morning he couldn't get out of bed. Heidi had to go upstairs to wake him up and tell him it was time to go to work. Rolf said it was like having the worst nightmare of his life to have his boss come, wake him up in bed and tell him it was time to go to work.

Rolf worked for us for a time after college and then went off to California. He came back after several years and went into business for himself. Years later we called him in desperation to take over the Landscape Department when we had lost both of our designers. One designer lived in New Jersey and found a job close to home. He said he couldn't take the commute anymore and battling the George Washington Bridge traffic twice each day was wearing him out. The other designer decided she wanted to go into business for herself. This all took place just before the launching of the new spring season. Rolf was reluctant to leave his business and the customers he had been dealing with for years. but he decided to help us out. After several years he found the job to be very stressful and went back to his less structured lifestyle and his old customers. People still talk about his designs and his ability to transform their property. He left a positive impact upon many Sprainbrook Nursery customers and helped me write and develop a numerical rating system for deer-resistant plants.

When I decided to write this book I called him to do some of the illustrations. We thank Rolf for capturing the meaning of this book with his incredible sketches. We also admire his self-reliance and his decision to live a productive stress-free life. He grows plants and vegetables and maintains lots of animals on his farm. His customers love him and his lifestyle is tied to nature. He has great talent and has learned survival skills that will serve him well.

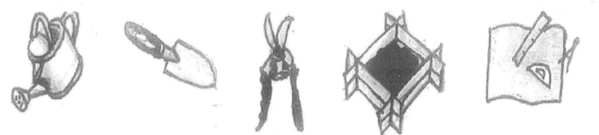

ADD YOUR GARDEN STORY HERE

32. DROUGHT SURVIVAL MANUAL

SECTION 1: INTRODUCTION

We are all aware of the possibility of water shortages. There are a number of simple procedures to follow that can both conserve existing supplies and add new sources at little additional cost. The biggest problem that you may face in a drought situation will be the water restrictions imposed on you.

Today, the average person uses approximately 130 gallons of water per day—four times a person's consumption back in 1900. Much of this water is wasted, much of it can be easily recycled for garden use and additional supplies of rainwater can be collected and stored for use.

With proper care and planning, we can plant as usual in a drought situation and not deny ourselves the beauty of our own environment. We can still maintain the quality of our lives with the pleasure provided by spring and summer gardens and lawns.

Because at any point we can be faced with a water crisis, we must learn to conserve. Conservation will teach us to become better gardeners. When all is said and done, even during a water shortage our gardens can turn out to be more beautiful than ever. Gardening provides a recreational activity that bonds us more closely to nature. Survival is one of nature's underlying forces. Beauty is one of its byproducts.

This section is filled with watering alternatives and advice on methods of conservation. My purpose is to stimulate your thinking. We know that if we can reduce our water use we will become better stewards of our environment. Implementing all of these measures may not be necessary, but there is security in knowing that they exist and are easily put to work should the need arise.

However, we cannot stand back and leave it all up to the other person. Conservation will only work if we start doing it ourselves right now.

SECTION 2: GOOD GARDENING PRACTICES
* Plant, seed, fertilize early
* Mulches
* Antidesiccants
* Soil additives
* Weed control
* Pruning
* Efficient watering

PLANT, SEED, FERTILIZE EARLY
Plant early. Short days, snow, cooler weather and spring thaws are all factors affecting soil moisture. Early in the season, a minimal amount of water is needed to get plants established. Try to push your planting schedule up if a drought is in the forecast. Don't get caught trying to plant during the hot, dry summer. If you plant early and use at least 3 in. of mulch (see below), you will be surprised at how little water you are going to need. While 2 in. of mulch is all you need under normal conditions, 3 in. works best in a drought situation. Woody plants can be planted as soon as the ground thaws.

* **SEEDING LAWNS.** Best time to seed lawns is in the early fall. Cover seed with 1/8 in. of soil. Soaking seed overnight speeds up germination, reducing water consumption. Seeds need to be watered three times a day until they germinate. Dormant seeding, adding seed prior to the first big snowfall, will often work without any additional water required to germinate the seed. Spring seeding requires soil temperatures to reach 50 degrees before germination takes place. By applying seed

early, you subject it to spring rains before it breaks dormancy. This conditions the seed so that when germination temperature is reached it germinates faster.

* **FERTILIZING.** Fertilize early to ensure good plant growth. The stronger your plants, the greater their ability to withstand drought. The spring rains will make the fertilizer available to your plants. Every precaution should be taken to protect your investment. Don't neglect to fertilize!

* **WATERING.** It is recommended that you hold back on watering early in the season and water sparingly. If you do not, you may encourage heavy growth, which may not be able to survive later if water is in short supply. Keep in mind that if water is held back, plants may be somewhat smaller.

MULCHES

The greatest technique to conserve moisture in your garden is to spread a 3 in. layer of suitable mulch around the base of your plants.

Mulches protect the soil from the direct rays of the sun and from moving air, practically eliminating water evaporation. During the great drought of the mid 60's, the Brooklyn Botanical Gardens, in a quest to salvage their existing plants, adopted a complete and heavy mulching program. Not only did they save their plants, but it turned out to be such a great horticultural practice that they have continued it ever since. Mulching also helps reduce weeds that compete for water. If you had to choose one method of conserving water, mulching would be it.

In periods of rain, mulching prevents erosion and reduces runoff water, allowing it to be absorbed into the soil. Mulches are often used for their aesthetic value, but in a water crisis they are a necessity to protect your plants and your investment.

ANTIDESICCANTS

These are products which form a protective coating over the foliage of the plant, reducing the plant's rate of water loss. Evaporation through the plant's foliage can be reduced as much as 80%. For shallow-rooted, broadleaved evergreens facing the rigors of a drought, this can mean the difference between survival and death. Antidesiccants can be safely used on herbaceous as well as woody plants and have even been recommended for use on turf.

SOIL ADDITIVES

* **HYDRO-GEL.** Hydro-gel tremendously increases the water-holding capacity of the soil and is consistent with organic practices. Gravitational forces are strong enough to take up the water as the plant needs it. Hydro-gel absorbs 130 times its weight in water, with 95% of this water available to the plant.

* **WETTING AGENTS.** These products are non-ionic wetting agents, which means that they reduce normal soil moisture retention to permit an increase in available water. This prevents plant loss during dry conditions. Dry soils and soil mixes take in water

rapidly when treated with a wetting agent. In addition, water will wet more uniformly in the root zone and water use can be reduced by 30%–50%. Wetting agents disperse dew on turf, allowing it to run off rather than evaporate. In a drought situation, every drop counts. Spray on or mix into the soil.

❋ **GYPSUM.** Gypsum opens up pores in heavy clay soils, increasing water penetration. Usually the product is applied on the surface of the soil.

❋ **MYCORRHIZAE.** Plants treated with mycorrhizal fungi are more drought tolerant than untreated plants. The fungi effectively increase root mass, improving water absorption.

❋ **PEAT MOSS.** Peat moss loosens the soil, increasing water penetration and it has an enormous water-holding capacity. This product is usually mixed into the soil before planting.

WEED CONTROL

Weeds are one of the greatest competitors for moisture in your soils. They should always be eliminated, especially in a crisis year. The best preemergent weed control in an organic garden is corn gluten covered by a mulch. This should be done immediately after a new planting or as soon as all the beds are cleared of existing weeds. In a drought situation weeds cannot be tolerated and must be removed immediately.

PRUNING

Hopefully, you have applied a generous mulch, are watering carefully and have eliminated all weeds. Next on the list is pruning shrubs and trees in order to reduce the leaf surface. Since the leaf is where virtually all of the water is lost, reducing the foliage can help conserve water.

EFFICIENT WATERING

Perhaps the greatest amount of water can be saved with the least effort when we are as efficient as possible in our watering methods.

Lawns use 90% of all water in the garden. You may decide, or be forced, to let your lawn go dormant. A good organic lawn can turn brown in the summer heat and drought and bounce back when rains return. Grass seeded with turf-type tall fescues and treated with mycorrhizae will withstand drought better than traditional lawns. If you have to choose, let your lawn go dormant and use the little bit of water that you have available to maintain shrubs and trees in your garden.

You want to have a system of watering that provides water to the plants without any runoff or waste. Drip irrigation is a watering system where water oozes out of tiny openings at a slow enough rate that will allow water to penetrate the soil before it runs off. All the water gets into the soil. There are lots of drip systems on the market, including ones that will water your hanging baskets. You will be using only 1/10 of the water compared to normal watering methods. The best time to water in a drought is between sundown and sunrise. This minimizes losses due to evaporation and allows the plant to absorb the moisture in the ground.

I have always advocated that thorough, deep waterings are more efficient than frequent, shallow waterings. Let your drip system run for longer periods of time at less frequent intervals. I emphasize this even more so in a drought situation. Plants will root deeply if they have to reach for water and develop a degree of drought tolerance. Shallow surface roots dry up rapidly.

SECTION 3: SAVE SOME RAIN FOR A SUNNY DAY

* ❋ Rain barrels
* ❋ Sump pumps
* ❋ Cisterns
* ❋ Wells
* ❋ Waste water is better than no water

RAIN BARRELS

Rain barrels have been used for centuries to collect earth's purest form of water—rain water. Today, 60 gal. plastic cans are replacing 54 gal. rain barrels. It is easy to place some under your downspout and watch them fill up. Downspouts can easily be disassembled and barrels can be hidden behind shrubbery.

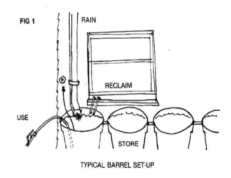

TYPICAL BARREL SET-UP

You might like to know how much water you can collect in a rainstorm. Measure the square footage of your house at floor level including the garage. One inch of rain delivers approximately 625 gal./1,000 sq. ft. When you realize most homes exceed 2,000 sq. ft., it becomes clear that a great deal of water can be collected by rain barrels alone.

An interconnecting system of barrels, as shown in Fig. 1, is a simple method to start with. Locating a cistern, discussed later, is a more permanent but costly approach. A sump pump can be added to the system to pump water from your rain barrel or cistern via your garden hose to your garden. The system can easily be set up and you will be surprised at its simplicity.

SUMP PUMPS

There are many types of water pumps which allow you to attach them to an ordinary garden hose. They are completely portable and easy to use. Simply set your pump in your water reservoir (rain barrel, bucket, cistern, etc.), plug it in and water your garden. It makes a simple job of moving the water from your rain barrel to your garden. (See Fig. 2). If you have a rain barrel located at each of the four corners of your house, a sump pump makes the watering of the plants around your house an easy task. It can also pump bath water out of a bathtub to within 1/8 in. of the bottom for use in your garden.

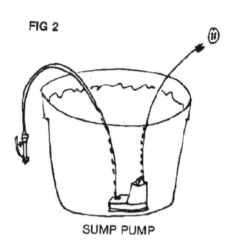

FIG 2

SUMP PUMP

When additional water is needed in the garden during periods of prolonged drought, this pump can help you through most of your watering chores. In a drought situation, this pump is a must to have as it makes salvaging water easy and the process worth the effort. It becomes equally useful in flood situations when it can be used to get rid of too much water.

CISTERNS

Cisterns are artificial reservoirs for storing water. They are often located underground. Frequently they are set up to collect rainwater from a roof. They can also be set up to collect runoff water. An old abandoned oil tank, if properly cleaned out, can make a great cistern. An old-fashioned well can be built out of rock and cement, adding charm to your property while acting as a storage system. There are numerous other ways to build a cistern. Run easy-to-use PVC piping from your downspouts to the cistern. Pump the water from the cistern to your garden when you need it. In the long run, a cistern is a wise investment. There may be safety and health issues and regulations that apply to cisterns in your area—do the research.

WELLS

There is a great deal of useable, untapped water down in our earth. Some people have wells drilled when they face water restrictions f0r public water use. For owners of extra-large gardens, this may be a good answer. However, be warned that in periods of drought, when the water tables drop, wells run dry—especially if under excessive use. In areas where there are not many wells in existence, the draw or water may not be as heavy; in areas where there are many wells, the draw of water may be too great and restrictions are often imposed to preserve the water table.

WASTE WATER IS BETTER THAN NO WATER

Waste water is better than no water and there is enough of it available to allow normal gardening. Most of us send more waste water away from our household than a garden would ever need. What we do need is some good old-fashion American ingenuity to reclaim this water for use in the garden. It may be an old wives' tale, but many farmers swear that soapy water was the secret to their success in gardening.

Containers for water accumulation must be devised along with a method for moving water to those containers. This system can be aboveground, underground, or in a basement. It can be as simple as purchasing 45 or 60 gal. plastic garbage cans and adding as many as you need with overflow piping inserted to fill the next in line. The system can be an old abandoned oil tank pumped out and cleaned or it can be an elaborate cistern system located someplace on your property. It is important to locate these collection areas in a lower portion of your property so simple PVC piping can carry the waste water there by gravity. Once the water has been gathered, a sump pump with a garden hose attached can be used to pump water to the garden.

THE WASHING MACHINE

The washing machine is the simplest source to tap for waste water. The outlet valve is usually dropped into a waste line and without any plumbing you can lift this waste line to a new line leading to your water barrel or reservoir. It would be possible with proper use of solenoids to automate the separation of laundry cycles. This way, if you so desire, only rinse water could be reclaimed. On the rinse cycle alone, for an average family of four, 80–100 gal. of water can be reclaimed each week. If you set up a simple filter system, all laundry water could be utilized from your washer. (See Fig. 3).

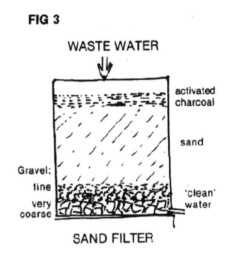

FIG 3

WASTE WATER

activated charcoal

sand

Gravel: fine / very coarse

'clean' water

SAND FILTER

Two chemicals in laundry water are harmful to plants. They are boron and chlorine. During a drought situation, when you plan to use laundry water, avoid bleaches and detergents with high levels of boron and aerate your water to eliminate chlorine. Hold the water overnight before using on your plants. Remember, water, even waste water, is better than no water. Toxicities in soil usually build up over long periods of time. There is less chance of injury over the short haul; therefore, use waste water for a short one- to two-month period. To aerate the water, place a mist nozzle at the end of the hose, direct it back to the barrel and let the pump recirculate for 5 minutes before using. Don't let your plants dry up. As long as you are using water in your household, there is water available.

If you have bare ground where mulch has not been applied periodically, rake the soil surface to prevent the buildup of a crust.

THE DISHWASHER

The dishwasher is equally simple to tap for waste water. However, a more complex system has to be developed for this purpose. A large amount of water can be reclaimed without the use of a plumber. A normal dishwasher uses about 10 gal. per washing. The rinse cycle uses about 2/3 of this. I would recommend that you use our filter system (Fig. 3) before recycling the water.

WASH AND BATH WATER

Each house has its particular plumbing system, but if wash, bath and shower water is diverted before it reaches the waste lines, you again tap into an abundant supply of water for the garden. Any soaps that are safely used on human skin are safe for use on your plants.

WATER FROM DEHUMIDIFIERS

One of the easiest sources to tap for waste water is the dehumidifier. This water is often conveniently accumulated in a portable reservoir, which can be readily carried to the indoor plants or outside for garden use. A dehumidifier in an especially damp basement fills up rapidly and can provide a dependable source for additional water.

SECTION 4: PLANTS THAT WITHSTAND DROUGHT

Most annuals are very tough when it comes to withstanding drought. One of the greatest culprits we face in growing quality annuals is excessive overhead watering from sprinkler systems. Although most plants do fine with good mulching and minimum amounts of water, here is a list of some of the more drought-resistant plants. If you are on a hill or have shallow, dry areas on your property, try adding some of these plants. Keep in mind that when plants have roots deep into the soil, they will draw moisture from deeper levels and will tolerate dry weather better. Developing deep root systems is achieved by less frequent but deep and thorough watering.

ANNUALS

* Cosmos bipinnatus (Cosmos)
* Gazania rigens (Gazania)
* Helichrysum bracteatum (Strawflower)
* Lobularia maritima (Alyssum)
* Pelargonium x hortorum (Geranium)
* Portulaca grandiflora (Portulaca)
* Tagetes species (Marigold)
* Verbena species (Verbena)
* Vinca rosea (Vinca)

PERENNIALS

* Achillea filipendulina (Yarrow)
* Anaphalis triplinervis (Pearly Everlasting)
* Artemisia abrotanum (Wormwood)
* Asclepias tuberosa (Milkweed)
* Coreopsis verticillata (Tickseed)
* Dianthus plumarius (Pinks)
* Echinops ritro (Globe Thistle)
* Eryngium umbelliferae (Eryngium)
* Gaillardia grandiflora (Blanket Flower)
* Hemerocallis species (Daylily)
* Lavandula angustifolia (Lavender)
* Potentilla cinerea (Cinquefoil)
* Salvia nemerosa (Sage)
* Santolina chamaecyparissus (Lavender Cotton)
* Sedum species (Stonecrop)
* Sempervivum tectorum (Hens and Chicks)
* Stachys byzantina (Lamb's Ears)
* Thymus vulgaris (Thyme)
* Veronica incana (Speedwell)

SHRUBS

* Arctostaphylos uva -ursi (Bearberry)
* Berberis thunbergii (Barberry)
* Chaenomeles speciosa (Flowering Quince)
* Cotinus coggygria (Smoke Tree)
* Cytisus scoparius (Scotch Broom)
* Hamamelis intermedia (Witch Hazel)
* Juniperus species (Juniper)
* Kolkwitzia amabilis (Beauty Bush)
* Myrica pensylvanica (Bayberry)
* Potentilla fruticosa (Bush Cinquefoil)
* Rhamnus cathartica (Common Buckthorn)
* Rhus typhina (Staghorn Sumac)
* Rosa rugosa (Landscape Rose)

TREES

* Betula populifolia (Birch)
* Koelreuteria paniculata (Golden Rain Tree)

THE SIX MAGIC RULES

In the event of drought, employ the Six Magic Rules below to ensure the survival and health of your plants:

1. Mulch all plants to a depth of 3 in.
2. Set up enough rain barrels to satisfy your watering needs.
3. When the rain barrels start running low, add waste water from alternative sources, such as baths, dishwashers, washing machines and dehumidifiers.
4. Water less frequently but thoroughly, making sure you employ a system where there is no runoff. This promotes deep water penetration, which in turn develops deep root systems.
5. Sacrifice lawns over your garden. Ninety percent of all water used in the yard is for the lawn. Only 10% is used in the garden. Lawns have a chance to come back and can be renovated. Dried-out plants don't come back.
6. Use sound horticultural practices at all times: weed control, wetting agents, anti-desiccants, proper soil additives, etc.

NOTES & OBSERVATIONS

.....THE DROUGHT YEARS.

During the 80's, Westchester County along with most of New York State faced the drought years. In the nursery industry our livelihood is based on people's ability to buy plants. During this dire period the Horticultural Industry in New York State was bracing for difficult years as the reservoirs reached record lows. The press was on the bandwagon covering the big story of the time. They sounded the warning to all their readers and raised the level of alarm. Water restrictions would have to be imposed and if we didn't get rain, a bleak picture was painted. Everyone's garden plants would die; farmers would not be able to harvest their crops; food prices would soar and if things really got bad, we would run the risk of not having enough water for the bare essentials. All of us in the nursery industry were worried. If people were not allowed to water, they would not buy plants.

Facing devastation, our industry became desperate. In order to survive we needed to use good old American ingenuity. As an industry we needed to come up with ideas to convince the public that they still could plant their homes with beautiful flowers and enjoy a great summer in their garden. The press was killing us. We needed a plan to counter the fear building up in people's minds. We needed a plan where we could assure the homeowners that we could provide them with enough water to save their plants; a plan to encourage people to plant and continue enjoying the beauty of outdoor living; a plan that homeowners could follow and the press could endorse. We needed a plan that would bridge the drought until the time when rains would come again. We knew the problems and needed to find solutions.

With no rain in the forecast, Jan Berends, my landscape designer and I spent countless hours researching for pertinent information related to droughts. We racked our brains on ways to come up with salvageable water. We played out in our minds every garden scenario to find solutions to this problem. We had to save our customer's plants and get homeowners to garden again. Together Jan and I wrote the Drought Survival Manual. I was president of the New York State Nurserymen's Association at the time and the Drought Survival Manual was published and distributed throughout New York State. It was a great success and helped many people get through a difficult crisis. I have included this manual in my book because I want my readers to have a reference tool to help them if they should ever face a drought situation.

At the Nursery we drilled a well to make sure we had enough water to water our plants. . Time restrictions and an alternate day watering schedule would not allow us enough water to grow our crops. The water restrictions were not kind to our industry. I got involved in organizations to fight for less restrictive water regulations to be imposed on those whose livelihood depended on growing and maintaining plants. We advocated that growers and homeowners use drip irrigation as a method to conserve water and to provide enough water to save their plants. Many gardeners had valuable specimens that they had nursed for a lifetime. I became part of the Westchester Countys' Water Task Commission and fought for legislation so that our industry could survive and homeowners could use enough water to save their plants. We were in an atmosphere where police were patrolling our streets and neighborhood handing out large summons to anyone caught watering on days not assigned to them. Watering restrictions varied to odd and even numbers assigned to odd and even houses usually on odd and even days. Strict time restrictions were enforced with only early morning and late evening hours being allotted for homeowners to water. Watering of lawns was prohibited and homeowners were told to let their grass go dormant and it would come back again next year. Anyone breaking the law was thought of as a criminal and everyone was encouraged to be a good citizen and report neighbors not abiding by the strict water restrictions. The cry was 'if we don't conserve water there will be nothing left for the bare essentials'. There was fear and a heightened state of frenzy as the drought became longer and more severe. My daughter always says "everything always happens for a reason". In this case her theory proved to be correct. It takes a change to create a change and this widespread drought in the Northeast was a big changer for our industry. After the 80's the Horticultural industry was never the same. We thought differently and operated differently. .

It amazed me that during this period of time some of the most beautiful floral displays were thriving and were more beautiful than ever. The overhead watering by sprinklers and heavy rains that cause poor flower quality did not exist. Drip irrigation became popular because it was a more efficient way to water, conserved on water use and you could water without anyone seeing you. While trying to save our plants we found methods to increase flower quality. Mulching became a necessity to prevent moisture loss. People were scrambling for any type of mulch and a whole new mulch industry sprang up. Byproducts from trees that ended up in the waste stream became a sought-after product and were in great demand. After the 80's gardeners never stopped mulching.

Forcing us to conserve brought about change. When the drought was over we adopted a new set of gardening practices because we found it made for good gardening. Good gardening is the strength of any Natural Garden Program. In the Nursery we found ourselves in a new gardening era where more information was needed. We produced a very informative catalogue which later became an informational website, Sprainbrook.com. Gardeningthings.com, our organic retail site was conceived and later launched. The seeds were sown in the 80's for us to move toward an organic approach to gardening.

Mother Nature is there for all of us. We need to learn to follow in her footsteps. If we work together with her we can develop quality that we never thought was attainable. Mother Nature is our partner working day and night for us and if we understand the dynamics of organics in Natural Gardening we will understand how to grow beautiful plants. Neither wind, pelting rain, scorching sun, nor drought should deter our ability or inspiration to have a beautiful garden. If we follow Mother Nature's principles we can develop beauty in our garden no matter what the circumstances. We proved this point during the drought years of the 80's.

ADD YOUR GARDEN STORY HERE

33. CONCLUSION

Hermine Krautter "Mrs. K"
1913 - 2008

My hope in writing this book is to stir a desire to restore the balance with nature that has been undone by the use of unnatural processes and chemicals. There is much that we can give and there is much that we can receive in the natural process. Giving and receiving builds up the strong bond that sustains us. When this relationship becomes imbalanced, the bond is weakened. We need to treat nature with respect or she will revolt. Nature speaks to us in many ways but most of us have not taken the time to listen and observe the signs. We are not giving back our fair share to preserve that vital relationship.

We, as Americans, have some of the richest farmlands in the world but our chemical dependency is ruining them. Our soils have become weakened; our bee population, which pollinates our crops, is dying; our livestock is caged and supported with antibiotics and hormones. The general population remains unaware of the damage chemical fertilizers, sprays, herbicides and genetically engineered seeds can do. The agricultural system of today produces farmers that follow the programs handed down by our colleges for greater yield and labor-saving techniques at the expense of our future.

Restoration requires a philosophical change. Natural Gardening is where restoring balance begins. It starts with individuals taking the natural path and radiates out to the community. As we have done many things wrong in our own gardens, this is where the grass-roots change needs to take place. By bonding with nature we gain a strong ally that will sustain us.

I have written this book with the help of Sprainbrook Nursery employees past and present. It has been a lifetime accumulation of facts, methods, learning curves, mistakes and successes. Each chapter was originally a handout, addressing horticultural problems and answering customers' pressing questions and concerns. This book is a home-grown book with illustrations and writing all coming from within a family-owned company. I have done all the writing with help from Rosella, Fred, my wife Heidi and other Sprainbrook employees who have made corrections and suggestions. The illustrations are all in-house from present or former employees. You will find their names mentioned in our stories. Even my two grandsons, Tyler in third grade and Brody in first grade, contributed illustrations to Grandpa's book. I guess this bears out my theory "The greater the mix, the better the results." I thank them all.

This book is meant to be interactive. I have left room for you to make notes and record your observations. You learn from your successes and your mistakes. Record them and make each gardening year a better one. I have left room for you to write your own gardening stories. I have written many of mine. This will personalize your book and make it YOUR book.

Keep gardening; it is good for the soul, the body and the mind…and it is good for our nation.

THE AUSTRALIAN BIRD

I found that writing a book was not an easy task. I had plenty of information at my fingertips and most of the information I had already written about. However, once I created a chapter, I found myself revisiting and rewriting each piece of written information over again. My winter months were spent staying up into the wee hours of the morning working on my book. My editor suggested that I add personal stories to the text. I liked that idea and came up with a format where a story followed each chapter. I probably went overboard, but once I started writing, it was difficult to stop. I found myself reliving the road I traveled and I am grateful to have had the chance to share it with you.

I wanted my book, 12 STEPS TO NATURAL GARDENING, to be representative of Sprainbrook Nursery's commitment to natural gardening. To stand for more than just plants, shrubs and trees. It stands for the awesomeness of nature and the natural resources our world provides to those who live in it. It stands for love, support and hard work. It stands for commitment, devotion and loyalty. It stands for family, community, hardship and growth. It has always been our family's goal to bring the beauty of nature into your home, your yard and your heart.

While designing this book, I knew that illustrations would aid in the dispensing of important information to the reader. I wanted past and present Sprainbrook Nursery employees to draw them. Rolf Svensson, a former designer, drew most of the full-page illustrations. Rosa Mendoza filled in as we needed more and the rest of the illustrations within the text were drawn by several Sprainbrook Nursery men. I was amazed at how artistic each person is and I want to thank them and recognize their talent.

When I was looking for volunteers to draw various illustrations for my book, my daughter, Tonja, told me that Tyler, my grandson, was doing some incredible sketching. His classroom teacher was amazed at his skill for detail at the age of eight. I told Tonja to have Tyler sketch something that I could put in my book. She asked me what I would like him to draw and I said, "How about a bird to add to my chapter on "Plants that Attract Birds?" Tyler was thrilled to be a part of the book.

Later that night, Tyler looked through his bird book and picked out the one that he wanted to sketch. After school the next day, he sat down to draw the bird he selected. He worked the whole evening without going to dinner. He was meticulous on detail and couldn't wait to show it to me. Brody, his younger brother, got wind of the project and decided he wanted to draw something for the book as well. "Sure," I said, "I would be thrilled to have my grandson's first grade drawing in my book as well." I have always advocated that the greater the mix of things, the better the result. In this case, I had the privilege and opportunity to mix the artistic talents of all ages, genders and cultural backgrounds.

The next day, Tyler and Brody sent me their drawings. Thanks to the Internet, I received the drawings from California to New York in an instant. Tyler's detailed sketch of an exotic bird was beautiful. Brody's sketch of a butterfly was fantastic. I couldn't believe that both of my young grandsons were so talented. I was thrilled to have both their drawings in the book. I was especially in awe of Tyler's bird sketch. It was truly a piece of artwork. However, there was one major problem. One of my employees noticed that the bird Tyler chose to sketch was not an American bird. My heart sank. I didn't know what to do. I knew that a drawing of a foreign bird would not be appropriate for my book. I felt terrible. I was going to have to tell Tyler that I could not put his beautiful rendering in my book. When I did, he was devastated. I don't know who was more upset Tyler or his Grandpa who loves him very much. My grandson worked so hard on something that would not be published. However, to his credit, he understood the problem.

Tyler decided to look up the bird in his bird book and figured out that he sketched an Australian bird. He then looked up birds found in North America and agreed to draw a Woodpecker. I was proud of him. His sketch of a Woodpecker was wonderful, but I couldn't stop thinking of his original sketch of the Australian bird and all the hard work he put into it. However inappropriate, I kept wondering if I should put the Australian bird in the book anyway. I thought, "How many people would know it migrated from Australia?" No matter how I tried to figure it out, I could not come up with an acceptable solution.

Talented artists were not the only people I found to help me with the creation of my book. When Charlotte rented Mr. Young's former cottage called "Happy Valley", I found out that she was an editor and I immediately knew she was destined to help me with my book as well. She has made wonderful suggestions and has done a great job editing. She let me tell it in my own way. It is amazing to think that from this little spot on earth, a seed was planted and 12 STEPS TO NATURAL GARDENING grew.

One always hopes that well-thought-out ideas and approaches will provide excellent results. I never liked copying other people's work. I always preferred coming up with original thoughts on projects and designs. For example, whenever customers ask me to bid on an already created landscape design, I dread the task. I prefer creating my own design. Therefore, this book had to become my way of leading others into natural gardening. My book is my own home-grown product and reflects my burning desire to lead people down a path to do what is right for the earth and future generations.

I decided in the end I had to make the right decision and invite a beautiful bird to leave Australia and emigrate to America. I found a place for her in both my book and my heart. Everything happens for a reason and maybe Tyler's bird can act as a symbol for a way for us all to move forward. The Australian bird reminds us that it is important to do what is right. It cheers us on in flight and carries our spirits high as we spread the word that we must all work together with nature to help restore our world.

We fight for what we believe are just causes with bullets and kill innocent lives. There has got to be a better way. The one common denominator every person in the world knows is nature. Let's nurture this fact. Earth is one small planet in a great big universe. In our little section of this universe we need to bond together, realize that our similarities are greater than our differences and accept that there is more that we don't know than what we do know.

We need to embrace the meaning and the journey of the Australian bird and help spread the word.

329

34. BIBLIOGRAPHY

❋ Bradley, Fern Marshall and Barbara W. Ellis and Ellen Phillips. RODALE'S ULTIMATE ENCYCLOPEDIA OF ORGANIC GARDENING. Emmaus, Pennsylvania: Rodale Press, 2009.

❋ Bradley, Steve. THE PRUNER'S BIBLE. Emmaus, Pennsylvania: Rodale Inc., 2005

❋ Dirr, Michael A. MANUAL OF WOODY PLANTS. Athens, Georgia: Stipes Publishing Company, 1990.

❋ Ellis, Barbara W. and Fern Marshall Bradley. THE ORGANIC GARDENER'S HANDBOOK OF NATURAL INSECTS AND DISEASE CONTROL. Emmaus, Pennsylvania: Rodale Press, 1996.

❋ Graph, Alfred Byrd. EXOTIC PLANT MANUAL. East Rutherford, New Jersey: 1974

❋ Hartung, Tammi. GROWING 101 HERBS THAT HEAL. North Adams, Massachusetts: Storey Publishing, 2000.

❋ Lowenfels, Jeff. & Wayne Lewis. TEAMING WITH MICROBES: A GARDENER'S GUIDE TO THE SOIL FOOD WEB. Portland, Oregon: Timber Press Inc., 2006.

❋ Martin, Deborah L. and Grace Gershuny. THE RODALE BOOK OF COMPOSTING. Emmanus, Pennsylvania: Rodale Inc., 1992.

❋ Paungger, Johanna and Thomas Poppe. GUIDED BY THE MOON. Munich, Germany: Marlowe & Company, 1996, 2000, 2002.

❋ Pollan, Michael. IN DEFENSE OF FOOD. New York, New York: Penguin Books, 2008.

❋ Smith, Jeffery M. SEED OF DECEPTION. Fairfield, Iowa: Yes Books, 2003.

❋ Tompkins, Peter and Christopher Bird. THE SECRET LIFE OF PLANTS. New York, New York: Harper Perennial, 1989.

❋ Wolverton, Dr. B. C. HOW TO GROW FRESH AIR. New York, New York: Penguin Books, 1997.

GLOSSARY

ALKALINE: A substance with a pH greater than 7.

ANAEROBIC: An environment with little or no oxygen, or organisms that require little or no oxygen to live.

ANNUAL: A plant in which the entire life cycle is completed in a single growing season.

BALLED AND BURLAPPED: A field plant whose roots have been dug out from the ground and wrapped in burlap as a means of transporting it.

BARE ROOT: A plant that is sold or shipped dormant, with no soil surrounding its roots.

BASAL BRANCHING: Branching that occurs close to the base of the plant.

B HARPIN: Harpin protein is the first scientifically proven trigger that amplifies every plant's inherent ability to protect itself and thrive. This breakthrough technology was discovered at Cornell University. Treated plants are healthier, more vigorous, better able to resist stress from adverse weather or pests and are more productive.

BIENNIAL: A plant that completes its life cycle in 2 years.

BLEEDING: The excessive flow of sap from spring-pruned plants.

CALLUS: The tissue that forms as a protective cover over a cut or wounded surface.

CHLOROPHYLL: The green pigment, located in the chloroplasts, which is necessary to the process of photosynthesis.

CHLOROSIS: Loss of normal green color in plants.

C/N RATIO: An abbreviation for carbon/nitrogen ratio. A ratio measured by weight of the number of parts carbon to each part nitrogen.

COIR: Fibers from the husk of a coconut, used as an ingredient in potting and planting mixes.

COMPACTION: The pressing together of soil particles by foot or vehicular traffic.

DAMPING-OFF: A disease caused by various fungi that results in the shriveling and collapse of seedling stems at soil level.

DEADHEAD: The deliberate removal of dead flower heads of seed-bearing plants.

DECIDUOUS: A plant that drops all of its leaves in autumn.

DORMANCY: A state of reduced biochemical activity that persists until certain conditions occur that trigger germination of a seed or the resumption of growth in a plant.

ERICACEOUS: Members of the Heath family, includes mountain laurel, azaleas, rhododendron and blueberries.

EROSION: The wearing away of soil by running water, wind, ice or other geological forces.

ESPALIER: A tree trained to produce several horizontal tiers of branches from a vertical main stem.

EUTROPHICATION: Excessive nutrient enrichment of ponds or lakes, causing the accelerated growth of plants and microorganisms and the depletion of oxygen.

EVERGREEN: A plant that retains its foliage year round.

EXOGENOUS: Originating externally. Derived or developed from outside the body of the plant.

FOLIAR FEED: To supply nutrients to a plant by spraying liquid fertilizer directly on plant foliage.

GERMINATION: The beginning growth of a seed.

GIRDLING: The removal from a woody stem of a ring of bark extending inward to the wood; also called ringing.

GRUB: The larvae of a beetle.

HARDSCAPE: Elements of a landscape other than plants and soil, such as paved pathways, walls and woodwork.

HERBACEOUS PERENNIAL: A perennial that dies back to the ground at the end of each growing season.

HOGARTH'S S CURVE: The shape of an S or partial S curve incorporated into a landscape design, suggesting that objects arranged within an S-shaped line portray grace and beauty.

HUMATES: The result of decomposed prehistoric plant and animal matter. They provide at least 70 trace minerals for plant health.

HUMIFICATION: The biological process of converting organic matter into humic substances.

HUMUS: A dark-colored, stable form of organic matter that remains after most of the plant and animal residues in it have decomposed.

HYBRID: The organism resulting from a cross between individuals differing in one or more genes.

LARVAE: Immature stages of an insect.

LEACHING: The process of removal of nutrients from the soil by water moving downward in the soil.

LOPPERS: Long-handled pruners used for pruning thick branches.

MICROBES: The oldest form of life on earth. Some types have existed for billions of years. These single-cell organisms are invisible to the eye, but can be seen with a microscope. They include bacteria and fungi.

MICROORGANISMS: Animals and plants that are too small to be seen without the use of a microscope.

MILKY SPORE DISEASE: A disease caused by bacteria that kills the grub stage of the Japanese Beetle. The milky spore bacteria infects and then multiplies within the grub host. When the larvae die, the disease is spread to surrounding areas of the lawn.

MONOCULTURE: Producing or growing one single variety of crop in a specific area every season without variance.

MYCORRHIZA: A symbiotic association of plant roots and fungi in which the roots supply a protected environment and secrete sugars as an energy source for the fungi while the fungi, in turn, help extract nutrients and water from the soil to nourish the plants.

NEMATODE: A microscopic, unsegmented, threadlike round worm.

NITROGEN FIXATION: The capture and conversion of atmospheric nitrogen gas into nitrogen compounds that are stored in the soil and can be used by plants.

NPK RATIO: A ratio of three numbers such as a 10-10-10 that identifies the percentage of three major nutrients—nitrogen (N), phosphorus (P) and potassium (K)—in fertilizers.

OMRI: Organic Materials Review Institute. Products that pass review are OMRI rated.

ORGANIC MATTER: Various forms of living or dead plant and animal material.

OEVERSEED: To seed an area that is already planted (such as a lawn).

PATHOGEN: An organism that causes disease.

PERENNIAL PLANT: A plant that comes back the following year, flowers and sets seeds for two or more seasons.

PH: A measure of acidity or alkalinity expressed as a number between 0-14, with 7 being neutral. High numbers are alkaline; lower numbers are acidic.

PHENOLOGICAL CALENDAR: A calendar that keeps a record of blooming dates and seasonal change. Many consider this to be a more accurate calendar for gardening use.

PHLOEM: In vascular plants, phloem is the living tissue that carries organic nutrients, particularly sucrose, a sugar, made during photosynthesis, to all parts of the plant where needed.

PHOTOSYNTHESIS: The process whereby the manufacture of carbohydrates from carbon dioxide and water, in the presence of chlorophyll, uses light energy and releases oxygen.

PINCHING: Nipping out the end bud of a twig or stem with your fingertips to make the plant more compact and bushy. Pinching entire side shoots makes the plant less bushy.

PORE (OR LEAF PORE): A small opening, as in the surface of a leaf or in the matrix of the soil.

POROSITY: The space between soil particles. The ratio of the volume of all the pores in a material to the volume of the whole.

RESPIRATION: The oxidation of food and the release of energy; may be either aerobic or anaerobic.

RHIZOSPHERE: The area of soil in immediate proximity to roots or root hairs of plants.

ROOT BALL: The combined root system and surrounding soil.

SCARIFICATION: Nicking or wearing down hard seed coats to encourage germination.

SEED: A plant embryo and its supply of nutrients, often surrounded by a protective coat.

SEEDLING: A young plant grown from seed. Commonly, plants grown from seeds are termed seedlings until they are first transplanted.

SNOW MOLD: A cool-weather fungus causing matting and suffocation, occurring usually after snow cover.

SOIL STRUCTURE: The arrangements of soil particles in the soil.

SOIL TEXTURE: The relative proportions of sand, silt and clay in the soil.

SPORE: An asexual reproductive unit, usually single-celled.

STOMATE: A microscopic pore on the surface of a leaf (usually on the underside) through which air and nutrients (dissolved in water) enter and water vapor escapes.

SYMBIOTIC: A relationship between two organisms, usually obligatory and of mutual benefit.

THINNING CUT: Cutting a limb off at ground level or at a branch collar to improve the quality of those remaining.

TOP-DRESS: To apply compost evenly over a bed of plants.

TOPIARY: Plants trained into shapes by frequent pruning.

TRANSLOCATION: The movement of food, water, or mineral solutes from one part of the plant to the other.

TRANSPIRATION: Loss of water from leaves through stomates.

UNDERPLANTING: Planting plants beneath other plants.

VEGETATIVE REPRODUCTION: A form of asexual reproduction using plant parts to clone and multiply an existing plant.

WHORL: The arrangement of three or more leaves, buds, or shoots arising from the same level.

XYLEM: One of the two transport systems in the plant. It conducts water and dissolved minerals from the roots to all parts of the plant.

Published by FastPencil
http://www.fastpencil.com